POPEYE

How a Young Immigrant's Arrival in the U.S.
Led Him Into the World of Street Gangs

Sully

Copyright ©2024

All rights reserved. Written permission must be secured from the author to reproduce any part of the book.

Printed in the United States of America

ISBN: 9798330398782

10 9 8 7 6 5 4 3 2 1

EMPIRE PUBLISHING
www.empirebookpublishing.com

So, here you are. Too foreign for home, too foreign for here. Never enough for both."

-Ijeoma Umebinyuo

DEDICATION

This book is dedicated to my father, my hero and my guide. To my mother, my angel, who was always with me and never let me face my trauma alone. We shared it.

To my wife and children. You are my oxygen and my nourishment. To infinity and beyond…

To the men and women, who have served and experienced the savagery of war, my deepest respect.

I would also like to express my special and heartfelt gratitude to P2, Corey L. and to my publisher, who was invaluable in helping me through the process; thank you, Francesca Maria, and the team at Empire Publishing.

To anyone who has arrived and is in this moment reading this very sentence… thank you. I hope my story resonates with you. I hope to somehow have impacted your life with my words.

PROLOGUE

Part One

April 2000 - 25 years old

The revolver, inches from my face, slowing the steady flow of time to a near crawl. To my right I noted a wood and glass table, commonly seen at thrift furniture stores. An equally cheap looking floral- patterned sectional, placed to my left and behind me. The furniture created a boundary, allowing only two escape routes to consider.

The man behind the gun, Danny, also known as "Playboy", wore a blank yet oddly calculated look on his face. His expression sent an instant fight-or-flight response surging through my veins.

Danny had just moments ago shot our mutual friend Mike Jackson at point blank range. His deranged attention was directed at me now. Mike was on his back and motionless on the floor, bleeding out. He was moaning, and his breath was labored. The moment caused a split-second reminder on the fragility of life, sobering me up from the shock of the moment.

The delayed flow of time felt familiar. Unfortunately, I had often felt this sensation during moments of high stress: a slow-motion, frame-by-frame depiction, happening in real-time. An exaggerated sedate effect caused a unique hyper-awareness of every nuance, smell, sound, and detail as it unfolded around me.

I noted the dim light in the small apartment. The light reflected off the short barrel of the revolver in Danny's hand. Its black metal frame created a faint and dark-hued kaleidoscope, as it mixed with the smoke lingering from the gunshot. Cordite overpowered my sense of smell and added to the foreboding in the room.

My vision, laser-focused on the dark chasm of the firearm bore. It's dark, and small barrel demanding my full attention. I stared deeply into its lethal depth, expecting to see the spark of the gunpowder lighting, indicating the hammer striking the primer and sending a round at my face. "Will I feel any pain?" I wondered.

Thankfully, and suddenly, I snapped out of my fatalistic trance, the need to survive overwhelming. I began breathing techniques to calm myself and avoid hyperventilating, which prevents oxygen from accessing your brain, causing your heartbeat to increase, and resulting in a panicked feeling, sometimes even fainting; I could not let that happen. I focused on my breathing, slow in, hold, slow out. I began to feel my heart rate slow and my breathing returning to a more normal range. Once I was in control of myself, I slowly continued to survey the room. Emotions fleeting, preventing full-focused thought.

I noticed Mike's shoes remained in place on the floor, slightly skewed, but exactly where moments ago, he had been standing in them. The force of the gunshot caused Mike to fall out of his shoes. A visual I will never forget.

Mike was on his back and moaning softly. Blood visibly pooling on the floor near him. He was breathing but wheezing, causing him to intake oxygen in short, intense gasps.

He was dying, and Danny's entire attention remained fixated on me. I could not help Mike, not with the gun pointed right at my dome. I felt helpless.

I noticed Danny's girlfriend, Sara, in my peripheral vision. Sara was pregnant and standing near the kitchen. She held her hands up to her face, trying unsuccessfully to shield her eyes from the gruesome image in front of her; I quickly realized she was in complete shock.

Earnest, Mike's wife's friend, was standing slightly to her left, fearfully looking from Mike to the stand-off between Danny and me; Earnest was also nervously frozen in place.

I had just met Earnest that night, to be exact. Earnest was visiting Mike and his wife Nora after completing Marine Corps boot camp. He was a close family friend of Nora's, and she insisted he accompany Mike, for a fun night out.

Earnest was not having any fun. He was having the exact opposite emotion. Earnest was clearly having a tough time processing the violence which had just unfolded right in front of him. Earnest stood frozen in place, shifting his gaze, mouth slightly agape, and standing rigid, like a statue.

I shifted my stance slightly to keep Danny and Mike in my field of vision and felt the front of the couch lightly touching the back of my leg. I understood my position in the small apartment and realized I was in a precarious and extremely dangerous position. I did not have a safe avenue of escape.

A small pathway between the couch and the coffee table remained my only option. Unfortunately, Danny stood at its end, blocking my only exit with his gun.

Part Two

Five hours earlier, as I cruised south on the I-15 from Ely, Nevada, into Las Vegas, I noted the familiar landscape of downtown Las Vegas and the famous Las Vegas Strip.

The Stratosphere tower, always prominent in its unique shape and incredible height, was a local boundary of sorts separating the touristy areas of Las Vegas from its darker, more sinister side. In the 1990s, the Stratosphere was more than a landmark for locals. For gang members and law enforcement, it was an unofficial demarcation line from safety to danger.

The area around the Stratosphere was known to criminals and gang affiliates as "Naked City." A California and a Las Vegas gang splintered and created their own. They claimed the area around the Stratosphere as their turf. They affiliated with the surging Sur-13 Mexican Mafia chain of criminal enterprises and called themselves "Naked City." It is how the area became known. A fitting name for a dangerous section of Sin City.

I was arriving in Las Vegas to celebrate my birthday; my family and I had recently moved up north to Ely, Nevada. The move was exciting; I was hired into my first law enforcement position since leaving the United States Marines. I applied for and was offered employment by the Nevada Department of Corrections, a position at the only Super Max facility in the state. Ely State Prison (ESP) housed death row inmates and the most violent criminals in Nevada.

Mike had put together a celebration for my birthday and to celebrate the positive changes in my life.

I was expecting to see individuals from my past and was experiencing some anxiety over it. Mike was adamant about putting the whole thing together and would not accept any of the excuses I used to try and circumvent the celebration. I did not feel comfortable going, but I also felt obligated because Mike was going out of his way to make my birthday memorable.

I drove straight to our prearranged meeting place: "Playboy's" apartment. I do not know how or why he received the moniker "Playboy," but my guess is that he assigned it to himself, thinking himself a savant when it came to women.

Danny lived in a low-income housing area near the University of Nevada Las Vegas (UNLV) campus, just off Maryland Parkway and Tropicana Avenue. The apartment homes were behind a Las Vegas Athletic Club and across the street from a 7-11 convenience store—an area inhabited by a primarily Hispanic and African American community. The area caused me consternation. This was an area controlled by a street gang known as 18th Street. I had a long history of violence with 18th Street and nearly lost my life during violent interactions we had in the past. I felt serious apprehensions about entering the area, and more than once, I touched my right knee... remembering.

During the four-hour drive into Las Vegas, I reflected on how life had changed for me. Only seven years ago, I was on a completely different path.

CHAPTER 1

Las Vegas, Nevada - 15 years old

We arrived in Las Vegas, Nevada, in the summer of 1991. The heat in the desert valley was as shocking to our systems as the cold in Chicago. We had just moved to the United States from Quito, Ecuador—our first stop on our journey, Chicago, Illinois. Chicago was the first stop because my dad's roots and origins came from the city of Chicago, and thankfully, we had support from his family as we transitioned. We lived in Chicago during our first year in the United States, but we headed west to Las Vegas when my dad received information about more job opportunities and a lower cost of living. In terms of weather, we went from one extreme to another. For fifteen years, all we knew was the near-steady 80-degree weather we enjoyed year-round in Ecuador.

We moved into an apartment complex behind a Phar-Mor Pharmacy off Tropicana Avenue and Pecos Road. My older sister Denise, my younger brother Kevin, and I shared one room in a two-bedroom apartment. As cramped as it was, we did not mind. In Chicago, we were forced to live in one tiny room, all five of us fighting for space and privacy, between two beds, placed in one room and somehow managed to share one bathroom. So, this was an unexpected luxury, and we enjoyed it.

My time in Chicago awakened me to inner-city subcultures, but I remained socially shielded and protected. I was not a typical teenager in a big city. While in Chicago, I attended an all-boys Catholic High School and was tepidly introduced to the realities of the streets—unfortunately, not enough.

By no fault of their own, my parents were ill-equipped to properly respond to the challenges I was about to face and the type of life I was about to embark on. They were not aware of the warning signs, and they did not understand street mentalities and street gangs; none of us did. It was too late when they gained full comprehension through a crash course from my own experiences.

My dad was hired as an English as a Second Language (ESL) teacher at Chaparral High School, which is located on the East Side of Las Vegas and the one I would attend.

My mom was able to quickly get a job as a cashier at the Phar-Mor Pharmacy by our house. Before we were even fully unpacked, both my parents were already working.

The cultural transition was hard on my sister and me. We remained in a state of confusion and sadness. Leaving Ecuador the way we did, with nothing, was not something our young brains could consider from a logical perspective. I attached all my confusion and sadness to emotions, emotions which I repressed. The reality of how we arrived at this point in our lives was too much to process. So, I kept the obvious resentment and anger at bay in my repressive confusion. Never allowing myself to feel any negativity towards the people I loved the most in this world, my mom and my dad.

My sister was starting university at the University of Nevada Las Vegas (UNLV). Kevin and I, set to have our first experience with the American public-school system. My dad told me I would be going to Chaparral High School, where he taught the entire summer, so I was relieved to have support. Knowing my dad would be available to me under such intimidating circumstances calmed my anxiety. But as usual, and a common theme in my life, things just did not develop as planned.

A brand-new school opened ahead of schedule, and they needed students to fill it. In a move no parents in the valley agreed with, the school district decided to bus students from different areas of the city to open the massive new school.

The new school was in Henderson, a suburb of Las Vegas, approximately 20 minutes southeast of the Las Vegas strip. It was a prototype of a new architecture for future campuses in the city and was built in the Green Valley neighborhood of Henderson. Green Valley was a wealthy area in the city of Henderson. Unsurprisingly, they named the school "Green Valley High School." The new school's color scheme was grey and green, and the mascot was a gator, the Green Valley Gators.

My first school bus ride experience was one I will never forget. I waited with at least seven other kids at the pre-arranged pick-up spot on Pecos Road. I quickly noted that I was the only one dressed like a skater, something which caused the familiar feeling of "I don't belong" to creep into my consciousness.

This was my first school bus ride. At Cotopaxi, in Ecuador, I lived close enough to ride my skateboard. At St. Patrick's, in Chicago, I lived too far for school bus services, so I walked and took the city buses; now, at Green Valley, I was going to experience my first yellow school bus ride.

I watched the yellow school bus approach, and I was so excited to get on the bus. I was going into tenth grade, and I was riding on an actual yellow American school bus, like the ones I had seen in movies for so many years. For me, the experience was surreal.

The bus arrived, and we all piled into it. I waited to board last. Other kids were already on the bus, and there were no unoccupied seats, so I found one next to a cute Black girl who smiled politely at me.

The bus took off, and there was a level of palpable excitement in the air. We were all on our way to our first day of school at a brand-new school. No one knew what to expect.

As the bus lumbered slowly down the road, making a couple more stops, a commotion broke out in the back of the bus. Two girls, both Hispanic, started to fight with each other. Suddenly, it was chaos; kids were out of their seats and yelling, the bus driver was trying to gain control but failing miserably, and the girls were in full-fledged hand-to-hand combat. I had never seen girls fight before (add it to my list of new experiences), and they were vicious! They both held a death grip on each other's hair, and both used their free hand to hit each other wherever they could.

They tossed each other around the entire bus, and everyone was cheering them on. Mental!

The bus driver finally pulled over and walked to the back of the bus to separate the girls. He took one of them to sit next to him in the front of the bus and told the other to remain in the back. There was some continued back-and-forth bickering between the two girls, but they listened. Everyone settled down, and we got back on the road. While everyone seemed entertained by the fight, I was quietly anxious and terrified.

Minutes later, we pulled into Green Valley High School. The campus was enormous. Tall grey walls made the school look like a fortress. Green metal gates at the points of entry/exit were visible, and students slowly walked through. Every student, looking around, curious of their new surroundings...

Our bus pulled in behind a lengthy line of buses arriving at the school. Once we reached the drop-off area, the driver opened the door, and everyone excitedly piled out of the bus like cattle. We were all ushered into the school's giant gymnasium.

Once all the students sat and were calm, they broke us up by grades and last names. We were handed a syllabus and a school map and sent to our corresponding home rooms.

I arrived at my homeroom for class and sat in the front because no other chairs were available. More students trickled in after me, and once the teacher counted heads, she began calling out students' names. When she finished her task, she asked us to stand up, one by one, and introduce ourselves to the class. She instructed us to say something unique about ourselves or what we had done for the summer.

A kid named Brian went first; he was Mexican from his mom's side, but his dad was white, and he lived in North Las Vegas. Dennis went next, he blinked his eyes repeatedly, some kind of nervous tick, the blinking was almost nonstop, and I felt bad for him. He said he was Italian and originally from New York. Natalie went after Dennis; I remembered her from the bus ride to school; she was full of attitude but cute. She had blonde shoulder-length hair, long legs, and full lips. She reminded me of Anna, a Finnish girl I knew in Ecuador, who was also the first girl I kissed.

All Natalie said was, "Hi, my name is Natalie, and I'm from Las Vegas."

Hugo went next, he was a short and skinny, dark colored Hispanic kid, and when he stood up, he said, "My name is Travieso, I am from the East side of Las Vegas, and I am from 28th Street Raskals Chapter 3!"

Before sitting back down, he made funny hand gestures, and Brian stood up to give him a weird pre-rehearsed handshake. I noted the teacher became visibly upset over their interaction. She sternly stated, "We will not have that in my classroom, gentlemen!"

I did not understand what was going on at all; the kids were laughing, but I also noticed other Hispanic kids in the class who appeared visibly upset and gave Brian and Travieso dirty, mean mugging looks.

The entire exchange in the classroom was beyond weird for me. I was completely and utterly clueless.

When my turn came, I stated my name and said, "I just moved to the United States from Quito, Ecuador." Someone yelled out, "Where is that, Africa?" Everyone laughed.

I spent the rest of the day just trying to find my way around the massive school. It was enormous and very confusing—there were so many hallways, stairs, and lockers. I had never been around so many kids at once. It was shoulder to shoulder and hard to move around. It was overwhelming.

I made it to lunchtime. I was too nervous to eat, and the line for food in the cafeteria was too long. I walked outside into the quad area and saw Brian and Travieso sitting with a bunch of other Hispanic kids at one of the outdoor tables.

The other Hispanic kids from my first-period class, who had appeared to get mad at Brian and Travieso during their weird exchange, sat inside the cafeteria with another large group of Hispanic kids. I looked around carefully and noticed about four distinct groups of Hispanic kids, all sitting away from each other.

The same tribal behavior, I noted, happened with the Black kids as well. Three groups of Black kids sat away from one another, easily distinguishable. One of the groups wore red clothing or accessories, the other wore blue, and the last wore green.

All these subsets of groups sat separately and were careful not to cross each other's paths. It was clear to anyone observing that the separation of groups was based on an adversarial element. The tension in the air was palpable.

As I tried to comprehend what was happening, I spotted a group of kids dressed like me sitting at a table. They looked like skaters and appeared friendly enough; I did not know what to do or where to go, so I just walked over to the table with the people who looked most like me and sat down.

To my relief, they were friendly and immediately introduced themselves to me. The two kids I had spotted were Mike and Chip. Soon, the kid from my homeroom class, the Italian from New York, Dennis, came over and sat down with us. They were all friendly, and we talked about how massive the school was. Everyone was new to the school, and it was a strange situation for everyone. The energy clouded in confusion.

Suddenly, as if out of thin air, Natalie, the cute girl from the bus and our homeroom, arrived at the table with a couple of other girls. My heart skipped slightly as she smiled at me. They all knew each other, and as they sat down, they immediately started gossiping about people I did not know. So, I sat quietly, listening and observing. I caught Natalie looking my way at times. Each time our eyes locked, I looked away shyly.

The day finally ended, and Mike sat with me on the bus ride home. He dressed like a skater, so I asked him if he skated. He told me he did not skate but was a "stoner," and most skaters considered stoners. I nodded, acting like I knew what "stoner" meant. I had zero clue.

Everyone was going to Mike's; his dad worked nights as a card dealer at one of the casinos and was usually never home. Mike had the house to himself, and it was a familiar hangout spot for everyone. I was nervous but accepted the invitation.

CHAPTER 2

We arrived at Hasson's house, and when we entered his home, we all made ourselves comfortable on his couches.

His house smelled like cigarettes. The smell was overpowering and permeated into every corner of the home. I could see the yellow discoloration on the walls and blinds from the cigarette smoke. If tar and nicotine could permanently stain benign, sturdy objects like walls and furniture, what did it do to the lungs of smokers? I found the habit disgusting. Always have and always will.

The shades at his house were closed, and the ambiance was dark and gloomy. The furniture was old but well-kept. It consisted of two couches, a recliner (which was his dad's, and no one could use it), and a cheap wooden kitchen table with four chairs. Hasson was an only child and lived at the townhome alone with his dad.

As we sat and made ourselves comfortable, Hasson ran upstairs and came down with a bottle of vodka. As I was trying to process the implications of the introduction of alcohol, Chip grabbed a pipe from his backpack, along with a bag of marijuana, and started to "load the pipe."

I was quietly becoming apprehensive about joining them at Hasson's; I was feeling the beginning of stress and anxiety emerging.

My entire life, drugs equated to evil and aligned to the devil. They caused you to do "evil" things; even being around them was a sin. Alcohol, well alcohol played a unique, violent, and sad part in my childhood. So, exposure to it by kids my age, by friends I just made... was a situation I was not equipped to manage.

I will say this about religion and the fear of eternal damnation: it worked.

As they passed around the bottle and the weed, I could feel myself entering a dark place mentally, causing me to judge all my new friends in a sinner/evil type of visualization. I was nervous and all I could think about was, do not sin.

Thankfully, before either the bottle or the weed got to me, it passed over to Dennis first, and to my total surprise, he politely declined.

I was pleasantly shocked when no one said anything, and no peer pressure applied to Dennis.

Witnessing this acceptance of allowing others to be comfortable with any decision, calmed me instantly. It gave me renewed courage to follow Dennis' lead. When it passed to me, I politely declined. No one cared.

I got through my first drug-related experience. I almost passed out from anxiety, and I was visualizing everyone going to hell, but I made it.

A Hispanic-looking girl named Phoebe approached Dennis and me and started asking me rapid-fire questions. "Where are you from?" "I heard you are from Ecuador?" "Where is Ecuador?" "Do you speak Spanish?" "Do you have a girlfriend?"

As I tried to answer all her questions, she sat on my lap and leaned close to me. She whispered into my ear, "Do you want to go upstairs with me?"

Before my brain could formulate a coherent response, Natalie, watching the exchange, rose off the couch, walked up to us, and swiftly took Phoebe by the arm. Natalie whisked Phoebe off my lap and into the kitchen, where they chatted.

I think Dennis could feel I was uncomfortable. He told me he was going to be leaving soon and asked if I wanted to walk home with him. I was so relieved because this visit to Hasson's was overloading all my senses.

We said our goodbyes, exited the home, and walked toward my apartment complex. As we walked, I felt sinful and dirty by my entire experience at Hasson's. A part of it terrified me, but other parts, like Phoebe and Natalie, stirred specific emotions in me. I was exposed to things I only saw in movies, and it was only the first day of school.

Dennis told me a little about himself as we walked towards my apartment complex. He had a younger brother named Salvatore, but everyone called him Sal. His parents were divorced, and he had been in Las Vegas since elementary school. He grew up with Hasson, Natalie, and all the other kids. They all attended the same Elementary and Junior High Schools. Dennis was friendly, and I noticed he dressed differently than the other "stoners," who dressed more like skaters.

Dennis not only dressed differently, but his overall style was unique. He dressed like a "cholo" (I learned this was a term used to describe Hispanic gang members); he wore the same style of clothing but mixed it with a skater flair. The way he wore his clothes was baggy and sagging, but he used skater-like accessories, like the wallet chain, which hung by the side of his shorts.

The stoners styled their hair, like skaters. Long at the top, trimmed at the sides, and combed downward and to the side—a typical Tony Hawk cut.

Dennis, on the other hand, had a long "tail" or wisp of long hair flowing from the back of his head and his long hair on top, slicked back against his head. His sides and the back of his head were all shaved except for his tail. It was a balance of both styles, straddling both youth cultures in a way that made it look cool. I dug it.

He asked about Ecuador and my family. I gave him a cleaned-up version of both. When we reached the main gate to my apartment complex, he pointed and said his house was the opposite way, across Tropicana Avenue, not too far from my apartment. We shook hands, and he walked away. Dennis was my first official friend in Las Vegas. I walked to our apartment, still attempting to wrap my mind around the eventful first day.

CHAPTER 3

As the first month of school wore on, I began to slowly learn the subculture and social dynamics that kept me in a state of confusion at school.

The stoners were potheads, but also known to experiment with other drugs. Stoners were the main source for obtaining narcotics at school. Chip was the biggest weed dealer at GV High School and made a business out of it. Chip was smart and came from a wealthy family. His dad was a professional sports gambler but was slowly dying of cancer. Chip took all advanced courses and used his superior intellect to build himself a weed empire. Chip was the weed guy.

Stoners did not affiliate with anyone, but with everyone. You could see Chip and his friends sitting and talking with every group at the school, the jocks, the Crips, the Bloods, the multiple Chicano gangs, the cheerleaders, etc. Stoners were easygoing and free-spirited. They had a good relationship with everyone. The fact they controlled the weed at the school made it easy.

The groups I needed education in, which I knew little about and had never been exposed to, were gangs.

My new friends took the time to explain all the Green Valley High School gangs. How to identify them, and why they hated each other.

The "Crips" wore blue and were usually Black kids, but not always. The Crip gangs in Las Vegas were mostly from the North Las Vegas area.

The "Bloods" wore red and were usually Black kids, but not always. The Bloods in Las Vegas were usually from the West and Northwest Side of Las Vegas. Bloods and Crips were mortal enemies.

The final gang of Black teenagers at Green Valley wore only green, and I learned it was a locally originated gang that called itself "Gerson Park Kings," or GPK. GPK controlled an area northwest of Las Vegas, well known for drugs and violence. There was a housing project next to a city park called "Herbert Gerson Park," which is how the name of the gang originated. GPK was a hybrid gang made up of both Bloods and Crips, who came together back in the seventies to form GPK. GPK is the oldest local Las Vegas Gang. Crips, Bloods, and GPK's all hated each other.

The Hispanic gangs were the most complicated. San Chucos (North Las Vegas), Little Locos (North Las Vegas), 28th Street (East Las Vegas), 18th Street (East/Central Las Vegas), Echo Park (California-based, but with a presence in Las Vegas), Los Primos (California based, but with a presence in Las Vegas), Naked City (Central Las Vegas), etc. All were part of Sur-13 (South-13), a street-level alignment with the Mexican Mafia.

There were limited Norteño gangs in Las Vegas. Norteño gangs are (Northerners), and the differentiation stems from a dispute between the Mexican Mafia and an offshoot of the Mexican Mafia, which formed in the California Prison system, called "Nuestra Familia." Those who pledged allegiance to the Mexican Mafia were considered Sureños (Sur-13), and those pledging allegiance to Nuestra Familia were considered Norteños (Nor-14). Sureños use the number 13 because the letter "M" is the 13th letter in the alphabet; Norteños use the same system and use the number 14 because the letter "N" is the 14th letter in the alphabet.

It is all complicated, but for my story, it is important to reiterate how the Clark County School District in Las Vegas implemented the destined-to-fail idea of: "Let's bus kids from across all areas of the valley to open up the new high school!"

All the gangs I described were funneled into one school. Prior to the Green Valley High School experiment, gangs remained in the schools assigned to their zoning district.

They did not anticipate the explosion of gang culture in the nineties, and by the time they realized their mistake, it had infested the entire community. They were infiltrating all areas regardless of money and status and creating a violent sub-culture that inspired the identity of an entire generation.

Green Valley High School was a box of matches waiting to ignite. The unpredictable and volatile nature of the experiment had unattached and distant similarities to my childhood experiences in Ecuador.

CHAPTER 4

Quito, Ecuador

Quito, Ecuador, South America, is a peaceful country on South America's Pacific coast, nestled between Colombia to the North and Peru to the South. To the East lies Brazil's dense Amazon jungle, and to the West, the Pacific Ocean.

Quito, the Capitol City I grew up in, is high up in the Andes Mountains. It is built in a valley surrounded by beautiful green mountains and multiple active volcanoes. Quito is known because the Earth's equatorial line runs right through it, dividing the Earth into northern and southern hemispheres.

The equatorial line is special because the Earth's natural bulge runs around the equatorial line, making any land on the line closer to the sun than any other place on Earth.

This also results in nicer temperatures all year round. Like other countries on the equator, Ecuador experiences the shortest sunrises and sunsets, due to the sun's daily path being perpendicular to the horizon.

Ecuador is considered a poor, Third-World country, but is also recognized as one of the most beautiful places on Earth. The Galapagos Islands belong to Ecuador and were made famous by Charles Darwin, who wrote his theory of Natural Selection based on the wildlife he found on the islands. The Galapagos remains protected and untouched, a treasure from which our basic evolutionary science stems from.

I arrived in Ecuador before I was a year old. Ecuador was the only place I knew as home. I loved Ecuador. My dad arrived with the intention of a short visit but ended up loving it and chose to make Ecuador his home.

My dad, John Bernard Sullivan, was an intimidating presence. Standing over six feet tall, wide-shouldered, with an athletic, muscular build and a stern but handsome face, he created a special aura around him anywhere he went.

He stood out mostly due to his unique walking style, which was aggressive and determined. His shoulders and back were straight, his chest out, and his body erect. His gait was purposeful and long; he was always the fastest walker in any group.

My dad's walk was the product of serving in the United States Marine Corps. The Marines are known for having the best drilling ability (Marching in unison with weapons while performing synchronized movements). Hours upon hours of marching and moving a platoon as one unit, hammered into Marines daily. It is one of their most effective and subtle tools for teaching teamwork, discipline, and precise execution.

Walking straight, keeping your body rigid, and moving with purpose are all foundational hallmarks of a Marine. The result is always a beautiful collective of discipline in motion. Repetitive maneuvers, conducted on an endless daily repetitive loop, cause young men like my dad to adopt the posture into their personal lives.

The Marines sent my dad to Vietnam. He met my mom shortly after returning. Riddled with the kind of guilt and mental illness only war can create.

When my dad left for the Marines, he was only seventeen years old, so special permission, or a waiver from my grandma, was the only way to facilitate his entry.

He was seventeen when he was shipped off to Boot Camp at Marine Corps Recruit Depot (MCRD) in San Diego, California, and he was seventeen when he deployed to Vietnam.

My dad's time in Vietnam caused him to develop a deep mental illness, now known as Post Traumatic Stress Disorder or (PTSD). My dad was seriously injured from a gunshot wound and almost lost his life in Vietnam. When he returned home to Chicago, he was not the same kid/man who had left. He was different, and only an unfortunate group of people with shared experiences could fully understand the reasons associated with his trauma. My mom, who I consider to be one of the most empathetic and caring people I know, tried hard, investing her heart and her life, to understand and dispel my dad's mental demons.

My parents met at a Mars Chocolate Factory in Chicago, where they both worked. At the time, my dad remained mentally and emotionally unavailable. Numbing his mental anguish from Vietnam with alcohol and was unable to show commitment to any relationships he had.

My mom always tells us she noted our dad's walk first. It is what caught her attention. A work-related romance quickly ensued, and ignoring the signs of trauma my dad certainly displayed, my mom chose to look beyond them. She saw a good man who was troubled. She fell deeply in love and believed she could help him. She believed she could permanently extinguish all the pain and anguish he carried with him from Vietnam.

She spent his entire life trying.

CHAPTER 5

Ecuador - Martin Cerere Elementary - 7 years old

The initial warmth always felt strangely satisfying.

First contact with my skin as it spread down my leg, oddly comforting.

The comforting warmth of my pee always only lasted a second or two; the pee cooled quickly as it traveled down my leg or pooled in my pants, making it wet and uncomfortable.

I would sit still, too afraid and embarrassed to move. I would stare at my desk or my notebook, avoiding eye contact with anyone, somehow believing if I ignored it, everyone else would too. Sometimes, when it was quiet, you could hear my pee dripping off my seat and onto the floor.

Sometimes, when dehydrated, the smell made it impossible to ignore.

At school, I loved PE days. I loved PE days because competition and athletics have always aligned with my core makeup. But I also loved PE because when I peed, the dark color of the uniform hid it perfectly.

Peeing my pants was a daily occurrence for me, at school and at home. I know my parents worried because I could obviously feel it was not normal, and I often overheard their worried and hushed discussions with teachers and with themselves.

At Martin Cereré, I started learning to speak English under my dad's tutelage. English is a difficult language to learn, and I had problems with it. This caused my dad to worry, and I could feel it was important to him, I speak English fluently. Having English class only once a day was a problem, and my dad actively sought to place us in one of the American schools in Quito.

In the meantime, I continued to enjoy my childhood and time at school. My peeing problem continued unabated but was thankfully offset by a special and popular girl who accepted me and kindly included me in her large group of friends.

Her name was Sofia, and for the rest of my life, I will never forget the kindness and acceptance she showed me. Without her empathetic nature, the suffering and embarrassment during such grim times would have been impossible to manage.

Sometimes, small acts of kindness and the courage to act on them can change the entire trajectory of a person's experience. Sofia, due to her popularity and high social hierarchy, made it possible for the other kids in my class to see past my uncomfortable accidents and see me through a lens void of the judgment peeing in your pants would normally cause.

This unexpected social acceptance allowed me to thrive in certain areas. I excelled at soccer and track and field. My dad was also the track and field coach, and I remember his pride as my sister, and I won every event. We inherited his athletic abilities, and my dad loved to watch us compete.

My sister even started competitive gymnastics, and she was good and surprisingly skilled. She received an invitation to practice at the Ecuadorian Olympic Center, which was an impressive feat. Unfortunately, my sisters' priorities became boys and singing. My family in Ecuador is a conglomerate of exceptionally talented musicians, singers, and inventive minds; it was a natural path for my sister to follow. She was also an incredibly talented singer. She forgot about sports and never followed through with her gymnastic dreams.

My time as a kid in Ecuador was spent with neighborhood friends, outside and unsupervised. The era is drastically different when compared to today's or even previous generations.

I do not believe the era we experienced in Ecuador, will ever be replicated. All the fears associated with unsupervised children did not exist. Corporal punishment was real and applied often; there were no rules for who could administer it: family members, teachers, and even random adults.

The entrapments of technology we see today were simply not a part of the equation. We roamed freely and fended for ourselves. There were no cellphones or a way to track us once we left the house. The level of trust in youth and society was unprecedented.

CHAPTER 6

While teaching at Martin Cereré, my dad continued his college education. He completed his bachelor's in education from a local University (Universidad Catolica) or Catholic University. He worked during the day and attended university at night.

His lack of a degree was the hurdle he needed to overcome to gain employment at one of the American schools in Quito. As soon as he graduated, he applied for open teaching positions.

His resilience and hard work paid off.

He was hired at "Academia Cotopaxi," or "Cotopaxi" for short.

Cotopaxi, considered the best school in Quito and modeled after American schools, was the crown jewel for foreign teachers. The program was the opposite of Martin Cereré. Cotopaxi was entirely in English, with only one hour of Spanish. It was a highly coveted private school, and only the super wealthy, or kids with diplomatic parents, went to Cotopaxi.

One of the benefits for teachers employed at Cotopaxi was free tuition for their children, which enabled us to attend the school.

Our lives were about to make a sudden and abrupt change.

My first day at Academia Cotopaxi was memorable. My sister Didi, my dad, and I arrived on campus in our new car, an "Andino."

I remember the Andino because it was everything a car should not be. It looked like a large box on wheels. Imagine the first car you ever drew on paper as a kid. Think about it and picture it in your mind. Well, the Andino could be your drawing.

It was square, with zero smooth edges. It included two front bucket seats, which were set lower than the back of the vehicle, so you had to step down from the back to sit in the front. The back of the car was noteworthy due to the lack of any safety features during its design. The back of the vehicle was completely open, and there were only two features: two benches made for two people per bench, set on either side of the car. The benches had no backrests, and they were placed above the rear wheels and running along the sides of the vehicle.

This design incorporated no traditional safety belts, and the middle of the back of the vehicle was wide open. My sister and I faced each other as we sat in the back. Traveling in the Andino was always an adventure. It was an exercise in balance and strength to keep from flying around the back of the car.

My dad, excited about his new purchase, drove with complete disregard for the death trap we found ourselves in. He drove fast, showing off the speed of the car and how well it took corners. While my dad practiced evasive driving, my sister and I flew around the back of the car.

The Andino, painted light cream, a light brownish color, with black and orange racing stripes running down the sides, was an ungodly sight.

Picture the ugliest car you have ever seen; the Andino was uglier.

Later, I found out that the Andino was so cheap that its engine had horsepower comparable to that of a motorcycle. It must be up there with one of the most unsafe vehicles ever created in the history of car manufacturing.

As we drove into Cotopaxi's parking area, I noticed the large white walls with blue edges surrounding the entire school. The front gate was a large black iron gate placed on the northwest corner of the perimeter walls. Armed guards stood outside the gates, and you could see more patrolling inside.

Mind-blowing!

I noticed nice cars dropping off well-dressed kids. Volvo's, Mercedes, etc., some of the kids dropped off, even exited their vehicles with their own armed personnel. It was all very strange. We entered the school, and begun our day.

When recess finally arrived, I found an empty blue wooden bench and sat alone, watching kids play soccer. The kids playing soccer were skilled, but while focused on the match, I failed to notice three girls' approach.

One looked Asian (she was Finnish), with straight dark long hair. Her friend standing next to her had short hair, shorter than mine, and she was sucking on a lollipop. She looked like a boy, and I had to do a double-take to make sure it was a girl. The third one was dark-skinned, short with dark hair, and appeared to be the shyest one in the group.

They approached me, and the Asian girl asked, "Are you new to the school?" I responded with a barely audible "yes." She asked me my name, and I answered, "Jonathan." She smiled at me, and I could tell it was genuine; she was nice. She said, "Hi, Jonathan, my name is Paulina, this is Fiona (pointing to the girl with the short hair who was still loudly sucking on her lollipop), and this is Monica (pointing to the shorter dark-skinned girl).

I looked up and smiled at each of them. I did not know what to say next or what to do. There was an awkward silence, which made me super uncomfortable and embarrassed; thankfully, my dad appeared out of nowhere, somehow summoned by the gods of new shy kids at new schools.

"Hi Jonny-boy (what my parents called me), how are you liking Cotopaxi so far?" Before I could answer, he turned to the girls and said, "Hi girls, how are you doing today?" They smiled politely and retreated.

My dad asked me to follow him. Dad with the save!

We walked along the concrete walkway, which paralleled the soccer field. At the end of the walkway, at the last classroom before you had to turn left and head towards the front gate, he stopped.

"This is my new classroom," he stated. He opened the door, and we stepped inside. His classroom was much bigger and nicer than the one at Martin Cereré. He showed me around his room and reassured me everything would be ok. He told me if I ever needed him, to come to his classroom. He made me feel safe, and I began to feel better.

I spent the remainder of third grade in Ms. Dee's class and made lasting friendships. Fiona, Paulina, and Monica were friendly. Fiona and Paulina eventually became my best friends, and I remain close to both. The bonds we created have lasted a lifetime.

I became friends with the soccer players and athletes and hung out at school with Mario, Paul, Patrick, Bill, and Steven. Steven was one of the only Black kids in our class and the entire school. Steven liked to be addressed by his last name, "Scruggs," so that's what we called him.

Even though everyone was friendly and accepting, I did not fit in. My mastery of the English language was severely lacking, and it showed in my grades. Everyone at Cotopaxi was also in a different socioeconomic class system. They were all wealthy. They traveled to the United States and Europe on vacation, their parents drove nice cars, and they lived in big fancy houses. Fiona, for example, had a seven-floor house. Let that sink in for a second; her house had seven levels.

We, on the other hand, were considered low-middle class. While most kids at Cotopaxi dressed in Benetton and Lacoste brands with fancy Swatch watches, I shopped at local Ecuadorian stores with cheap local brands. The differences were noticeable. I certainly felt them.

I did not belong. This was an all-too-common theme in the history of my existence. I was always out of place from Martin Cerere to Academia Cotopaxi and fast-forwarding to St. Patrick's High School and Green Valley High School. I was never comfortable in my skin, searching for the kind of acceptance I never found.

CHAPTER 7

Las Vegas, Nevada - 15 years old

When I started my sophomore year at Green Valley High School, I aspired to return to playing soccer and to try playing basketball for the school.

I spent hours playing basketball at the park during my lone year in Chicago. Playing basketball daily elevated my game and gave me the confidence to attempt making the school team.

Barely three months into the year, I failed at both.

My first mistake was befriending Brian and his cousin Travieso (his real name was Hugo); once they realized I spoke Spanish fluently, they took a specific interest in me.

I continued my education on gangs and their culture. In the early 1990s, you could not avoid it. Gangster culture spread through every available outlet. In rap, in hip-hop, in dancing, in clothing and styles, and video games. The lifestyle was exploited in all conceivable mediums, forced fed into suburbia, and glamorized to reach all races and socioeconomic groups.

Gangs ran the schools and controlled all street-level criminal enterprises. You could not walk around as a teen or young adult without a form of harassment or threat of violence. School was more like a modern-day gladiator academy, with multiple fistfights daily.

Hasson, Chip, and Dennis helped me to navigate the complexities involved with gangs and their lifestyle.

Our group of friends grew, I created new friends, Blaine, Ivan, Eli, Aaron, and a couple of others. During lunchtime, I began to split my time between my group of stoner friends and Brian and Hugo. Brian and Hugo were from the 28th Street gang on the East Side of

Las Vegas. There were "chapters" to the gang or sub-groups, but they both belonged to Chapter 3 and called themselves "Raskals."

They spelled Rascals with a "k," replacing the "c," to avoid using the letters associated with a rival gang, the San Chucos, or "SC."

I felt more at home with Brian, who went by his street moniker "Huero" (White Boy), and Hugo, who went by "Travieso." (mischievous). They both spoke Spanish and though I was now comfortable speaking English, Spanish remained my native language.

Huero and Travieso lived in North Las Vegas, 28th Street was on the East side, but their families relocated to projects on Walnut and Owens in North Las Vegas. Geographically speaking, it was hard to hang out with them outside of school. I did not have a driver's license or drive a car; I spent my time with them at school, but on the weekends, I spent time together with my hybrid-stoner crew.

My crew consisted of Blaine, Ivan, Eli, Hasson, Chip, Dennis, Aaron, Natalie, Phoebe, and others. Blaine, Ivan, and Eli dressed more like Dennis, using the hybrid style and balancing both cultures. They blended the gangster hip-hop look with the stoner style, which became increasingly popular. I grew closer with Blaine, Ivan, Aaron, and Eli, and they were primarily the ones I began to hang out with.

At school, Blaine, Eli, and Ivan sometimes joined me at lunch with Huero and Travieso. Dennis hung out with us at school but was careful not to get too involved with gangs.

The year was speeding by, and I began to adopt the hybrid look my friends all sported. I was wearing the typical Latin gang-banger uniform of brown, blue, or black Dickie or Ben-Davis pants, with a plain white t-shirt and Cortez Nike's (Cortez Nike's where running shoes, co-opted by gang members, and referred to as "gangster Nike's)

I was slowly, without conscious intent, changing and adapting to my unfamiliar environment. Little did I know that the people I befriended at school and how I began to dress would cause an incident that would change my life forever.

Our apartment was on the Southwest corner of Tropicana and Pecos, which is considered centrally located but borders the East side of Las Vegas.

Las Vegas is divided by the Las Vegas Strip (where all the main casinos are located and the city's tourism location). The strip serves as an unofficial central border for Las Vegas.

I did not know it at the time, but the general area we lived in was controlled by 18th Street, a Latino gang that originated out of Los Angeles. They had established a strong presence in Las Vegas. They controlled the area around the University of Nevada Las Vegas and the area east of it. 18th Street's territory expanded as far east as Boulder Highway and south to Sunset Road, bordering the suburb of Henderson.

The primary location was in low-rent apartments in front of the Boulevard Mall on Maryland Parkway. The apartments and the area in general were considered the worst neighborhoods in Las Vegas and received the street classification of "Crack Alley."

I quickly learned that 28th St., and 18th St., hated each other. 28th Street originated from Las Vegas locals and is rooted in the projects on 28th Street and Bonanza. 18th Street, on the other hand, was one of a handful of transplants from California who had moved in to expand their control of the drug trade. 28th Street and 18th Street became mortal enemies.

CHAPTER 8

Since becoming friends with Huero and Travieso at school, unbeknownst to me, I was being associated by other gang members, as belonging to 28th Street.

"Guilty by association."

I can recall hearing my parents and teachers utter the exact same phrase before. It was used as a warning and learning moment, which none of us heeded. But they were right. You became the people you spent time with.

In my mind, I was spending time together with kids who spoke Spanish and made me feel more at home.

I learned a hard lesson about the repercussions of my associations.

My friends started to drive or knew someone who drove while I continued to take the bus. My parents did not approve of or allow me to drive with teenagers, so the bus was my main source of transportation to and from school.

As I walked off the bus one afternoon, my backpack slung over my shoulder, landing on the familiar sidewalk near Doris French Elementary School, I could not have predicted what was about to happen next.

I began walking east on Hacienda Avenue, towards Pecos Road. As I neared the corner, I was surprised and a bit alarmed when I saw five kids dressed in the now familiar "cholo" outfit preferred by Hispanic gang members (Dickie pants, with white t-shirts, and gangster Nike's) rounding the corner on Pecos Road, and walking west on Hacienda Avenue, towards me.

As they walked around the corner, I noticed one of them holding a bat—one of the short wood ones you can win at state fairs, not a full-size one. The small bat had become synonymous with gang culture. It was easy to conceal and a great blunt object weapon to have handy.

I recognized one of the kids from school; they called him Nacho. Nacho was a member of 18th Street and had recently fought Huero at school; Huero had beaten the much larger Nacho in the fight. I knew Nacho claimed 18th Street, and for a split second, a naive part of me believed it was only a strange coincidence we were meeting on the street like this.

As we closed the distance, I heard Nacho say, "That's him esse, the huero that hangs out with the Twinkies." (Twinkies being a put-down, or disrespect, for anyone claiming 28th street).

Immediately, on instinct, I thought of turning around and running away, but Hacienda Avenue was long and oddly deserted. Just my luck, where was an adult when I needed one?

I thought of crossing the street to avoid them, but the reality of the situation hit me in a depressing and alarming manner. Fear froze me. My legs felt heavy, and the blood in my body dropped to my feet. I was so scared that I could not run. My only choice was to stand in place.

I was not a gang member; I had no problems or "beef" with any of the kids approaching me. A thought flashed into my mind, thinking I could talk my way out of what was about to happen.

I came to a stop just feet from them, and they stopped too. No words were exchanged; we just stared at each other awkwardly.

They began to slowly step towards me. I tried to reason with them, saying, "I don't have any problems with you guys. I don't want to fight."

I began to back up, walking backward up a small dirt embankment next to the sidewalk. The embankment ran alongside the perimeter wall of my apartment complex and had trees planted every few feet. I backed up all the way to the wall, purposely doing it, so they could not get behind me. This was instinctual.

The kid with the bat was "Pitufo" (Smurf). I learned his name at that moment because he seemed to be the leader and the others addressed him repeatedly, as Pitufo.

Pitufo stared at me menacingly. He had short hair and a grown man's mustache. He was thin and clearly confident. He was light-colored, almost white, but I recognized a thick Latin accent as he asked me gruffly, "Where are you from, Puto?"

I told him I did not gangbang, and that I was not a gang member. He asked me, "Don't you hang out with the Twinkies at school?"

Before I could respond, Nacho, who had maneuvered to my left side, punched me hard in the jaw, and I went down, barely clinging to consciousness. Nacho was a big and strong kid; I felt every bit of his power. I continued to get punched and kicked against the wall, thankfully backing up to the small dirt embankment turned out to be surprisingly beneficial. They kept losing their balance as they attacked me, sliding and slipping on the dirt hill.

Through the flurry of fists and shoes, I caught glimpses of Pitufo raising his bat and striking me. The strikes were surprisingly soft-handed; he was directing his strikes at my legs and mid-section. I found it oddly encouraging he was not trying to kill me.

I curled up and tried to fend off the blows with my arms and legs. At one point, I brought my knees up to protect my midsection, and this is when one of Pitufo's strikes hit my right knee forcefully; I screamed out in pain—the moment, forcing a similarly violent and repressed memory to involuntarily surface. Causing a brief but vivid re-engagement with trauma, I actively repressed.

CHAPTER 9

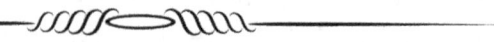

Quito, Ecuador - 14 years old

It was late, and I was the only one awake. I was not doing well academically, and a big test loomed the following day. I was sitting at our living room table, trying to study and memorize. I was under pressure to do well in school. My dad was one of the best and most beloved teachers at Cotopaxi. He was an extremely smart and hardworking individual, so similar characteristics were expected from me.

My friends excelled in school, were amazing students, and ranked at the top of the class. I, on the other hand, struggled. English continued to be a problem for me, and I wanted to stop disappointing people, especially my dad. I was feeling pressure to perform well on the test. I wanted to give my parents something to be proud of.

The living room window looked directly into our driveway, and I heard my dad's car pull up. I saw the lights of his car shine into the room, casting long shadows through our sheer white window curtains. His car door opened, and I heard him stumble out of the car; I could tell from the grunts and noises, he was in bad shape.

I caught a glimpse of my dad, barely able to hold himself up, using the wall for support. He drunk walked along the path to our front door. I should have woken up my mom, but I sat frozen in place, hoping he would go straight to bed when he walked into the house.

He entered our apartment like a bull in a China shop, unable to walk steadily; he stumbled over one of my mom's potted plants, one in a set of two, in our foyer. The contact with the plant caused it to drop to the floor with a loud crash. I heard my dad talk to himself, shushing himself for breaking the pot. He bumped loudly into every wall and continued talking to himself. How my mom did not wake up from his grand entrance remains a mystery.

I sat quietly with my back turned to him, staring at the white wall in front of me, silently wishing for him to walk by, turn right, and go down the hallway to his room. I tried to make myself invisible, sitting in absolute silence and remaining completely still.

"Please just go to bed," "Please just go to bed," I repeated over and over to myself inside my head.

I heard my dad pause where a crossroads of sorts in our apartment created a four-way intersection. He could go straight into the kitchen, turn right, and walk down our long hallway lined with our rooms, go back the way he came from, or turn left and come into the living room and dining room area towards me.

The pause at the intersection felt like an eternity, and there was no sound at all. I remained frozen in place, and for a second, I thought he had fallen asleep standing up and leaning on something; it wouldn't be the first time.

Then, just as I was beginning to think I may have escaped a drunk interaction with him, I heard him call out loudly, "Johnny Boy!"

I turned my head and watched as he staggered towards me. "Hi, Dad," I replied unenthusiastically. He asked what I was doing, and when I told him I was studying, he pulled out one of the wooden chairs, sat next to me, and wanted to help.

He was in a good mood. He was happy, which was unusual when he was this drunk. He tried to read my notes, and as he leaned in close to me, the stench of sweat, cigarettes, and alcohol engulfed my senses. He had trouble keeping his balance while sitting and had to brace himself on me or the table to avoid falling over.

Suddenly, he lost interest in trying to help me study and decided it was a suitable time to talk about Vietnam instead.

He started to talk about Huey City, a battle that cost him friends, and where he suffered his combat-related injuries. He began to tell me in detail how the battle began with an ambush.

The Vietcong was waiting for the Marines to arrive in Huey. While they were crossing the bridge into the city, the Vietcong blew up the backside of the bridge, preventing any retreat. They then dropped a large cloth banner from nearby buildings, which read, "Welcome, First and Fifth Marines."

The Marines, stuck in a choke point, were mercilessly attacked and overwhelmed with mortars and machine-gun fire.

With no cover or concealment on the bridge, my dad lay prone on the street next to one of the sidewalks, trying to use the sidewalk as cover, with rounds flying just above his head. He explained how the enemy funneled them into the bridge, creating a deadly and effective ambush location.

He talked about running out of ammunition for his rifle, just trying to prevent their position from collapsing. His squad was able to use one of their remaining tanks as cover and fought themselves off the side of the bridge into an embankment. They ran into a nearby rice field, which offered concealment.

My dad re-lived, how already injured on his back due to shrapnel from an enemy-thrown grenade; the Vietcong started to hunt them in the rice fields and into the jungle bordering the fields. He described intense, violent firefights as they moved from one position to the next, trying to retreat and seeking an exfiltration point.

While his platoon hunkered down behind a large, downed tree in the jungle, he recalled running out of ammo again (he had resupplied by grabbing ammo from dead Marines). The enemy kept moving in on their positions with relentless and violent motivation. He described how out of desperation, he took out his pop-flare and fired the flare into the face of a man (or "gook," as he called him) who was rushing him with a bayonet-mounted rifle.

The fighting at close quarters caused the flare to hit the man's face forcefully, knocking him down to the ground and causing the ignited flare, which had landed on top of him, to instantly catch his clothing on fire, burning the man alive.

He described this vividly, and I became enthralled by the story. I could only stare in a mixture of awe and terror. I was trying to picture my dad under such awful conditions. I could not.

He spoke briefly about how he tried sprinting away to a new position, but during the attempt, was shot in the left calf, causing him to fall to the ground unable to put any pressure on his leg. He remained in the open, forcing members of his platoon to move out of cover to help him back into relative safety. Shot with a 7.62-millimeter round from an AK-47, his left calf was destroyed and caused a near-fatal injury.

It was impossible for me to reconcile my dad to the person he was describing, suffering through such overwhelmingly horrible circumstances. My brain wouldn't allow it.

I felt a strong sensation my dad survived due to a sheer, uncontrolled savagery, a will to live.

He was a hero.

I continued to paint a mental picture of my dad as he was reliving his hell. I emerged from my thoughts with a profound and intricate respect and admiration for him.

As my dad continued to reflect, he kept pausing for short periods. The pauses were deliberate and intense, and I felt he was remembering things he did not want to verbalize.

His muscles visibly tensed, his jaw tightened, tears welled in his eyes, and he bawled his hands into tight fists. The air was pulsating in barely contained violent energy.

He was no longer talking to me about his experience in Vietnam. He was now alone in his head, quietly and intensely re-living something.

I watched him; that was all I could do. He was withdrawing. His breathing came in short, intense bursts of air, and tears were now freely falling down his cheeks.

He stared straight ahead at the same wall I had moments ago been staring at myself. Snot was now pooling around his nose, and he was becoming increasingly menacing with every breath.

He started to mumble incoherently, and I sat, watching him, terrified and unable to turn away or move. Not knowing what to do and being too afraid to do anything.

In a sudden burst of intense energy, he slammed his clenched fists on the wooden table with tremendous force and stood up abruptly. The chair he was sitting on slid backward across the floor, turned over from the force, and hit the back of the couch. He grabbed the table with both of his hands from its underside and flipped it over on its side, sending all my notes, books, and backpack flying.

I jumped out of my chair, and backed up by a potted plant in the corner near the window; the plant was tall enough to offer me concealment, and I stood behind it, too afraid to make a sound. I had never seen my dad in such a devolved state before, and I could tell he was experiencing a form of mental breakdown.

I finally heard my mom's footsteps running down the hallway as she yelled, "John?"

Then my dad turned towards me.

He stared at me, or through me would be more accurate. He was not seeing me; this was clear in the manner his eyes focused on me. There was unabated fury and fear in his eyes. His mouth curled in a menacing snarl, baring his teeth and making him look like a predator cornering his prey.

He took a step towards me and grabbed me by my left arm violently, pulling me from behind the plant and tossing me on the floor with a thud. He turned and faced me as I landed, his look feral and his body tense. He took a short step toward me and, without hesitation or thought, began to punch me. I curled up in the fetal position, with my knees tucked under me and facing the floor, covering my head and face with my arms, my forearms resting on the ground and bearing my weight. Getting into this position was instinctual, and my brain understood that this position would minimize damage.

My mom had made it to the living room and was screaming and crying, asking my dad to stop. Her long white pajama dress flowed in the periphery of my consciousness as she desperately tried to make him stop.

My dad was in an uncontrollable rage, and as she attempted to restrain him physically, he easily pushed her away. I remained on the ground, just waiting for it to stop. Then, without any queues or warning signs, it stopped.

I could sense, smell, and hear my dad standing over me, breathing heavily from the exertion. I could feel his gaze on me. My mom, now uncontrollably crying and under extreme stress and anxiety, continued pleading and whimpering, begging him to stop.

Was it over? I was too afraid to sneak a peek, but I knew I needed to. I cautiously unraveled myself from my protective shell, getting off my forearms and placing my hands directly on the floor. I lifted my head while staying on my knees and cautiously looked behind me.

I could only catch a quick frame before I went into complete darkness. My dad stood over me, his legs parted and my body in between his legs. He held the chair he had pushed back into the couch in his hands. He held the chair chest height, by two of its legs. The quick frame my brain registered, saw him in motion, bringing the wooden chair downward; the impact caused me to lose consciousness. My last memory of the incident was of my mom trying to protect me and clinging to one of his arms.

When I regained consciousness, I was upstairs in our landlord's apartment. Our landlord was a general family doctor, "Dr. Pita," and he and his family lived directly above us.

Dr. Pita was tending to my wounds, and I immediately noted intense pain when I took in a breath. Every breath was an exercise in pain management. My mom was sitting on the edge of the bed watching me carefully. I lay with my eyes closed, still aware, and heard my mom and the doctor talking.

My mom explained what had happened to the doctor. My dad brought the chair crashing down on the right side of my back, causing one of the legs on the chair to break—the impact caused deep bruising on my ribs. The doctor wrapped my injured torso with a bandage. He gave us a prescription for pain medication and told me I could not attend school for at least two weeks.

I was to stay in bed, immobile.

My dad's steady and sad descent into the depths of his trauma precipitously dropped and became increasingly more volatile. Violence began to manifest during intense alcohol-fueled memories of Vietnam.

Unfortunately, or maybe fortunately, when considering my siblings, the violence was directed solely at me.

His drinking, now intertwined with violence, placed a terrifying and paralyzing fear in my life. Violence inserted such an unexpected and unpredictable element in his behavior; when those moments arrived, it caused me significant anxiety and panic.

This violent episode holds a special recollection of my dad for me. Not because of my physical injuries, nor due to any psychological trauma I may have suffered.

It was one of the few moments my dad allowed the raw emotional pain he held in his mind and in his heart to break free. It was a moment in which he allowed his internal suffering to rage out of him. If it had to happen, I was relieved it was with me. Imagine if it had been my mom. Or my sister? Or even my little brother?

No. It could only be me, and in a very weird and unhealthy way, I will always remain relieved it was.

It is hard to express why I never felt anger and resentment, but somehow, I always understood my dad's complex emotional guilt and shame. His trauma touched my heart deeply.

I was picturing my dad's handsome but troubled face, his torment and his self-loathing, visible as he regretted his actions… but, as I was bringing the memory of his face into focus, my present arrived abruptly. As if suddenly coming out of a sort of emotional coma. I returned to the very real pain in my knee and the beating I continued to get from 18th Street.

Chapter 10

Las Vegas, Nevada - 16 years old

The last thing I remembered before mentally shutting down was Pitufo striking me with the bat on my right knee. The pain from the injury cleared my head. Fists and feet continued to rain down on me, but apart from my knee, I was numb to any of the incoming strikes. The numbness, I imagine, came from the trauma I had just relived. Causing a strange transition, almost catatonic.

Thankfully, on the other side of the wall, my friend Raul had arrived home from school with his mom. Raul recently moved to Las Vegas from Portland, Oregon, where he had been a gang member and claimed "blood," but he loved to smoke marijuana (which he called Motta) and was more of a stoner than a gangster.

As he and his mom exited their vehicle, they heard the commotion on the other side of the wall. Raul, curious, decided to check. He jumped on top of the wall and looked down. He saw the beating I was enduring and yelled, "Hey, Stop!" just to try and scare them off, and thankfully, it worked. Raul popping up over the wall was enough for them to stop. They took off running.

I tried to stand but could not. My right knee hurt in a way I never felt before. I could not move. Any movement, caused me extreme pain. I could feel blood dripping from my nose and my mouth, and I felt my lips beginning to swell.

I could see blood dripping on my shirt and pooling on the ground. I felt dizzy and nauseous. Raul jumped down to check on me and said he would call my parents. I was in pain and too scared to face my parents. I needed time to think of a plausible story. I asked him not to call my parents; instead, he called our friends Hasson and Mark for help. He jumped back over the wall, and thirty minutes later, Raul, Mark, and Hasson arrived with a grocery store cart. It was our version of an improvised wheelchair.

Between the three of them, they got me inside the cart. They pushed me all the way home and left me at my front door. We had concocted a tale, which claimed we were messing around with the shopping cart, pushing each other at high speeds, when during one of these playful episodes, while I was in the cart... It lost control, and I crashed against a brick wall, striking my knee and my face and causing all my injuries. It was a dumb lie, but we produced it on the fly. Raul, Hasson, and Mark were too afraid of my dad to stick around, so they wished me luck, rang the bell, and took off running.

My dad opened the door; his expression softened momentarily, and a look of worry crossed his face, but just as quickly, the Marine in him surfaced, and his face hardened. I wondered how seeing me beat up and hurt made him feel. Did he also experience playbacks of our shared trauma? Did he just keep it all locked away?

I attempted to have a conversation with him about it once, years later, when I was in Bosnia. He apologized, which I know was sincere, but he quickly changed the subject. He was never able to confront those demons and talk about them fully. For him, it was easier to pretend they never happened.

Once he saw I would live, he demanded to know what had happened to me and who had done it. I stammered through the fabricated story, but he was not buying it. I had little doubt he would have hurt every single one of those kids.

My parents were understandably in a bit of shock. I can only imagine the imagery of seeing your son a bloody mess inside a shopping cart at your front door. My poor parents, neither of them understood the gravity of what was happening. Neither did I.

We were completely ignorant of gangs and the path I was taking. Our collective naïveté, a problem which would prove damaging to our entire family.

At the hospital, the emergency room physician diagnosed me with multiple cuts, a concussion, multiple deep bruises, and a fractured right kneecap. The doctor, during his examination of my wound, pulled out a small shard of wood out of the cut in my knee, and my lie crumbled. A long, hard cast was placed on my leg, and I was told I would have to wear the cast for six months.

CHAPTER 11

Six Months Later

The air escaping from my lungs visible with each exhale. My heavy Raiders jacket cloaking my body and the uncontrollable shivering underneath it. Even under the usual cold Las Vegas winter conditions, I was sweating. I could feel my tail or a lone wisp of long hair, which remained on the back of my head, swaying in the wind. It had grown long, and I could feel it in the small of my back between my shoulder blades. I started to question if my shivering was more from fear than due to the frigid air around me. More than once, I asked myself quietly, "What are you doing?"

It felt wrong. This was not me.

Moments earlier, a group of us had walked to Doris French Elementary School. It was midnight, the agreed-upon meeting time. Five of us had walked from Chips' house, where we had all stayed the night.

Blaine, Griffin, Scooby (who had recently transferred in from Las Vegas High School), Huero, and I walked in silence to the school, jumped the fence into the playground area, and waited near a bench. The bench sat at the edge of the basketball courts bordering a large open grass field kids played on during school hours.

I imagined kids laughing, running, playing… the thought, a fleeting and momentary escape from the present. My good friend Blaine stood next to me. Blaine and I had become close, a friendship borne out of our genetic similarities and shared interests. We both had white fathers and Hispanic mothers. We identified strongest with our Hispanic ancestry and ethnicity. Unfortunately, we did not look Latino at all. Our complexion usually caused questions about our legitimacy. At least Blaine had his mom's dark, thick

Mexican hair and looked more Hispanic than I ever could. I looked like a white boy.

Griffin stood slightly behind us. He was the smallest of the group—thin, awkward, and short—shorter than Blaine and me, and trust me, we are not tall. Griffin would often behave in a macho manner when around Huero and Scooby, but it was an act. I recognized myself in Griffin often, not in his machismo but in his insecurities. I could see the fear in Griffin; his shivering, at least to me, appeared to be from fright.

Griffin looked terrified, the fear etched on his face. His eyes darted suspiciously around or looked down at the ground, unable to make eye contact with anyone. His expression was sullen, and he appeared deep in thought. His skin was pale, and his posture defeated. His shoulders slumped, arms hanging almost lifeless at his side, and his body was sagging, held in place only by his small skeletal frame.

Watching Griffin made me wonder how I was projecting myself to others. I instantly straightened my posture, not wanting to show how I truly felt. I had a bad habit of overanalyzing my actions in real-time. Sometimes, I distracted myself from conversations or activities, and I was unable to follow because my mind wandered.

"Why? Why did I have a need to suppress what I was feeling and create an image in the opposite? Why did I fight the urge screaming inside of me to flee?"

The thought came and went, quickly overwhelmed by my mounting fear of what was about to happen.

The battle raged within me, becoming harder to control—panic at the edges of my consciousness. The fear overwhelmed all my senses, coming in large powerful waves, creating an ebb and flow intense emotions. I wanted to run! To run home to the warmth of our small apartment. To my mom's welcoming hug and kiss. To my dad's stern look, which would often soften as he realized I was ok. I wanted to flee and arrive to hear my little brother Kevin playing and my sister Denise practicing her singing. The urge to run away was becoming unbearable. To run home and be safe.

I did not run, but I should have.

I fought the urge with every molecule inhabiting my body; at times, I felt I would falter and succumb to the screaming in my brain. My knees buckled slightly, and I felt faint. Again, I looked over at Griffin and hoped I did not look as scared as he did. I found solidarity in his fear. I did not feel alone.

Huero ("white" in Chicano slang) was the de facto leader of our small group. Huero had a shaved head; he was wearing khaki "Dickie" shorts with white socks pulled all the way up to his knees. He had an LA Kings beanie and jacket on. He was considered the toughest in our small group. His cousin, Oso (Bear), was well-known and feared on the streets. His family were gang members and most affiliated with 28th Street; it was an expected rite of passage. Huero carried himself with a unique confidence and swagger, a trait that commanded attention and respect.

Scooby was what most Americans would call a "typical Mexican." What racists would ignorantly call a "wet back." Dark skin, strong Mexican Aztec facial bone structures, and dark, long, thick hair. Most girls considered him handsome. Scooby also had a noticeable thick Spanish accent and a deep baritone to his voice. He met all the usual stereotypes.

Scooby was not raised in gang life the way Huero had been, and his lack of familial connection gave him less street credibility. Scooby deferred to Huero, but Scooby was wiser and measured in his responses and decisions. Huero, on the other hand, was dangerously impulsive.

While we waited for the others to arrive, blowing warm air into our cold hands and trying to stay warm, I considered my life.

Dots of specific circumstances woven into a pliable universe and connected in a series of events, leading me to this very moment. To a choice that would alter my life in a manner I could not have forethought or imagined. For a while, changing who I thought I was.

I began to mentally check out, something I do often. I reflected on how my life swung in a pendulum of uncontrollable and unforeseen circumstances, swinging on uninformed and naive perceptions and decisions of the world around me.

From a geographical and emotional perspective, I created a life I did not want or expect. I did not ask for any of this. Unexpected challenges were thrust into my path during a precarious developmental stage of my life. The shift would undo me to my core, changing me in ways that prevented me from returning to who I was forever.

CHAPTER 12

As I stood in the frosty winter night, lost in my thoughts, my reflection was cut short as lights from a car panned in our direction, momentarily highlighting us and waking me back into the present.

The amber from the streetlights cast long, ominous shadows, adding to the moment's darkness. I continued to argue with myself, "Why are you doing this? "Why don't you simply walk away? "Why?"

The answer was complicated, with layers upon layers of complexities, but for context, only one reason really mattered at the moment. Protection.

At least, that is what I convinced myself of. It is how I justified going through with it. If I wanted 28th Street to protect me at school and on the streets, I concluded I had to get "jumped in."

Huero, Scooby, and Travieso pressured this decision. The beating I endured by Pitufo and his crew had me scared and constantly looking over my shoulder. I was terrified of finding myself alone at school or somewhere on the street. I no longer took the bus. My parents were taking me and picking me up from school; the incident terrified them and caused them to be extra watchful over anything I was doing. I bummed rides with friends when I could, but fear of avoiding another attack was magnified every single day, simply by seeing members of 18th Street.

Huero, Scooby, and Travieso manipulated my fear and the potential of continued violence, steering me into joining their gang. With their protection, I would be untouchable, or so they claimed. Blaine and Griffin were with me for similar reasons; we were all there to officially get jumped into 28th Street. To become actual gang members. We all agreed to do it together. Finally, the day arrived, and I was sure we were all regretting it.

While waiting for others to arrive, I retreated into my memory bank once again. Going back to a part of my life, when being able to skateboard was my biggest concern.

Skateboarding consumed a part of my childhood in Ecuador. I was good and enthusiastic about it; I was skilled enough to win the city championship in Quito. It was a big moment for me: I was interviewed live on television by a popular children's show host called "La Tia" (The Aunt) on channel 4, Telejardin, a popular kid show.

These memories made me feel like an impostor. Like it all happened in another life, to another person.

I stopped dressing like a skater and metamorphosed into looking and acting like my new friends. Gang members, drug users, and dealers; how did I arrive at this moment?

My life in Ecuador was so simple compared to these violent complexities. Why did I have to get beat-up for twenty-eight seconds to prove my worth to the gang? To gain acceptance? Violence in and violence out.

They called it "Blood in; Blood out."

Huero and Scooby stood behind the bench on the opposite side of us. We were all waiting for Joker, Sleepy, and Sapo (Frog) to arrive. Sleepy was older, in his early twenties, and recently released from a short stint in prison. We had not met him yet, but we had heard stories about his violent exploits. None of the stories bode well for our future well-being.

Moments ago, the car that had highlighted us with its beam pulled up and shut its lights off. Three individuals emerged and jumped the fence into the school. They walked towards us.

Huero and Scooby met them halfway, at the basketball courts, and circled up as they discussed something. All we could do was watch nervously. We were too scared to say anything. Their meeting broke up, and they approached the bench. Scooby spoke to me in Spanish. I do not even remember what he said, but it was to validate I was Hispanic. I do not look like one, so there were questions. Once a nod from Sleepy confirmed I passed the test, Sapo looked at all three of us and asked, "Who is going first?"

I had been anticipating the question. It was a question I had been struggling with mentally since deciding to join. Now, the moment had arrived, causing waves of fight-or-flight with increasing intensity. I knew myself, and if I had to witness Blaine or Griffin beat-up first, fear would probably cause me to run away. If I did not go first, the emotional turmoil raging inside of me would crumble. I would end up running like a coward.

It was not something I was prepared to do. I had to go first. I knew with every fiber in my body that if I did not go first, I would run.

So, when Sapo calmly asked, "Who is going first?"

I instantly blurted out, "Me!"

"Me!" shot out of my mouth prematurely, like a scene from American Pie. I suspected Blaine, at minimum, was planning the same tactic, and Griffin, too. I thought myself clever for anticipating the question and being able to beat them both to the answer.

In retrospect, I was wrong. I would realize that when I thought I was being clever, I was operating on an illusion, created in panic as a way of self-preservation. But it backfired.

Patience was the virtue I should have sought.

As soon as "me" spewed out of my big dumb mouth, Scooby, Huero, Sapo, Sleepy, and Joker took off their winter jackets in unison. Instantly, making them look like gladiators. They all wore wife beaters (cheap tank tops) under their jackets. It was an intimidating sight. The amber light from the moon and the glow of the streetlights glistened off their shaved heads and ripped muscles.

"Gulp," I swallowed my spit with tremendous difficulty.

Blaine and Griffin quietly receded into the darkness, backing away and standing by the school wall, watching.

Scooby and Huero moved on my right flank. Sleepy and Sapo moved on my left flank. Joker remained in front of me and a couple of steps behind the bench. We were now on the grass field, and like a snake, they slowly tightened the circle around me, constricting any exit. I thought of taking my jacket off, too, but realized it was too late; if I tried now, they would use the moment to attack, leaving me completely vulnerable and unable to defend myself.

The energy was tense and palpable; I could see everyone's breath as it escaped their lungs into the frigid air. I sensed and could see the faster intake and outtake of everyone's rapid breathing, causing tiny wisps of white air visible all around me and steadily speeding up in anticipation, like a pack of wolves closing in for a kill.

They remained just out of striking distance, and I kept turning in place to ward off attacks. Suddenly, Huero lunged at me with a looping right-hand punch; I saw it coming and stepped back and out of the way. He missed.

I reacted and turned to face him, thinking I could at least get one good punch in before they overwhelmed me. This proved to be a costly mistake. Joker was waiting for me to commit, and as soon as I did, he took a running start and launched himself off the bench, up into the air, and landed a devastating right-hand punch. The punch landed with great force and precision on my left temple.

I remember feeling the blow to the side of my head and feeling intense pain for what seemed like less than a fraction of a second. Then I remember sensing an intensely bright and white flash in my brain, as if lightning had just struck me, then darkness.

I woke up a couple of seconds later, like two or three, and found myself lying face-first on the grass, getting pummeled with fists and kicks. Mental flashes of shoes and fists, an endless loop over and over in my field of vision. They struck me in the face and head repeatedly. I tried to stand a couple of times, but a swift kick to my face from Sleepy ended the idea permanently.

Getting "jumped in" to 28th Street is supposed to last twenty-eight seconds, representing the value of the street. Everyone later agreed: My twenty-eight seconds lasted close to two minutes!

All I could do was cover my head and my face with my hands and arms and roll up in a fetal position on the grass. My brain flashed white in pain from every strike, like a high-powered flashlight shining right into my eyes with every connection.

Horrible does not begin to describe the experience. It felt like it would never end.

Blaine later told me Sleepy was holding onto Joker's and Huero's shoulders and using them as leverage to launch himself in the air and land on my head, stomping me with his foot as he landed.

It finally stopped, but only because they got tired.

I was not feeling so clever anymore.

I remember lying on the grass, not sure if the nightmare ended. I could not believe it was over. I heard them all breathing hard from the exertion, congratulating themselves and high off the adrenaline. My eyes closed, but the now familiar feeling of nausea and dizziness began to manifest.

Not feeling clever.

I opened my eyes and found myself lying on my side. I could see the darkened end of the grass field, where no streetlights delivered their reassuring glow. For the first time in my life, the darkness was comforting. Looking at it sideways, I began reflecting on my life in Ecuador again. I turned on my back and stared up into the dark sky; I could feel the blood running down the sides of my face. I did not care. I did not feel any pain.

I thought of Fiona, Steve, Paulina, and Dror, my lifelong friends from Ecuador. What would they think of me? I looked up, stared into the universe's vast emptiness, and started to feel sorry for myself. A part of me understood; I had just made a terrible mistake. As I began to consider the implications of what just happened, legs and bodies appeared in my field of vision. I looked up to see everyone looking down at me, grinning.

Huero and Scooby offered their hands and helped me to my feet. They smiled broadly, and each hugged me, "Welcome to the barrio esse!" Sleepy, Sapo, and Joker all approached me and did the same. They congratulated me and showed me camaraderie. Oddly, it felt good to find acceptance from these tough, young men. I looked over to where Blaine and Griffin had been standing and noticed only Blaine remained. Griffin ran away after witnessing the mauling I endured. I did not blame him. I think I would have done the same thing. I respected and admired Blaine for fighting the fear I knew he felt. He stayed, and he was next.

Everyone surrounded me, assessing my multiple injuries, joking good-naturedly, and reliving the details of my "jumping in."

My left eye had apparently swelled to epic proportions, right where Joker landed his flying punch. Joker looked at his handy work closely and said, "I popped you good in the eye, esse!" He made a punching motion with his right fist and said, "Pop," as he slowly raised it to my injured eye, and then said, "Eye." Pop-eye!

Thus, my 28th Street gang moniker was born.

Popeye.

Months later, I got it tattooed on my back, with "Sur 13" on my left hand and "28 St.," on my right hand. There was no turning back.

Chapter 13

The initiation into 28th Street was equally horrifying and fascinating. My social status changed overnight. When I returned to school, it was like walking in as a different person. Everyone knew I was now "Popeye from 28th Street," not Jonathan or Jonny, but Popeye.

The pummeling I took to gain this new-found respect was whispered and talked about around the school. I was no longer ignored or looked at as indifferent. Kids feared me; jocks who never spoke a word to me now showed me respect. I received head nods as I walked down the hallways from stoners, athletes, and other gang members. Girls who never paid attention to me now looked at me with curiosity and interest. I loved the feeling. It intoxicated me. I went from being a no-one to being someone overnight.

It reminded me of one of my favorite movies growing up, "Can't Buy Me Love." I identified with elements from the movie.

Unfortunately, the attention was not always positive. Naturally, rival gangs now knew I was fully affiliated. San Chucos, Little Locos, and 18th Street showed the most interested in my new identity. For all the respectful nods and smiles from girls I received, I also received stern and intense stares from rival gang members. Tension was palpable anytime we crossed paths.

Kids, and by now school staff, were waiting for the proverbial shoe to fall. The violence in Green Valley HS had reached unreasonable levels. Lunchtime became an exercise in intentional avoidance. Otherwise, it could have become a version of the Roman Colosseum. Teachers, administrators, and School Police were always present and visible during lunch hours.

Multiple fights had already taken place. Including Huero's and Nacho's, the fight had been the precursor and the unintended consequence of what created the chain reaction to my journey as a gang member.

Crip and Blood fights had also occurred. Green Valley High School was quietly expelling kids involved in gang-related activities and fights. The administration was trying to quell the barely contained flame, which could result in a spreading and uncontrollable fire at any moment.

At least two fights were happening at school per day. Most fights happened at lunchtime, in the hallways, classrooms, bathrooms, parking lot, and on buses. The administration at Green Valley High School thought opening the campus for lunch would ease the tension created by having all the kids on campus during lunch. So, with great fanfare, we were now allowed to leave campus for lunch.

Since becoming affiliated, my circle of friends expanded. Multiple resources were provided for rides, and on the first day of off-campus lunch, a large group of us went to Rally's Hamburgers on Sunset Road.

As we sat down to eat our food, two carloads of San Chucos pulled up. Their leader was Marcelino, a heavy-set kid with big hands who looked like he was in his twenties. He drove an old-school 1965 Ford truck retrofitted into a lowrider. He was with his best friend Randy, a big Black kid who was affiliated with San Chucos. Randy was all muscle and cast an intimidating presence.

Behind them was the always popular "Green-eyes." Green-eyes was a known flirt, and popular would not be the right word to describe his relationship with girls at school. He had an athletic build, light brown skin, and bright, piercing green eyes. Girls thought him "beautiful."

With them walked in all the pretty cholas from San Chucos, Jennifer, Rokana, Christina, and Belinda. The men all dressed in the common gangster uniform of Dickie pants with a white t-shirt or wife beater and an open flannel buttoned only at the top. Everyone wore Cortez Nikes, known as "Gangster Nike's." Cholas wore heavy makeup and looked as intimidating as the men.

One of the San Chucos cholas, Belinda, had locked eyes with me a few times in the hallways. She was beautiful, with a great ass and an athletic body. I was not a fan of heavy makeup, but even the heavy makeup she wore, could not hide Belinda's natural beauty.

As they entered the outdoor sitting area at Rally's, Belinda and I looked at each other, and both shyly smiled.

The San Chucos sat with their food as we were finishing ours, and every student at Rally's grew quiet, expecting something to happen between our groups. They were not disappointed.

We were rolling deep; Huero, Scooby, Blaine, who now went by (Speedy), Eli, Ivan, Aaron, Patrick, and me. As we gathered our things and walked away, someone from the San Chucos crew threw a Twinkie our way.

Twinkies, the cream-filled pastries, were known as the most common way to disrespect anyone from 28th Street. The Twinkie, still in its plastic wrapper, landed right in front of Huero. He slowly bent down and picked it up. The San Chucos all laughed.

Huero, who was the last to get up and was bringing up the rear of our group, now found himself at the helm. As soon as he turned, he was immediately engaged in a fight with Randy.

Huero, with the Twinkie still in his hand, turned and faced Randy. The first thing Huero did, and with lightning-fast speed, was to smash the Hostess product on Randy's face.

Randy was much bigger and instantly grabbed Huero. Randy started throwing Huero around the outdoor sitting area of Rally's. Other kids started to run away in fear. Adults and the Rally's staff attempted to break up the fight, but our groups had tightened a circle around the combatants, and no one was getting in. Huero and Randy wrestled out into the drive-thru lane.

Here, in a more accessible area, Huero was able to use his speed and land a combination of punches on Randy. Randy was a monster but lacked speed. It was a good back-and-forth fight. Huero landed quick punches on Randy, the ratio about three to one, but the ones Randy landed had a more noticeable effect. Huero was wearing the damage visibly on his face. During the commotion, Green-eyes and

I locked into a wrestling match, but as soon as we began to turn into each other to fight, the police arrived.

CHAPTER 14

Everyone in the vicinity of Rally's took off running. Introducing the police into any teenage or gang-related situation tends to cause pandemonium.

We were bumming a ride with Patrick, a friend who associated with us. He was driving a Buick Regal and had parked the car in the Taco Bell car park just above Rally's. Henderson PD had blocked the exit out of Taco Bell, so Patrick backed up at high speed and hit the raised embankment separating Taco Bell from Rally's, launching his car in the air! His Regal landed hard on the back bumper, and everyone got whiplashed and banged up. To his credit, Patrick took it all in stride and maneuvered the car past a slew of running kids and other cars trying to flee the area. He got on Sunset Road, with half his bumper hanging off his car, and took off! We did not return to school; we headed to Hasson's house instead.

When we arrived, we were still high off the adrenaline and laughing about the whole thing. Hasson was already having a ditch party at his house, Natalie was there, and when we arrived, we told and retold the story feeling like heroes, celebrated by what had just occurred, somehow elevated in the eyes of our peers, Natalie in particular, found the story of our exploits impressive.

We drank 40oz of Old English Malt Liquor and smoked weed. We laughed, partied, and felt important. No one was sober, and the day quickly turned into late afternoon. Everyone started to leave to make it home, pretending they had attended school.

Hasson's apartment grew quiet. Most of the kids had left, but the ones who remained were either sleeping or making out. Natalie took advantage of the setting and grabbed me by the hand and took me upstairs. I did not resist. Once upstairs, in one of the bedrooms,

Natalie, in a move I did not anticipate, turned to me, and asked me out,

She just came out and said, "I want to be with you; do you want me?" I could only nod dumbfounded and mumbled a weak "Yes." As soon as the labels became established, we began to make out and dry hump, as only horny teenagers with little experience can do.

We spent the entire afternoon on Hasson's futon, exploring our new-found relationship and lack of boundaries. Natalie wanted to do more than explore and willingly expressed it, but I was still too afraid and intimidated. I was still a virgin, which was unheard of in my new circle of friends.

When we returned to school, someone snitched on Huero and Randy, who were both expelled. Tensions between San Chucos and 28th Street intensified, and the San Chucos sensed vulnerability and lack of leadership with Huero gone. They were not wrong. We were a bit lost without him. We lacked his intimidating presence and violent energy.

A few months had passed, and things with Natalie were slowing down. I was getting more involved in gang life, and she was more of a stoner/skater girl. She even attempted to have her mom recruit me into becoming a born- again Christian; their idea of trying to save my soul and guide me away from the destructive path I was on.

Natalie and her mom talked me into going to church with them, and like a dummy, I agreed. They both pressured me into getting baptized, but I politely declined. Natalie and I started to drift apart after the church incident, which Natalie's mom was not happy about. We remained together only out of convenience because we lived so close to one another.

Feeling the looming break-up coming, Natalie asked to come over one night. She wanted to talk. My parents were out, but my siblings were home. I met Natalie at our usual meeting spot, outside by the main gate into my apartment complex, and we walked back to my place holding hands. We beelined it into the bedroom;

completely ignoring my sister and my brother, as they watched Alf on the living room TV.

As soon as I closed the door to the room, Natalie locked it, turned towards me, and started to kiss me. She maneuvered me to the mattress I used as a bed and pushed me on it, following my descent and playfully falling on top of me. We kissed, and in that moment, I felt more for her than I thought I could. I became lost in the energy and emotions of the moment.

She undressed me, then she undressed herself. I was on my back, terrified and not knowing what to do. I had not even discovered masturbating yet! Do not judge me. I know it is pathetic, but religion terrified me. It's funny because I learned about masturbation after having sex. My whole sexual revelation was backward.

Natalie then slowly mounted me with obvious experience, and we started to have sex. She was rough and wild. Moaning loudly and moving aggressively on top of me, I knew my sister could hear us, but I did not care.

I was frozen in fear and shocked it was happening. I was having sex!

I was so out of my element and so inexperienced, I just watched as Natalie moved on top of me. Slowly, I allowed myself to relax and enjoy the moment. The first feeling of having actual sex is immortalized in my memory.

The soft moaning, the feeling of our naked bodies bonding, our sweat glistening and making our bodies shine from the ambient moonlight filtering in through the blinds. It was everything I expected and nothing like what I thought. It must have lasted five minutes, and that is being kind.

We finished, or I should say, I finished… and Natalie dressed and left. She had to get back home. I was still in the clouds as I walked into the living room, where Denise and Kevin were still watching Alf. My sister looked at me with a weird expression, trying to hide a smirk and failing. She asked me, "Why are you smiling so much?" She knew. I was no longer a virgin.

Chapter 15

Natalie and I remained together for a month after we had sex, and then she broke up with me. She knew I was too much of a coward to break up with her, just like I had been too afraid to ask her out. Natalie took matters into her own hands. I did not blame her; I had been ignoring her and paying more attention to other girls. So, with the confidence and courage I clearly lacked, she broke up with me.

I never saw her again.

Scooby and Travieso were also expelled for gang-related activity. Their departure left Blaine (Speedy) and me as the only 28th Street Raskals on campus. We had friends, but they were not gang members. Speedy and I stuck together more than ever.

Eli, who was one of our closest friends, and a human bear, became more involved with Blaine and I. Eli had the biggest hands I had ever seen—meaty, mitt-like hands that looked swollen. When he made a fist, his hands looked like sledgehammers. Coupled with his natural strength and surprising athletic ability, he was a problem for anyone.

Eli was Jewish, and loved hip-hop culture; so, him choosing to hang out with us created a welcomed buffer zone. We felt secure having Eli around. Most kids were afraid of him, and for good reason; I was afraid of him too.

Thankfully, we were friends. He was intimidating, but his physical appearance did not match his personality. Eli did like to fight, and he was good at it, but he did not search for altercations; he was usually the first voice of reason and a kind-hearted individual, but you did not want to be on the receiving end of one of his punches. I watched kids put to sleep behind those meaty hammers.

One afternoon, a bunch of us drove to Wendy's on Sunset Road and Marks Street for lunch. The campus remained open for students at lunch, and everyone continued to take advantage of the freedom. Eli drove with Speedy in the front and Ivan, Aaron, and me in the back. Chip, Dennis, Hasson, and other kids also went but drove in Chip's truck. We all went inside, ordered, and ate.

As we were walking out, belly full and talking... Marcelino, Green Eyes, Belinda, and a couple of the other San Chucos were walking into Wendy's. We were going to cross paths, and an altercation was unavoidable. We all knew it, and we could all feel it.

As Green-eyes and I approached each other, we stared at each other while intentionally slowing our walk. Since the near fight we had at Rally's, we both knew a confrontation was imminent. Our beef was going to play out at that moment.

As we walked by each other, we intentionally and violently bumped shoulders, causing us to take a step back to catch our balance. We turned towards each other and immediately began to fight.

Green-Eyes threw the first punch, which I was not expecting; I was expecting the usual shit-talking and posturing, which was common, but he was ahead of the game and connected solidly right on my nose.

The punch made my eyes water, and my vision became blurry from the tears. He followed up his first strike with more; I had to backpedal and try to dodge his strikes, simultaneously trying to blink the tears out of my eyes. Kids ran out of Wendy's to watch the skirmish, and a large crowd gathered.

We were on the pavement just outside the drive-thru lane and next to the parking area between the Chevron and the Wendy's. A large group of kids surrounded us as we battled each other. It was a good fight, we were both quick and athletic, and we were both landing on each other repeatedly. I could hear my friends yelling and encouraging me, and the same from the San Chucos for him.

We started the fight with a flurry of punches, and we both gassed out. With lactic acid building up, we locked up momentarily, tired from the adrenaline dump fighting creates. Our heads were on each other's shoulders, and we grabbed the backs of each other's necks and arms—a common wrestling starting point.

We were both breathing hard, and we were tired. While locked up in the wrestling embrace, I noticed the back of his t-shirt was halfway up his back. For an odd reason, this spurred a movie memory for me.

"Youngblood!"

"Youngblood," with Rob Lowe, was one of my favorite movies growing up, and I had watched it at least four times. It is a classic underdog story told through the experience of an ice hockey player. There is a buildup to the climax, where the underdog overcomes his foe. This is the part that sprung into my memory bank as I noticed Green Eyes' shirt pulled up.

In the movie, Rob Lowe, who plays Youngblood, can defeat his much larger enemy by pulling the back of his jersey over his head and trapping his arms inside the jersey. Once Youngblood had his enemies' elbows trapped, he was able to defeat him.

So, when I saw Green Eyes' shirt halfway up his back, I grabbed it and pulled the Youngblood move on him. To my total surprise, it worked!

I pulled his t-shirt over his head, and his arms locked in place in front of him. His elbows caught and unable to straighten them, his only option, to pull his shirt off.

As he struggled with trying to take his shirt off, I used the opportunity to create distance and unleash a torrent of combinations on his face and head, which dropped him. He was not getting up. The fight was over.

As we were celebrating and talking our shit, I looked back and caught Belinda staring at me. She smiled at me. I had just whooped her homie, but she chose to smile. I dug it. She did not care, and I smiled back. What we were doing was dangerous, and if we continued to flirt, we could find ourselves in trouble, but regardless, it was a precarious show of emotions. Belinda was unbelievably beautiful, and I could not help but smile.

We returned to school, and I felt a great high from the fight and the win. Word had already spread, and I was congratulated by people I did not know. Even Ivan's sister, Daisy, whom I idolized, came and hugged me. I felt like a rock star! But the feeling faded as soon as I went into the bathroom and looked in the mirror. You could not miss the two black eyes from the first punch Green-Eyes landed on my nose. I looked like a raccoon.

Since Huero, Scooby, and Travieso no longer attended Green Valley HS and lived so far away, we rarely saw them. None of us had cars, so we stayed within walking distance of our neighborhoods.

In the 1990s, gang culture became popular. Everyone wanted to be a gang member or associated with one. Gang culture was glorified and romanticized in Hollywood. Soon, across suburban America, you could find signs of the subculture. It did not matter if it was a small town, a big city, or poor and wealthy areas. You could find "wanna-be" gang members everywhere.

A movie, a cult classic, and a satirical comedy referencing this very thing, "Malibu's Most Wanted," captured generational behavior in a clever and ridiculous manner. But it was funny because elements of reality were displayed on the big screen in a mocking collaboration of jokes.

The anchors to our gang-related path were no longer at school, so Speedy and I had to adjust. Outnumbered, we decided the answer was to expand our ranks and recruit.

Speedy and I started to jump people into 28th Street at breakneck speed. Scott (Sad Eyes), Josh (a jock and football player, cannot even recall his moniker), and Raul (Motta), the kid who saved me from 18th Street.

Now, we had more numbers at school, and our association with Chip led to a strong partnership with the stoners. Speedy and I became leaders by default, and we entered a partnership with Chip.

We started to sell weed for him, and this created different relationships with separate groups.

Becoming a drug dealer was sadly not my first experience with intentional criminal activity, of purposely breaking the law and choosing to suffer the consequences later. I am not proud of this at all, but I broke into a school and burglarized it when I was about ten years old.

CHAPTER 16

Quito, Ecuador - 10 years old

Byung Ill Yoo was a friend I instantly connected with at Cotopaxi. He was South Korean, and we shared a love for the Japanese anime Mazinger. We both loved martial arts, specifically ninjas. We loved combat movies and often role-played as ninjas during recess.

One weekend, Byung talked me into a sleepover at his house. I say, "Talked me into," because I worked hard at avoiding sleepovers. I avoided them because I peed on the bed at night.

I had slept at my friend Patricio's house a couple of times, and every single time, I peed the bed. It was embarrassing and humiliating. Patricio and his family never even acknowledged it, and they did their best to make me feel comfortable, but I could not help but feel the shame and confusion that accompanied those moments.

Byung was an accomplished martial artist, even at a young age. He started training in Taekwondo at an early age and regularly practiced with his parents.

I had the unfortunate experience of being at the receiving end of Byung's Taekwondo skills. We were at our friend Anna's house, and we had created a homemade tetherball in the attached garage. I do not remember why it happened, but I did something to piss Byung off, and he unleashed a lightning-fast torrent of kicks at my mid-section. One of the kicks took my breath away, and ever since then, I was careful not to piss him off.

The movie American Ninja was released in theaters in 1985, and Byung and I idolized it. We played American Ninja at recess daily.

The night I stayed at Byung's house: he persuaded me to stay by telling me he wanted to sneak out of his apartment when his parents went to bed to play ninja outside on the street. Byung procured (I do not know how) a couple of Halloween-like ninja costumes, and the possibility of a fun adventure was simply too enticing to decline.

When my mom dropped me off, she quietly warned Byung's mom of my bed-wetting problems. It was so embarrassing.

The night was slow moving, like watching paint dry. We waited impatiently for Byung's parents to go to sleep, and of course, they wanted to stay up and interact with us all freaking night. They stayed in the living room with us, watching "MacGyver" and "The A Team" for what seemed like forever.

When eternity finally ended and his parents retired to their room, we waited another thirty minutes before sneaking out of his building. We put on our all-black Ninja costumes, with plastic throwing stars and swords, and made our way out to the dark, deserted street.

I do not remember what time it was, but it must have been late because there were no cars or people on the streets. Byung lived in a building near "Parque de la Carolina," which, on the street level, housed a famous pastry store in Quito called "Cyrano." I remember the lit Cyrano sign providing comforting light on the sidewalk.

We played in front of his building, playing an early version of parkour as we tried to climb walls and jump from object to object. Using our imagination as we killed bad guys with our throwing stars and swords. We were kicking ass!

Byung lived right around the corner from Cotopaxi, and he introduced the bright idea of playing ninja at the school. We ran to Cotopaxi's front gate, making plans to scale the fence, get on the wall, and jump the wall into the school—a solid plan.

Those plans quickly evaporated when we saw the armed guards awake and patrolling the campus.

We started to walk back dejected. As we walked down the sidewalk, back toward Byung's apartment, we began to pass the detached Cotopaxi kinder campus. We stopped and looked through the slits in the gate and could see no guards or guard house. There was no activity inside the gates at all.

Before I even took my face away from the gate, Byung started to climb the gate, he jumped up on the wall, and, with cat-like ability and silence, disappeared into the school side of the wall.

"What just happened?" He had moved so fast that I could not even ask questions or object. He was there next to me, then gone.

Reluctantly, I followed.

I could not believe we jumped into the kinder campus. We were on the other side of the wall, and I was really scared. The moment and the decisions we were making caused a strong yearning to turn back around, knowing what we were doing was wrong.

As would unfortunately happen too many times in my life, the excitement and adrenaline rush overrode any need to do the right thing.

I followed Byung as he tried to open the front door to the building, but we had no luck. We started to walk around to the back of the building, pretending we were Ninjas, keeping to the shadows and moving slowly and deliberately. No lights were on; the only light was the ambient illumination provided by the moon. Darkness slowly engulfed us as we continued around the building, and trees began to block the light from the moon. My mind registered how scared I would have been, if Byung wasn't with me. Probably frozen in fear from the darkness. My imagination, causing a deep sense of relief, Byung was with me. I instinctively inched closer to him.

I hated the dark; it terrified me. I associated darkness with evil, with the devil, and all his menacing theists created indoctrination rooted in fear.

My mom, my grandma, and my family in Ecuador, in general, used devil-related stories to create a very real and impressionable control mechanism based solely on fear.

My fear of the darkness and the devil played a significant role in my bed-wetting problem. I became psychologically traumatized by fear of the devil and the dark, and this ailment affected me well into adulthood.

I could make out the faint outlines of a playground in the back area of the school, as we continued exploring. We stayed close to the building, hugging the walls and checking every door and window. As we were nearing the end of the building, we finally found an open window.

We looked inside, and there was nothing but darkness and the faint dark outlines of desks and chairs. We stood silently on the threshold and listened for any sound. It was completely silent; the only noise was our breathing.

We paused as we contemplated our next move.

Or, I should say I paused because before I could even initiate a discussion, Byung was through the window and inside. He was very agile, and in one quick and effortless leap, he cleared the window frame and was inside the building.

Again, I reluctantly followed.

I landed on the wood floor next to Byung. He crouched against the wall, listening and watching. He motioned for me to stay still, and we remained in this position for a couple of minutes. Once we were both satisfied that we were alone and that our entry had not been discovered, we began to explore the classroom.

The classroom was small, with an open space and small desks for the children. Pictures and toys were visible. One of the walls was visibly lined with small cubicles for the kids' personal items and labeled with each kid's name. Byung and I explored the small classroom and made our way to the teacher's desk.

Here, we found our treasure trove. In one of the drawers, we located scratch-and-sniff stickers and cool animal stamps—you know, the ones teachers stamp onto your work to let you know you did a "good job" or "great work." For an odd reason, which I still cannot quite comprehend, we decided these items were things we loved and needed.

Mind you, prior to finding them, neither of us particularly cared for them. I never collected any stickers, and I certainly did not receive any positive stamps on any of my schoolwork. We began to fill our pockets and socks with stickers and stamps, filling them to the brim.

As we stole the items, we occasionally paused to scratch and sniff the stickers we had not seen before, completely oblivious to the noise we were making, giggling and forgetting we were ninjas. We lost all sense of where and what we were doing.

Suddenly, we heard a door open somewhere in the building.

Byung and I froze in place and stared at each other in paralyzing fear. We were both too afraid to move. There was a pause after we heard a door creak, but for long, paused seconds, nothing happened. We held our breath, waiting and unwilling to move. Then, our worst fear became reality: heavy footsteps started to echo off the wood floor, someone was approaching.

Our hearts stopped in unison. His eyes were as wide open as I had ever seen them, fear clearly etched on his face. I could only imagine what I looked like. We stared at each other, frozen in fear, not knowing what to do next. We were stuck, too afraid to do anything.

The footsteps continued, and heavy slow thuds, moved closer and closer to our location. The footsteps, the only noise piercing the heavy silence and echoing off the empty building like a heavy bass drum, mocked us with fear. As the footsteps grew closer, we scrambled and hid under the teacher's desk, carefully pulling the rolling chair behind us. I had never felt more scared in my life, my heart pounding out of my chest, and unable to catch a deep breath.

The steps reached the classroom where we were hiding. We heard the knob turn slowly as the door creaked open on rusty hinges. Whoever was checking the school was using a flashlight, the beam of the flashlight panning carefully through the classroom. When the person was satisfied, the heavy steps slowly entered the room.

"Clunk, clunk, clunk," the heavy, loud gait thundered for us on the hardwood floor. They suddenly stopped right in front of the teacher's desk!

My face was pressed against the floor, and I could see underneath the slit of the desk. I was able to get a clear look at the person's shoes.

I recognized those shoes! They were exceptionally large, black leather shoes. They were rounded at the toes, and slightly bubbled out; probably steel toed. What set these shoes apart though, were the wooden heels. The heels were distinct and belonged to an already very large and intimidating human.

Mr. Moy.

Mr. Moy was well known at Cotopaxi. He was a multi-purpose individual and was always around the school. He was a grizzly bear of a man; he towered over everyone, including my dad. If I had to guess, he was at least six feet seven inches tall. He was a big, burly old man who wore red suspenders to keep his pants up and used the thickest bottle-looking glasses I had ever seen.

All the students knew Mr. Moy because once a week, he taught "Square Dancing" in the gym to all the elementary kids. He stood in the center of the gym, with a microphone and a portable speaker, playing the square dance song on a record player. He sang along on his microphone, giving us instructions, like "put your right foot in; take your right foot out; put your right foot in, and shake it all about, do the hokey pokey, etc."

He was always dancing and demonstrating his moves with his huge, thick black leather shoes, which clunked loudly on the wooden gym floor. These were the only pair of shoes he wore.

Those shoes were now inches from my dumb face.

Mr. Moy stood in front of the desk for what felt like an eternity. We stayed completely still, in complete silence, hoping he would keep moving.

After too many seconds passed, Mr. Moy finally decided to move his search along, and we heard his heavy footsteps receding as he continued his search of the school. Byung and I exhaled loudly, like just coming up for air from underwater in a pool.

We had both been holding our breath!

As soon as we calmed down and felt safe, we quietly exited through the window, ran to the front, and jumped the wall back outside to the sidewalk. We sprinted back to Byung's apartment, breaking speed records along the way.

We were flying!

When we were back safely in Byung's room, we inventoried our loot. It was all fun and games now. We laughed and felt high from the adventure and the adrenaline. Who was scared? Certainly not Byung or me. We would have taken Mr. Moy out if he had found us. We were Ninjas, and he was lucky not to find us.

When we finally came off the high, we crashed on his bed into a deep sleep.

I peed.

I hid all my loot in my backpack, and when I got home the next day, I placed all the stickers and stamps under my bed mattress. This was a big mistake.

On Monday morning, Dror came over as usual, and we left for school on our skateboards; I did not tell him anything about my adventure with Byung. I was too scared. The religious fear of "Thou shall not steal" occupied my mind with visceral visions of eternal damnation. I did not want to say anything into existence.

The day was unwinding like most. I saw Byung, but we were both pretending nothing happened, hoping it would all just go away. Tied in a little nice bow, none the wiser.

After lunch, an aide pulled me out of class to see Ms. Prexl, the Principal, in her office.

Uh-oh.

As I arrived at the principal's outer office, I saw Byung walking out of the central office with his parents. He looked down at the floor and did not make eye contact with me. His parents looked at me with disappointment. I swallowed a hard lump of spit and prepared for what awaited me. My heart sank; I knew I was in deep trouble. Somehow, our ninja adventure was no longer a secret.

My mind raced with possible lies and excuses...

The secretary broke my thoughts with "Your turn, Mr. Sullivan," as she ushered me into Ms. Prexl's office. I walked in and lost my breath when I saw my dad standing beside her desk. He looked super pissed.

Any idea I was developing of lying my way out of the mess immediately evaporated. My dad looked livid, embarrassed, but mostly disappointed.

He was carrying a white plastic grocery bag, which he spilled its contents on Ms. Prexl's desk.

All the stolen items I hid under my mattress fell unceremoniously onto her desk. My mom found them while making my bed, called my dad, and the rest, as they say, is history.

Byung and I were both suspended for three days. This was the first of a handful of suspensions I would receive in my scholastic career.

Before going home, my dad walked me to his empty classroom. We entered the classroom, and he took off his belt. He did not say anything; he did not have to; I had it coming. My dad belted me in his classroom and then walked me home. It was not my first time getting belted, and it wouldn't be my last. The walk home was made in complete silence; I was holding my skateboard, not riding it, sore from the beating, but mostly, I was sad to have embarrassed and disappointed my dad at school.

Chapter 17

Las Vegas, Nevada - 1993

As much as I would love to blame my criminal inclination on gangs, trauma, and naïveté, I would be lying. I had a choice to follow Byung into the school, no one forced me to do so. Stepping into the role of selling drugs, in retrospect, does not seem quite as surprising as I would like it to sound. I always had a choice; I just usually made the wrong ones.

One of the groups I started providing marijuana for was a group of kids who hung out on Pearl Street, located on the Southeast side of the city and just a couple of blocks from my apartment. A kid named Joey lived on Pearl Street, and his house was a known party house. His mom and stepdad allowed kids in and out of the house at all hours. Drinking was an expectation. Joey's older brother and brother-in-law bought the alcohol for all the minors, and for a while, I was Joey's main marijuana supplier.

I enjoyed dropping off products at Joey's because it was always a fun time—filled with alcohol, music, and girls. Dennis was a friend of Joey's and hung out there daily. Dennis introduced me to the scene at Pearl Street, and soon, I started hanging out there as well.

I met Mike Jackson at Joey's (Mike was known as "Crazy," and he was from a local Crip gang called Donna Street Crips, or DSC). Joey had regulars who were there every day and every weekend. I became friends with them: Kevin, Ryan, "Duckie" from the Little Locos Gang, Wade, Glenn, and others.

A lot of girls spent time at Joey's on the weekends, two of them being sisters and their shared best friend. The sisters were Gina and Jenetti, and their best friend, Melissa, was always with them. On the weekends, you could find kids from all youth social cultures hanging out on Pearl Street. It was wildly chaotic and simmering with electricity from unsupervised youth.

Gina, Jenetti, and Melissa were also from the Little Locos gang or ("LL"), a North Las Vegas Hispanic Sureño gang. When I met Gina, I became infatuated on sight. Gina was easily one of the most beautiful girls I have ever seen. She commanded every male's attention in any room she walked into, and she knew it.

She was shy and confident, which made her even more alluring. Gina had mocha-colored skin, large almond-shaped eyes, full lips, long, curly dark hair, and a near-perfect shape. Every boy lusted over her. Mike, at the time, was dating Gina's older stepsister Jenetti. The more time I spent on Pearl Street, the more Gina and I connected.

Our different gang affiliation was a problem. 28th Street and Little Locos did not openly war with each other, not like we did with San Chucos and 18th Street, but considered rivals and enemies. The neutrality and diversity on Pearl Street created a safe space or unintended peace treaty. Plus, violent gang activity was happening in north, east, and west Las Vegas. Hardcore gang activity and gang members were only slowly trickling into our area.

My bond with Gina grew into my first true foray with love. We were both obviously physically attracted and emotionally connected, but we were afraid of what our "sets" would think or say. Gina, at the time, was dating a kid named Mark, who had recently been put into juvenile detention for a failed string of burglaries, so Gina was low-key available.

We flirted often, and our connection drew Mike and me into a close friendship. Gina and Jenetti were attached at the hip; they did not go anywhere without each other, and soon, so were Mike and me.

Chapter 18

Mike and I started to become inseparable. The constant time spent with Gina and Jenetti caused us to become brothers. A bond neither of us ever expected. A young black man of Jamaican descent who ran with the Donna Street Crips, and a Hispanic kid from Ecuador who looked white, and ran with a Latino gang from the projects on 28th Street. It was an unusual pairing to say the least, especially because 28th Street developed a partnership, borne from a prison agreement in the local drug trade, with the West Coast Bloods, who mostly operated out of a set of housing projects on the West side, famously known as "The Jets."

Mike and I started to spend our free time together. He lived near my apartments, and he slowly began introducing me to his circle of friends from Donna Street Crips. One night, while hanging out with Mike and a couple of his friends at the community pool at my apartment complex, I experienced my first shooting.

This was my first time meeting Mike's school friends, who did not hang out on Pearl Street. One of his friends was a kid named Doug. Doug was quiet, his interactions limited, and it was easy to forget he was even there.

He just faded into the background. While at the pool, we met two sisters, Angie and Mandy. We kicked it with them all afternoon, listening to the Ghetto Boyz and Too $hort. They were both very attractive and we were all crushing on them. As the sun began to fade, casting long orange glows across the sky, they invited us to continue the party at their apartment.

Hours earlier, a half-dozen white college kids from UNLV had arrived and were drinking beers in the jacuzzi with some girls. We had no interaction with them at all—no sideways glances or

90

aggressive posturing. They were clearly not involved in our lifestyle and noticeably older than us.

As we started to follow Angie and Mandy out of the side gate, which was directly in front of the jacuzzi, one of the college kids made a snide comment about us, loud enough for our group to hear it. I was walking in front of the group, already past the gate's threshold, and did not know what was happening; a verbal altercation began.

The entire exchange took about ten seconds, but even as I remember it, it still feels like a slow-motion movie scene.

Doug and one of the college kids exchanged words. The college kid stepped out of the jacuzzi and raised both his arms in the air in the common aggressive street motion of, " What's up?"

Doug and Mike continued to slowly walk out while turning their heads to talk shit back to him; it seemed like this would end as a back-and-forth verbal dispute. Doug and Mike continued slowly walking away, attempting to disengage and ignore the obviously inebriated young man. But, suddenly, unprovoked and to everyone's collective shock, the college kid yells out, "Niggers!"

Doug, Mike, and Tyrese are black.

As quickly as the words spat out of the college kids' mouth, Doug, who was last in line exiting the gate, turned around, pulled a gun out of his pants that no one knew he had on him, aimed it at the racist prick, and shot him. No hesitation, no talking, no warning... he just shot him.

Stunned silence.

The scene played out in front of me and left me in a state of shock and confusion. The college frat boy fell back violently into the jacuzzi, blood visible in the water as he sank beneath the surface. His friends quickly came to his aid and shouted something I could not process. I looked around, and I could see the shock in everyone's expressions and eyes; everyone was looking around in a state of confusion, somehow trying to validate that we had just witnessed someone shot. Was this real life?

91

Everyone was frozen in place. The only sound was the pounding of my heartbeat in my ears. My brain was unable to get past what had just happened. I froze in place. I felt a hard pull on my shirt, almost causing me to lose my balance. It was Mike. He was pulling me and yelling at me to run, but I could not hear him.

As my senses returned, I heard people yelling; Angie and Mandy cried hysterically. I could see the backs of Doug, Tyrese, and John as they ran toward Pecos Road. Mike continued to pull me in the opposite direction, and I finally started to sprint behind him.

Mike and I sprinted down the street. We did not know where Doug or anyone else went. I was following Mike purely out of survival instinct, my senses still overloaded and overwhelmed.

We ran across the complex, out across a patch of desert, and into a strip mall. We ran into the Phar-Mor pharmacy my mom used to work at, we could already hear the sirens.

Customers were shocked as they witnessed two teens sprinting full speed through the store while the faint hum of the police sirens grew louder. We ran through the back of the store and out to the loading docks, to an alley behind the store. But we both skidded to a stop as we noted the escape route blocked. Las Vegas Metro had both exits blocked with patrol vehicles and their spotlights searching.

Everything was devolving into a chaotic scene I could never have imagined being a part of. We sprinted back through the loading dock and back into the store, this time police lights visible through windows and sirens echoing loudly off the walls.

Customers and staff ran out of the store or got on the ground in a prone position, afraid and confused by what was occurring. As we reached the front doors, four Las Vegas yellow jackets (Metro gang squad) stepped into the store, guns drawn and pointed at us.

"Hands up! Hands up!" they yelled.

We put our hands up and obeyed their commands. They arrested us and put us into the back of separate squad cars. To their credit, the Yellow Jackets recognized we were juveniles and called our

92

parents. By the time our parents arrived, they had caught Doug and collected enough eyewitness testimony to understand Mike and I were not involved in the shooting.

They released us to our parents with a date to see the Juvenile Court Judge on two charges. The college kid, thankfully, was going to be okay. He was in the hospital with a gunshot wound to his shoulder, but survived.

I did not have to lie to my parents about this one. I was still in shock and still trying to process the entire thing. I was numb and just told them the truth in a strange and detached monotone, as if it was someone else who had experienced it. I was not involved. I had just met Doug that night. I did not know he had a gun on him, and I ran because Mike ran. I panicked.

Chapter 19

After days of being in trouble, Mike and I met up with Gina, Melissa, and Jenetti. Everyone wanted to hear details of the shooting. Once again, we were somehow revered for being involved in a violent act. These episodes of random violence created an immature and completely misguided aura, causing our peers to perceive us as tougher and increasing our street credibility. Kids respected us, and girls found a weird attraction to the bad boy persona.

When we met Gina and her girls, we met at a Children's Nursery parking lot on the corner of Hacienda and Pecos. We immediately started talking about the incident, and I could tell Gina was worried. As Mike told the story and answered questions, I pulled Gina away gently, and we walked away from the group. We stood silently, unsure how to navigate what we felt. We both looked down, embarrassed to lock eyes. I was so nervous; my heart was pounding out of my chest. I wanted to ask her out but feared rejection. I could not bring myself to verbalize it. The lack of conversation was becoming awkward, so just to say something, anything at all… I asked her, "Are you still with Mark?"

She looked down, but I could see she was smiling. I waited nervously for a response, sweating under my shirt and nervous as hell. Gina looked up at me and answered my question with one of her own, "Do you want me to be?"

I smiled and looked down embarrassed. Now, it was me who could not meet her gaze. Caught up in the moment, the word "no" evaded my vocabulary. So, instead, I shook my head. She looked at me and said, "I'm not."

Her reciprocation gave me the courage to ask her out, and I did. She said yes, and I was the happiest kid in the world.

94

I wanted to kiss her, but we were both so inexperienced in relationships and feelings that neither of us knew what to do or how to do it. We walked back to the group, touching shoulders as we walked side by side. Gina and I knew we had to keep our relationship a secret. But we were both grinning ear to ear and could not stop looking at each other, making obvious attempts to touch hands as we walked down Pearl Street.

There was not a day I did not get at least ten beeps from Gina on my beeper. We talked every night and all night on the phone. If our phone lines were busy, we would emergency interrupt whoever was using the phone. It was a thing back in the day that if someone's landline remained busy because someone was on the phone, you could call the operator and request an emergency breakthrough on the call. The operator would interrupt the conversation and say, "Will you accept an emergency breakthrough from…"

I used to love getting those from her. We would talk until we started to fall asleep on the phone, and then we would always have a lighthearted argument about who would hang up first.

One night, I walked Gina and Jenetti home from hanging out on Pearl Street. Gina told Jenetti to go inside the house and told her she would follow in a few minutes.

Once Jenetti disappeared through the front door, Gina and I walked to the corner of her street holding hands. When we got to the corner, we turned towards each other and slowly began to kiss. It was everything I had dreamed of and more. I do not know how long we kissed, but it was blissful. Under the stars and the ambient light of the moon, our first kiss was memorable. When we stopped, she said goodnight, and I watched her walk home. I was feeling something I had never felt before. A deep connection with another person and full of raw emotion. I was falling in love.

Gina was a virgin, which was great for me because I was only one body count ahead of her. We continued to get to know each other intimately, building on a young and immature relationship.

Both of us brand new with feeling this way about another person and unsure how to move forward.

95

As Gina and I grew closer and spent more time together, our bond became deeper. Then, in a move neither of us expected, her dad decided to move her family to the other side of town—to northeast Las Vegas, to be exact—and into low-income apartments on the corner of Walnut Road and Lake Mead Boulevard.

I was devastated. Gina went from being within walking distance to being completely unreachable. The only comfort from the move was that Gina's new apartments were two blocks away from Huero's and Travieso's projects. My homies lived at Walnut and Owens, right down the street from her new place.

Gina's moving so far away shifted my plans. Now, hanging out with Huero and Travieso, became my priority. I began reconnecting with Huero and spending my weekends with him at his house.

I was trying hard not to let the move interfere with our relationship. However, the environment, her new school, and being so close to her Little Loco friends did begin to cause distance between us.

We talked every day, and sometimes, she and her sister took the city bus to our side of town to hang out on Pearl Street, but those moments were few and far between. Eventually, they stopped completely.

Pearl Street continued to gain traction as the place to be on our side of town. Drugs flowed freely through Joey's house. It started with marijuana and alcohol but had graduated to methamphetamine, cocaine, and acid as well.

Joey began to ask for larger amounts of marijuana, which were out of my league. So, I introduced him to Chip and was relieved to stop being the go-between. Selling marijuana was not my thing. I began to slowly stop and disengage from doing it. I referred most people to Chip or Speedy.

Pearl Street was becoming a crazy atmosphere on weekend nights. Imagine ten to twenty teenagers hanging out in front of a home in your neighborhood, cars parked at every available curb space, and music bumping loudly from their speakers. Kids smoking marijuana and drinking malt liquor on the curb and coming in and out of the residence. It was crazy, and it started gaining momentum and a specific reputation.

One crazy weekend brought the fun on Pearl Street to a complete halt. Pearl Street was alive that night. A group of kids listened to music in front of Joey's house, blasting Cyrpess Hill and slowly swaying with the beat. Dennis, a regular sight on the venue, was sitting on a swing chair on the front porch with Joey's sister Karen. The crowd, larger than usual, included people I did not know and had never seen before. Chip, Hasson, and all the stoners became regulars on Pearl Street as well. It was good for business. Everyone was chill; Duckie from Little Locos, who lived nearby, had also become a regular on the scene. We were from different gangs but got along well.

Duckie had left with a kid named Zach to make a run for more alcohol. Zack drove a pick-up truck, and I watched them leave on their way to seven-to-eleven.

About forty-five minutes later, I watched as Zack and Duckie pulled up to the house at a high rate of speed. Duckie got out of the truck and made a beeline for me. I saw he had just been in a fight as he neared me. He said, "Popeye, we just got jumped at the seven-to-eleven by a bunch of 18 Streeters, and bitch ass Pitufo was there!"

I had been waiting for an opportunity to catch up with that Smurf, the injury to my knee, still fresh in my mind. I got Mike and the three of us got into Zack's truck. Mike got up front with Zack and Duckie and I jumped into the bed of the truck.

We arrived at the strip mall where the 7-Eleven was located on the Southeast corner of Tropicana and Pecos. We entered the parking area and slowly rolled through it, trying to find Pitufo and his crew.

We found nothing; they had left the area. We made plans to drive around the immediate area to search for them because, according to Duckie, they had been on foot... but those plans changed instantly.

A Las Vegas Metro cruiser suddenly appeared behind us. He was probably summoned over the fight, lit us up with his lights, and bleeped the siren to gain our attention.

Zack started to pull over, but Duckie panicked. He punched the window and yelled, "Go, bro, go! I am on parole and cannot go back to jail!"

Zack, who was just a normal, nice kid, more of a skater/surfer type, completely shocked all of us. I do not think any of us expected his reaction. Without hesitation or questioning anything, Zack took off down Tropicana at a high rate of speed. My first police chase unfolded in a way I could never have imagined—especially not while riding in the back of a pick-up truck!

The way the pursuit ended made the local Las Vegas news.

Zack was driving recklessly, which was terrifying for Duckie and me. We were violently tossed around the bed of the truck and barely able to stay inside. Experiencing something like a police chase in real time feels surreal.

You know it is happening, but a part of your brain keeps you in awe of how everything unfolds. I could see the patrol car driving aggressively behind us, its sirens wailing loudly, and I even noted the stress and fear on the police officers' face. I was sure this would end badly, and I started to consider the real possibility of dying.

Zack sped east on Tropicana Avenue and suddenly made a violent right-hand turn on Sandhill Road. By the time we started speeding down Sandhill Road, three Las Vegas Metro patrol cars joined the chase. Their lights and loud sirens were disorienting. I could see cars pulling over as my vision flashed by them. I could not believe I was in an actual police chase. As scary as it was, it was also exhilarating!

I was not mature enough to really understand what was happening. The consequences of our actions were not even a consideration. We barreled down Sandhill Road, taking up both travel lanes. Everything was a violent blur of speed and sudden movements, and every slight input Zack made to the vehicle sent Duckie and me in the opposite direction, causing us to dangerously collide with each other and changing our visual perspective continuously... causing disorientation and confusion.

I knew the general area where we were and knew a four-way stop was quickly approaching. On the last input, I had landed near the tailgate and was able to look up and catch a glimpse through the back window of the truck as Zack tried to make a left turn on a side street at a crazy speed.

He tried to make the left because a Las Vegas Metro squad car was approaching from the opposite direction. The problem was that we were moving too fast, and as he tried to apply the brakes, we began to skid, causing the back of the truck to lose traction and slide on the street... making it feel like one of the tires left the ground.

Zack lost control, and to avoid a rollover, he tried to correct it by turning into the skid. This caused us to jump over the curb and crash head-on into the perimeter wall of someone's backyard!

The impact was thunderous! The truck's momentum took us through the wall and halfway into someone's backyard pool. Then, the truck came to a complete stop in a sudden and very violent fashion. The impact sent me flying from the back of the truck and caused me to slam forcefully against the rear window.

As usual, everything began to slow down for me. I looked up and saw Duckie with a massive gash on his head, blood freely pouring out of it, soaking his face and his shirt. He yelled something at me, but I could not hear him. He turned, jumped out of the bed of the truck, and disappeared, sprinting down the street and into the night.

I looked through the back window and noticed Mike's door was wide open, and his seat was empty. I turned my gaze and saw him running and disappearing around a corner. I then shifted my gaze to check on Zack and instantly felt overcome with a feeling of alarm and worry for him. Zack was slumped over the steering wheel. I could see blood on his face and head, and he was unconscious. He was not moving.

I stood up with tremendous difficulty. I could immediately tell something was not right with me. I could sense police officers moving around me, their lights casting ominous shadows as they moved past them, cautiously approaching us and the vehicle. My senses were severely delayed, and the lights and sirens added to my confused state.

I reached the side of the truck, used my right hand to support myself on the driver's side bed panel, and attempted to jump off, thinking I could also flee.

That is the last thing I remember.

I woke up at Desert Springs Hospital days later with what felt like intense pain coming from my crotch area. As I regained consciousness, a nurse was finishing the task of pulling my catheter out of my penis. It was not a pleasant experience, and she had not fully deflated the balloon. I do not recommend it.

My mom and dad were there, worried looks on their faces. They both came to my side, kissed, and petted me. I could sense they had been under tremendous anxiety. I asked them what happened because I could not remember.

When I hit the back of the truck, I broke a rib. When I jumped from the truck to try and run, the broken rib collapsed my lung, and I stopped breathing.

The first Las Vegas METRO Officer to get to me, checked me for vitals and immediately began CPR when he noted I did not have a pulse and was not breathing. From what my parents relayed to me, the officer continued CPR until Emergency Medical Units arrived.

Wow. I could not believe it. I was dead. In the medical definition of a person dying, I fit the criteria. No pulse and no breath. Crazy.

I wish I could tell you I saw a light or my life flash before my eyes, but unfortunately, it was nothing—a dark void in my memory. My parents told me everyone involved was going to be okay. That was a relief. I remembered Zack motionless over the steering wheel and was glad he would be okay. I never saw Zack again.

After days in the hospital, they finally released me back home, but I was bedridden for a couple of months. I was okay with that because it hurt just to breathe. I was on a liquid diet for the first week and under a strong narcotic because I spent my time sleeping. Normal movements caused me extreme pain.

My poor parents were now only beginning to understand, through the resources they received from police and juvenile courts, about my path and the challenges ahead. They did the best they could to help me.

Pearl Street shut down after the incident. Police patrolled the area often and prevented large groups of kids from congregating.

Chapter 20

During my recovery time, Gina and Jenetti, became deeply entrenched with Little Locos gang. Gina and I continued to talk on the phone and maintained a semblance of a relationship, but I could feel a difference.

Our conversations grew shorter, and there was an obvious resistance to any emotion associated with our relationship. Her journey into becoming a gang member, causing a new side of hers to emerge, one I had never seen before. Uncaring, uninterested and an aloofness, which worried me deeply.

Gina's timidity, and caring nature, slowly evaporated. Replacing it with a hard exterior and embracing a disconnect from her youthful personality; making her appear cold and emotionless.

Gina tried hard to make this updated version of her, the central part of her life. She was obviously going through tumultuous transitions I knew nothing about, she was confused, and all she started to care about, was getting high and escaping her reality.

I knew little about Gina's past. She was never open to talking about it and was always very private. I knew she had an older sister in Hawaii, where her mom was from. She had lost her mom at an early age, and her dad became her sole parent.

To this day, I do not know what her dad ever did for a living. My interactions with him were always positive ones, but limited. I liked him, but could tell he remained distracted by his own problems. I heard rumors he had connections to the Italian Mafia in Las Vegas, but that is all they were… rumors.

During this phase Gina was experiencing, it almost felt like she did not want to remain in a sober state. Her thirst for feeling high led to strange moments for her and me, and she introduced me to new methods of getting high, that in retrospect, I can't believe I actually participated in.

One of the methods she introduced me to was huffing spray paint. We would walk to Walmart, buy gold colored spray paint, and then find a quiet and private place to sit. We would then spray the paint onto one of her old socks, fold it and then we would begin inhaling the fumes through the sock.

It gave us an instant head high, but the high ended quickly and usually followed by a headache. I never enjoyed it, but Gina loved it.

Gina also introduced me to something I cannot believe I took part in. I was so in love with her, I would have done anything for her, and with her.

We were out of paint one day, and she took me outside of her apartment, and asked me to follow her. We walked around her apartment complex, and she introduced me to getting high off vehicle gas fumes.

Yes, you read that right.

Gina showed me the process, which I do not know where she learned; she would find a car, usually picking one parked far away from any buildings or prying eyes. Once she found the right vehicle, she would begin to push it, causing the shocks on the cars to shake the vehicle back and forth. This, to my total surprise, created pressurized vapors inside the gas tank. When she was satisfied, she opened the gas tank, placed her mouth where you would normally pour gas through, and inhaled the gasoline vapors!

I did it with her. What can I say?

I did totally feel like a crack head, but in a fucked-up place in my mind, I was simply happy to be spending time with her.

Gina sadly continued her descent down the path, and I remained so attached to her, I was willing to go along for the ride.

Even with my willingness to engage in behavior I did not want to participate in, the distance and growing differences between Gina and I became too vast.

As hard as I tried to ignore it, I could tell she was no longer feeling the same way about me. She told me she was, when we talked about it, but her behavior proved otherwise.

One night, I decided to stay the night at Huero's house, who lived just blocks down the street from Gina's. Gina and I had recently been reconnecting a bit, and I was growing optimistic we could survive these growing problems.

She told me her dad would be gone all night, and she wanted me to come over. She explained she would page me when her dad left, letting me know it was time to come over.

I went to Huero's and hung out with him and his cousins. His family dynamics were strange to say the least. Travieso, Huero's cousin, lived next door to him in the low-income housing projects. Travieso's older brother, Gus, was also a gang member, but instead of following the family lineage, Gus was a San Chuco. Make it make sense.

They were family, so they got along, but technically they were enemies. They were always ribbing each other about their sets, but they made it work somehow. (Gus, sadly died in a shooting at their housing projects years later).

We were sitting outside on plastic crates, listening to Lighter Shade of Brown, when two random white people walked up to us, and bought drugs from Gus. Gus gave them something wrapped in tin foil, which I had never seen before. I asked Gus what it was, and he said, "Watch."

I watched as the two individuals he had just sold to, carefully opened the tinfoil and removed two cigarettes. The cigarettes looked like regular cigarettes, except for a weird shine to them, almost making them look wet.

When they held them up, the cigarettes were not as sturdy as you would expect them to be, but sagged a bit, as if dipped in a form of liquid. The two men, started to share one of the cigarettes; they sat in the grassy area near the projects parking lot and took long deep puffs of the cigarette.

They allowed the smoke to fill their lungs, keeping the smoke trapped inside their bodies as long as possible, causing them to expel it in a fit of coughing. They took about three long deep puffs each, and then they put the cigarette out, and back in the tinfoil. I watched with amused curiosity as these individuals sat on the grass and appeared to be in another universe.

Oblivious to anything happening around them, they sat stuck, almost appearing to be unable to properly move. Gus, Huero and Travieso laughed at them, but I was low key concerned.

They looked weird, making slow exaggerated expressions with their faces and arms, and when they did speak, it was a slow and deeply slurred speech.

Finally, Gus told me, "Those were Sherm-sticks Popeye, we get cigarettes or joints, and dip them into embalming fluid or PCP, it gives you a long lasting high, and these crackhead fools can't get enough."

"Did you just say embalming fluid?" I asked in concerned astonishment. Gus replied, "Yeah fool, the same shit they use on dead people."

I thought he was lying, that they were clowning me, but Huero and Travieso affirmed what Gus said, and I was shocked.

As I watched these two individuals sitting on the grass, behaving in a severely delayed and weird manner, I finally got the beep from Gina I had been patiently waiting for.

Huero, Travieso and Gus made fun of me as I started walking towards Gina's apartment. "You are whipped esse! Make her a sandwich, she is tired of waiting!" They made the whiplash sound with their mouths, and I could hear them making fun of me until I walked across Owens Avenue and out of hearing range.

As I walked towards Gina's I was thinking about the possibilities the night might bring. I had been dating Gina for two years. Gina was still a virgin, and I respected it. I knew her boundaries, and never crossed them. She was intoxicatingly beautiful, and I wanted to be her first, but remained intimidated by her beauty and by the fact she was a girl.

I had only experienced sex once, and Natalie had done all the work. I did not really have any actual experience; I was still a total rookie, and I was in my head about it. I did not want to suck.

As I walked into her apartment complex, I became optimistically nervous. I knew I loved Gina; I had never felt this way about anyone before. Gina was the first person I thought about when I woke up, and the last person I thought about before I went to bed. Every decision I made was rooted on how Gina would feel or what she would think. She was my first true love.

I arrived at her apartment, and nervously knocked on the door. When she opened the door, my optimism grew in intense leaps and bounds.

She had her make-up off, which she knew I preferred, her beautiful long curly hair just washed, and it hung down past her shoulders and back. She was wearing her Dallas Cowboys jersey, which she knew I hated, but that is all she was wearing.

I gulped, and told her, "You look gorgeous." She smiled, grabbed my hand, and led me into her apartment and into her room.

It would be impossible to describe the experience of making love to Gina that night. It was a beautiful dance. A beautiful and deliberate coexistence of two people momentarily becoming one.

When done, we clung to each other for a moment. Neither of us wanted to let go. Deep down, I think we both knew our young romance was starting to end.

When we finally let go of each other, we shared a look, and simultaneously said, "I love you."

At the time, we both deeply meant it.

Chapter 21

Even though I knew things were ending with Gina, I wanted to try to salvage it. I remained deeply and emotionally connected to her. She meant everything to me. We continued to see each other, but spending time together became a lost cause. The few times we did meet up, the disconnect was obvious.

During my time dating Gina, her friend Melissa and I bonded in a unique way and became good friends. I loved Melissa, she was genuine and funny. I trusted her, and she was a source of information for me with anything regarding Gina.

Melissa was the one to break the news to me. Gina wanted to break up, and she asked Melissa to tell me. I was devastated.

It was my first experience loving someone intensely, and then losing them.

The heartache it caused me was something which still clings to my heart, like an emotional scar unwilling to heal.

Gina, for two years, had been the foundation of my motivation for life. The young, naive, and tender first loves; they remain forever, imprinted in your heart.

I was sad, in a depression over it, but Huero, Oso (Huero's older cousin), and the crew, helped to redirect my feelings.

They turned my emotional vulnerability into anger.

I started to hang out exclusively with Huero, Oso and Travieso. Oso was older, an OG (Original Gangster), and had a reputation as a person you did not want to cross paths with. In previous gang related fights, he endured a stabbing, and a gunshot wound. He had legit street credibility.

Oso was massive; easily three hundred pounds and standing about six feet two inches tall. He was a big man. If bears could have ethnicity, he would be a Mexican Grizzly.

Oso was older than us and drove a low-rider Impala. Trying to stay close to Gina caused my relationship with Huero and Travieso to strengthen, and soon, a friendship with Oso, also blossomed. He started to pick me up on the weekends to hang out.

Speedy, at the time, was going through his own issues, he was in a serious, but turbulent relationship with a girl I had dated, Caramia. His parents had recently divorced, and he was going through personal difficulties. So, we did not pressure him much on hanging out with us. He spent his time with Eli, Aaron, and Ivan.

My weekends, now mostly spent on the east and north sides of the valley, began to increase in violence, drug use and criminal activity.

Gang violence was getting worse, and at times we rolled five cars deep and I felt indestructible. We attended 28th Street parties and picnics held at Freedom Park. I began meeting other homies from 28th Street, and slowly began engrossing myself, deeper and deeper into the lifestyle.

There were unwritten rules and/or expectations with every street gang. There must be structure and leadership, otherwise there would be no cohesion. One of the rules 28th Street adopted, was that any new member jumped into the neighborhood, could endure another beat down; or others, "getting their hits in." "Getting your hits in," meant any members who were not there during the original "jumping in," or original initiation, had the opportunity to hit you or beat you up.

Suddenly, I became mortified to be around my new friends. Any party or picnic came attached with the possibility of another mauling.

Thankfully, most guys in the neighborhood I had met were chill, and none expressed any desire to get their hits in. But there are always exceptions.

There was a little fat garden gnome, who went by Gordo. Once, while Speedy and I were leaving Lisa's apartment, which was in the same complex I lived in, Gordo and his crew showed up.

It was Gordo, Foxy, and Drifter. They stopped us on one of the walking paths, and told us they wanted to get their hits in. Neither of us wanted to get beat up again, and Speedy and I could have beat them all up, but rules were rules.

Blaine went first this time, but I was not as fearful as I had been the first time. Gordo was short, fat and simply not athletic. Foxy was short and so skinny; he must have weighed a hundred and ten pounds with his clothes on. Drifter was the only one who seemed like he could be a problem, but he did not appear to be enthusiastic about participating. So, I stood on the path as they moved into the grassy area and started the process. Speedy, was already getting the best of them, all by himself.

Suddenly, I saw my little brother Kevin walking down the path towards us. When he saw us, he stopped and processed what was happening. A worried expression crossed his face, and he took off sprinting towards our apartment. On instinct, I took off after him, trying to catch him before he made it home and snitched.

I caught him as he was rounding the corner to our apartment building, but as I caught him, he yelled, and my dad came out the front door in a hurry. All my recent experiences had my parents on edge. He immediately demanded to know what was going on, and Kevin said, "He was about to get jumped again dad!" My dad grabbed me by the arm firmly and took me inside. He put me in my room and advised me not to leave; he grounded me.

Gordo took the incident as a sign of weakness and disrespect. He thought I was afraid of him, and felt I ran away from fear. It is a moment in my life which I wish I could do over. Gordo talked a ton of shit and was spreading inaccurate accounts of what had happened. Thankfully, Speedy saw my brother and understood what had happened; he vouched for me.

Oso and Huero also had problems with Gordo and Foxy, so just to avoid any set-on-set drama, we started hanging out with a California set which had arrived in Las Vegas; "Los Primos."

One night, we headed to a Los Primos kickback in Naked City. Los Primos were new to the city, but they had already created a name for themselves, cutting California to Nevada drug pipeline deals, with the local gangs.

They aligned with Naked City and were able to operate freely on their turf. They had not made any enemies yet, and we kept a loose relationship with them, unfortunately so did 18th Street.

Before driving to the kickback, Oso told us he had a surprise for us. We drove to a random house on the east side, he parked the car in front of the house and honked the horn. Out came an older cholo I had never met. Huero, Travieso, and Oso exited the car and gave him daps and hugs. They showed him respect. Oso and Huero introduced him as their cousin, "Orco," who had just come home from a five-year stint in State Prison.

Orco was quiet, he barely spoke. He was muscular, with a shaved head, but a patch of thick black hair on the back of his head braided all the way down to the middle of his back. He had a long bushy go-tee and was an intimidating presence. Orco teemed with an unpredictable energy, he seemed tense and was always looking around, weary of his surroundings.

When we arrived at the kick back, we were surprised to see "Yoyo" (Yolanda), from 18th Street. Yoyo was one of the few people I knew, who could casually commingle with different gangs and not have a problem.

She was friendly to everyone, and I knew her brother Robert from Pearl Street, so we had interacted quite a bit in the past.

Yoyo was close with Pitufo and the crew who had jumped me, but we never mentioned it. Yo-yo and I got along and coexisted.

It was a fun night, and even though Yoyo was technically an enemy, she was always cool with me. We drank, danced, and smoked weed, and we were all crushing on one of the girls from Los Primos called Patty.

We left Naked City, all of us a little high and a little drunk.

We were hungry and decided to go to Sonic. There was a Sonic near Eastern and Washington, on our turf, and we decided to head there.

When we arrived, there were multiple cars parked and waiting on orders or already eating. We parked Oso's Impala, we ordered and then we all exited the car to stand around listening to music. More than once, I checked my pager hoping I may have missed a page from Gina.

Nope.

I noticed a light grey van circle the Sonic slowly before pulling into one of the parking spots across from us to order. The van was an older model, the kind which had curtains on the windows and gave every kid a creepy vibe. A Ford or Chevrolet, American made.

As the van parked, I noticed the driver and passenger were affiliated with a Hispanic gang. They were young, Hispanic males, with an intense look on their faces. I did not recognize any of them, but Oso and Orco did. They were from 18th Street, and the driver shared my moniker, Popeye.

As soon as they stepped out of the van, Oso tensed up as he recognized them. We stared at each other across the Sonic center island, and Popeye from 18th Street yelled out, "Fat ass Oso, of course you are eating!"

There were only three of them, so when Travieso, and Huero came around the corner, they instantly rethought their aggressiveness.

We started to walk across towards them, and they hurried back into the van, Oso, had grabbed a crowbar out of his car, and as they backed up and drove away in a hurry; he hurled the crowbar at their van hitting the back window and shattering it. The crowbar clanged on the ground loudly.

The van sped up, and turned right on Eastern and we thought had left the area for good. They were on our turf, near 28th Street, and it was already strange they had chosen to eat at that Sonic.

The customers left after the exchange. We received our food and sat at one of the outdoor tables offered at Sonic. We talked and laughed and were discussing plans for next weekend with the fine girls from Los Primos, Patty in particular.

We were deep in conversation and did not notice the van creeping up into Sonic, lights off and driving slowly, this time from the opposite direction.

It was Huero who noticed them first, and yelled, "Get down, get down!"

We all looked up, and saw the van creeping, with its side doors wide open. Visible inside the door, was one of the vatos from 18th Street, with an automatic machine gun.

We all hit the deck.

"Brrraaap, Brrraaap, Brrraaap!" The sound of the machine gun cycling three to five round bursts. Thankfully, we were the only ones left at the Sonic, and it was late, almost closing time.

The van sped up and turned around the sonic at a high rate of speed, and then disappeared again down Eastern Avenue. The exact same way they had left the first time.

We checked ourselves to make sure no one suffered any injuries. Everyone was fine. We checked on the staff, who thankfully, were also all fine, but clearly shook up. We all were.

We left in a hurry, knowing Las Vegas METRO was certainly on the way. We spent the next few hours looking for them, hoping to find them. Oso kept handguns in the car, and I became afraid of what would happen if we found them.

When Oso finally tired of driving around and searching, I was immensely relieved. The imagery of what would have happened, had we been able to find them, played out in my head in violent fatalistic ways. It would have ended badly; death or having caused it. Neither ending boded well for any of our futures.

Moments like what happened at Sonic created a strange mental dilemma for me. I felt warring energies, and a sense of dualism, raging inside of me. It almost felt like I was living two lives.

I knew deep down; I did not want to be involved in anything I had been doing recently. I felt like I was slowly inching close to a steep drop. A precipice, which I reluctantly kept stepping closer and closer to its edge.

I was consciously afraid I would lose myself in this life if I did not somehow disconnect. I was remarkably close to taking that step over the edge, I recognized, if I did… my life was over.

What was I doing? I was just a soccer player and skateboarder from Ecuador. What was happening?

For brief moments, when logical thought entered my mind, I realized I did not fully comprehend why I was making these decisions, displaying this type of behavior, and accepting these people as my friends. Everything happening in my life at that point was moving in the opposite direction of everything I believed in. Against the very nature of my personality and who I thought I was.

The realization slowly began to dawn on me; I did not know who I was anymore. Feeling like a stranger in your own skin is one of the scariest and most confusing things a person can feel.

Moments of deep and meaningful reflection, like I was having on the ride home after almost dying, overwhelmed me mentally. It caused me to slip into a mental cocoon and causing me to slip away from reality and return to moments in my life I cherished… My flashbacks always took me back to the best, and worst times of my life. My childhood in Ecuador …

Chapter 22

My first memory of my dad's "darkness" is vivid. The first time I saw my dad become violent is ingrained into my memory bank. I know being over six feet tall does not sound super tall, but when you consider the average height of Ecuadorian males, which is around five feet six inches, over six feet sounds gigantic.

I remember my sister Denise and I were in the car with my dad, stuck in traffic. The car was a small compact car, a San Remo, it was a piece of crap. A cursory glance could cause people to wrongly assess my dad's size while he was sitting in the small car.

We were in heavy traffic near Quito's biggest park, Parque de la Carolina, or "Carolina" for short. Carolina was centrally located and connected to major thoroughfares. It was Quito's equivalent of Central Park in New York.

At some point, as traffic began to move in bursts, the car in front of us slammed on his breaks, my dad following too closely, reacted in similar fashion, making our tires skid and abruptly come to a stop, causing our front fender to gently tap the rear fender of the car in front of us, a taxi.

My dad, already annoyed by all the traffic, became visibly upset. His face turned red, and his jaw clenched. He was able to see no visible damage occurred just by looking out the window, and he took out his hand and waved to apologize.

The driver of the vehicle did not appreciate the love tap. He put his car in park in the middle of traffic and exited his vehicle.

He began to walk aggressively towards our car, yelling and demanding money. My dad put the gear in neutral, pulled the emergency brake handle, and rose out of his seat.

As my dad stretched to his full height, I saw the small Ecuadorian man almost stumble backward, trying to stop his aggressive forward motion. He instantly reconsidered his aggressive approach and ran back to his car. He made it into his car and locked his door. The man could not drive away, because all the traffic landlocked us.

My dad was in a bit of a rage. He approached the man's driver's side door and attempted to open it, but he could not. He yelled for the man to get back out and fight. The man refused. I then saw my dad take a step back and kick the man's window. He kicked it a couple of times until it finally shattered. The man in the vehicle was yelling for help.

My dad dislodged the remaining glass with his hands, grabbed the man by his shirt, and lifted him out of his seat and out of the broken window.

Once out of the car, the man was terrified. He was cowering and not resisting at all, but my dad felt the need to punch him in the face, causing him to fall unconscious. Taxi drivers who were landlocked with us intervened and separated my dad.

By this time, my dad had returned to our car, and room had been created in the traffic. My dad drove away. I do not remember him saying anything or talking about it at all. I simply remember being afraid. It was a side of my dad I did not know existed.

It scared me, but life just continued, and the incident receded. Soon, I forgot about it. Until the next time.

CHAPTER 23

One afternoon in the summer of 1983, I was outside on the street in front of my house, playing soccer against the neighbor's wall. We lived in the "Las Casas" neighborhood, a low to middle-class neighborhood on the west side of Quito and on the skirts of "Pichincha," a well-known mountain range and natural western border to the city.

My sister was riding her bike and giving my younger brother Kevin a ride. Our maid, Susana, was outside with us, supervising.

Yes, we had a maid, and no, this does not mean we were in any way wealthy. You must understand that in Ecuador, everyone, apart from the extremely poor, has maids. Maid services in Ecuador were dirt cheap (this no longer applies since the country now regulates payments for maid services), but back then, it was to the point of being morally and even criminally wrong, but it did provide the poor with the opportunity to work.

I continued to kick the soccer ball against the wall, imagining myself the hero of the World Cup, scoring the game-winning goal. My sister continued to give my brother Kevin a ride on her bike when, out of nowhere, we heard loud, panicked screaming from the neighbor directly across the street from us. It was a woman screaming. She sounded desperate and was yelling for help, "Ayuda!" (Help!) "Alguien ayúdenme Por favor!" (Someone, please help me!).

I stopped kicking the ball and held it under my foot. Susana took my brother Kevin with her and ran inside our apartment. My sister got off her bike and came and stood next to me. We stood silently, listening to loud thuds, objects breaking, and more yelling.

My mom and dad came running out of our apartment, followed by Susana, who was still carrying my brother. My mom was crying and begging my dad not to get involved. She tried tugging at his arm unsuccessfully, but he broke free and ignored her.

He walked with a focused purpose and opened the front pedestrian gate of the neighbor's interior patio. We followed my mom up to the gate and stood with her on the threshold.

We watched as my dad loudly knocked on the front door. The female continued to yell and plead for help, but no one answered the door. He tried a couple more useless knocks, then, like he did when he broke the car window, my dad stepped back and delivered a thunderous kick at the door. The door burst open in an explosion of wood and glass. My dad disappeared inside.

We ventured inside the front patio to hear and see better. We heard a loud scuffle, and then a lady ran out of the house. Her hair was a mess, her dress was torn and bloody, and her face was red and swollen. She went up to my mom, and my mom asked Susana to take her into our apartment.

My mom was still crying and now yelling for my dad to stop and come out. Suddenly, the man who had been beating on his wife ran out of the wreckage, which was now their front door, my dad hot on his heels. He was trying to run away, and the look on his face was pure terror.

My dad, unaware of my mom's yelling and crying, cornered the man in the front patio area. The man attempted to resist, and a wrestling match ensued. My dad quickly overpowered him and had the man on his knees against the fence. He controlled the man and kept him unable to move from the position; my dad then began to punch him with his fists.

The man, completely defeated, halfway sat on the floor while doing his best to cover himself from the staccato of blows my dad delivered. Fists flew, blood spattering and the thud of every heavy blow landed on the man's face and head, echoing in a hypnotic rhythm.

I watched the entire incident, not knowing how to feel. It is possible I was in a bit of shock, but I was also equally fascinated.

Finally, my dad stopped, not out of pity but because he appeared too tired to continue. My mom felt comfortable enough to approach him and gently pull him away by the arm. The wife beater slumped to his side, like a sack of rice, laying awkwardly on the cold patio floor.

Before we walked back home, I took a moment to examine the man. He was breathing, but he was out cold—a bloody mess of flesh and clothes, unconscious on the patio floor.

Instinctively, I felt bad for him. It is in my nature to seek altruistic perspectives and always cheer for the underdog.

A part of me, though, understood why my dad had just unleashed this level of violence on the man, and the duplicity of my young, inexperienced ability with a grounded perspective made my head hurt.

I recognized the adrenaline pumping through my body. I looked at the man again, but this time, I remembered his wife's screams and her bloody face as she ran towards us. I did not feel as bad for him anymore. A small part of me registered the deserved retribution. I was confused by the mix of emotions, but the one that remained defiant and at the forefront, unwilling to move away, was fear.

A sudden stop from the motion of Oso's car woke me from my deep slumber. I had fallen asleep.

While Oso drove everyone home, I passed out. I was the last person he dropped off, giving me ample time to consider parts of my childhood in the comfort of his backseat as he casually coasted around the valley in his Impala.

The memories of my dad, of the violence, and Ecuador slowly receded, and in a moment of raw panic. I remembered the incident at Sonic. Close to losing our lives, but it just felt normal. What?

Chapter 24

Las Vegas, Nevada - 1993

The incident at Sonic, where the vatos from 18th Street tried to kill us, was in an endless loop in my brain. I could not shake the feeling of... feeling like an impostor, living someone else's life. I was living a life in a parallel universe and living another version of myself. It began affecting my core personality, the things that made me who I was.

I started to slowly disengage from hanging out with anyone from 28th Street. There were no cellphones back then, only beepers, and my geographical location in the city helped. We spoke on the phone and sometimes saw each other at the waterpark (Wet &Wild), but I started to stay closer to my area of the city, closer to home, with Mike, Dennis, Speedy, and the others.

Most of the gang members had been removed from Green Valley High School, only a few remained, and they watched us with a microscope, looking for any excuse to get rid of us.

Things had simmered down considerably. I was still selling marijuana here and there, mostly to friends and to an OG Crip from Hoover Street in Los Angeles, who went by "Ty-Bud."

Ty-Bud had recently moved into my apartment complex with his wife and young daughter. He hit me up at the community pool once and asked me if I could get him weed. He was new in town and could tell I could find it for him.

Ty-Bud quickly became a regular customer. I would sit and smoke with him in his apartment sometimes, and he would tell me crazy stories about gang life in Los Angeles.

Chip continued to provide me and everyone else I knew with the product. Chip got big and became well known. Soon, he had a new truck and a new girlfriend. He was living large.

"Chip, was aware the police were surveilling him and actively trying to press charges on him. But, he was smarter than most. Chip was very careful and very clever, he consistently outsmarted the police. The only reason they got him was due to a missing mud flap in his truck. It was the "Probable Cause" for a traffic stop, which changed his life forever.

Since things were calmer at school, and only a couple of us remained, I finally found the courage to ask Belinda out, the San Chucos chola.

Our once cautious and distant flirting became more intentional. I bumped into her in between classes and asked her for her number. I was so happy when she smiled shyly and wrote it in my notebook. She drew a heart next to the number, and I knew we both felt the same.

Belinda and I began to talk daily. We grew close and set up a date to attend a kickback together.

I had recently started working at Vons and, with the help of my parents, was able to buy a white Chevrolet Caprice—my first car. It was a boat, but I loved it.

I drove my Caprice to pick up Belinda at her house in North Las Vegas. Belinda lived by the elementary school where my mom and dad worked, Lincoln Elementary.

Belinda came out of her house in burgundy creased Ben Davis pants and a white crop top shirt showing her flat belly. She looked incredible. I know I must have had my mouth wide open; she was a head-turner. I opened the car door for her, and we left on our date. Belinda was nervous about her homies catching her with me in the area, so she sat low in the seat. We had an awkward conversation until we got to the kickback, which was in Green Valley.

It was a big party, cars parked everywhere, but as we pulled in, people started running out. A fight had already broken out, a knife was introduced into the fight, and the party was over.

Belinda and I never even exited my car. We watched with curiosity as people ran, trying to see if we could find anyone we knew. We saw big Kevin, Ryan, and Glenn running into the street. I honked my horn and yelled out for Kevin while motioning them to come towards us. They ran to my car, and I told them to get in. They all got in, and we took off.

They told us the fight had involved Gabe and his brother Jandro, who were both from Los Primos. They did not know who their adversaries were, but it had been a violent fight.

I formally introduced Kevin, Ryan, and Glenn to Belinda. Kevin and Ryan had seen her at school but did not know her. Glenn went to Valley High School, and he had no clue who she was, but one thing was immediately clear: They could not believe she and I were together.

Not only because we were from different sets and sworn enemies, but also because Belinda was so beautiful, they immediately started joking about how she was out of my league and only with me because I had a whip.

We ended up buying forty's (40-ounce malt liquor, which comes in large glass bottles) and going to a school's playground to drink and talk. We were having a fun time. Belinda and I held hands, and we kissed. It was great.

We all finished our drinks and were feeling lovely, all of us buzzing. We decided we needed more alcohol, so we drove up to Circle K on the corner of Pecos Road and Tropicana Avenue. I parked next to a pump, acting like I was going to get gas. Belinda would do the dirty work and try to get an adult to buy us beer.

Belinda walked into the store, and as she entered, two big Reet Boys (a Henderson area blood gang) walked around the corner. These guys were massive—over six feet tall—and adults in their late twenties. They were men. I could immediately tell they were drunk. Their balance was off, and they each had a 40-oz bottle of Mickey's in their hand.

They threw up their arms and challenged us as soon as they spotted us. They were big and intimidating, but there were four of us, and they were clearly very intoxicated, so I was not worried; plus, big Kevin stood six feet three inches himself, so I felt confident.

I threw up my hands as well, yelling, "What up?"

The Reet Boys immediately started to walk fast towards us and, when in range, chucked their beer bottles at us. Luckily, neither of them struck any of us, but the bottles crashed into the gas pumps, causing glass and malt liquor to fly everywhere. As soon as the bottles left their hands, they rushed us.

It is important to note that I am describing the scenario using the plural word "us."

Rushing four of us, for a second, felt odd. Yes, they were bigger, but there were four of us; these guys were either very drunk, nuts, or on drugs.

I took a split second to look behind me to make sure Kevin, Glenn, and Ryan were with me and ready to scrap, but I was utterly shocked and confused to catch a glimpse of their backs as they all sprinted across Tropicana. I could not believe it; they had just left me. But it also explained why these guys rushed me so confidently.

I turned back around just in time to duck one of their punches. I was able to push the one who threw the punch off me; he was so drunk that it did not take effort. He took a few steps back, and I used the short pause to disengage and determine what to do.

Running away would have been an option, but I could not leave Belinda. So, as the second one stepped forward, I began to engage him in a fight.

What happened next will forever make Belinda the downest, most courageous girl I know.

While I was fighting two grown men, Belinda came running out of the Circle-K with a large bounty of beers and Boone Farms. She saw what was happening and, without any hesitation or pause, ran over to help me.

As she approached us, she removed one of the Boone Farms bottles from the bag and held it in her hand by its slender neck. She did not even slow her pace. She came right up behind the first Reet

Boy in her path and violently hit him on the back of the head with the bottle.

The Reet Boy went down and stayed down. He was out of the fight. I could hear him groaning and complaining. He was bleeding from a head wound, but he was ok.

This caused me and the Reet Boy I was engaging with to turn our heads in unison, stunned by what Belinda had just done.

The most incredible part of the incident was that Belinda held on to the rest of the liquor and saved the rest of the bottles. While I continued to fight my larger opponent, Belinda, jumped into my car, turned it on, and drove to the next gas aisle where the fight had moved to. She rolled down the window and yelled, "Get in Popeye!"

I could not believe it. Three of my male friends ran across the street, but Belinda not only saved me and took one of them out of the fight, but she was also now commandeering my car and saving me again. What a keeper.

I jumped through the passenger's side open window, and Belinda took off. The entire incident was incredible, and I was in awe of Belinda.

She drove across the street to pick up the fuckboys who bailed on me, and we went back to the school. I could not believe they had bailed and left me to fend for myself. I had watched them all get into fights and knew they were capable and not afraid. To this day, I do not really know why they ran, but intoxicated by the adrenaline and by Belinda, I just laughed it off.

It was impossible to be mad with Belinda around. She just clowned them the entire rest of the night, and it was wildly entertaining. They could not say anything back; they just took it.

Belinda was relentless and so funny about it that she had us all rolling. We drank and laughed until the sun came up. I took everyone home, saving Belinda for last.

I parked in front of her house, and we kissed as the sun rose. She said she had fun, and we laughed about what had happened. I watched her walk into her house. She paused before entering and turned to look at me; she gave me the sickest, most beautiful smile a girl has ever given me—a smile I will never forget.

What a night and what a girl.

CHAPTER 25

Belinda and I continued to talk on the phone. We both liked each other, but she was too afraid of what could happen to her if we were found together.

Belinda and I stopped talking after they expelled me from Green Valley HS for fighting. I would not even consider it a fight, more like a wrestling match, which happened during a disagreement at gym class, but I was a known gang member, so it was an easy decision for them... The purge continued.

It was almost summer, so I did not have to attend school for the rest of the year. I was free to do as I pleased.

Summer came, and Pearl Street was back in action. Once things died down, the police stopped patrolling the area, and summertime brought everyone back. Pearl Street was the default place all the kids in the area returned to.

Pearl Street picked off right where it left off. Joey and his family continued to allow drugs and alcohol to flow freely through the house. Not long after word got out, Pearl Street was back; a drive-by shooting took place while a bunch of us were outside. A vehicle had approached at a high rate of speed; there must have been at least twenty of us standing outside when someone from inside the car shot at us and at the house multiple times. Everyone instinctually ducked for cover.

Thankfully, no one suffered any injuries, but it was a sobering reminder of how quickly things could turn horribly wrong.

Mike brought his friends from school to Pearl Street and proposed holding a large BBQ at Paradise Park.

We set it up for the following weekend. It was a large gathering of mixed teen cultures. Crips, cholos, and stoners. The usual suspects were there, Dennis, Ryan, Kevin, Wade, Mike, Glenn, Tyrese, and a couple of others.

To my surprise, Gina, Jenetti and Melissa showed up as well.

It had been a hot minute since I had seen or talked to Gina. All three of them had made a hard turn into gang life; they were openly gangbanging, dressed in typical chola fashion, and acting hard around everyone. The only one who said hi to me was Melissa.

I was a rival and an enemy. Seeing Gina was hard; I wanted to leave. I still loved her deeply, but having this manufactured anger and tension after everything we had been through was emotionally taxing.

The BBQ was going well, another large group of teens arrived, and they had their own BBQ., There was no tension, and we pretty much stayed at opposite ends of the park. They did not seem to be gang-affiliated, just a large group of kids enjoying a summertime BBQ.

A basketball game on the outdoor court was creating a buzz. I walked over and began watching, trying to minimize my interactions near Gina, and trying to keep my thoughts in order. It was hard to be in the same place with her. I just wanted to go over to her and hug her and hold her, like old times. It was breaking my heart.

The basketball game drew increased attention. The attention was due to a girl, who was a part of the other group of teens at the park. She was a skilled player and killing everyone on the court. She dazzled the crowd with speed, athleticism and dribbling moves which kept the crowd oohing and aahing. Everyone was amazed at how good she could ball. She had legitimate skills. I was impressed, and it was fun to watch her; it was a needed distraction.

When the game finished, and as she walked back to her group of friends, Mike approached her and said, "I bet you $20, my boy there (pointing at me) can beat you 1vs1."

She took one look at me and said, "Bet."

I really did not want to play. I was in my head over the whole situation with Gina, sad and just not in the mood, but Mike put me on the spot, so I had to agree.

We decided to play to eleven, make it take it at three. Now, everyone was watching. The half-court we were playing on was surrounded by spectators.

Any dumb thoughts of "taking it easy" on her immediately left my body when she drove hard to the hoop and landed a well-placed elbow right to my throat.

That elbow hurt. She made the first point, and she was clearly not messing around. She was good and very tough. She used her elbows and hips very well if I tried to be physical with her. She had a good shot, too, so she was dangerous from anywhere.

I was playing my hardest, and drenched in sweat. Desperation began to affect my game, losing to a girl, at the time, would have been embarrassing.

Something my friends would make fun of me repeatedly and forever.

It was a back-and-forth battle. The heat was getting to us both, and every possession felt like the final possession. It was intense. People cheering, the sun beating down on us, and before I knew it, it was 10 to 10, her ball, and the next point wins.

I was dead. She had already been playing, so I imagined she was also feeling the effects.

The temperature was over 105 degrees that summer afternoon and the heat affected us both. The last point took forever. We both fouled each other hard, and neither of us wanted to give the other an easy point. There were no layups. If a drive to the basket happened, it immediately resulted in a hard and intentional foul. We both employed this tactic.

It became a battle of attrition, endurance, and skill. The crowd was into it, my friends cheering loudly and her friends doing the same.

Both of us were soaked in sweat. The ball stayed wet from the perspiration on our hands, and our faces were etched in stern concentration. Both of us zeroed in and committed ourselves to winning. Driving the ball to the basket was not an option.

Neither of us conceded an inch, and we both understood the last point was something we would need to earn. It was going to have to be a shot, and we were both exhausted. Face guarding every possession and relentlessly bodying each other up to prevent any room for a shot to release.

She had the ball at the top of the key. She dribbled through her legs, faked a hard drive left, and then dribbled the ball back through her legs as she stepped back right, creating a tiny bit of distance to release a fadeaway jump shot.

I was expecting the move. She had tried the move multiple times already; it was her go-to jump shot: on the right elbow, fading away. It was a hard shot to defend. I stepped to my left and jumped as high as I could, using my right hand to block the shot as she was releasing the ball from her right hand.

As I stretched to my full height (which is not saying much), my fingertips barely grazed the ball as it left her hands, flying in a high arch through the air towards the basket.

My defense had been on point. I had anticipated the move and the shot and could not have played it any better. After she released the ball, I turned and faced the basket; we both temporarily froze, watching in anticipation.

I was prepared to rebound the miss. She and I both stared at the ball, moving towards the basket in perfect rotation; I thought for sure that because I had grazed the ball with my fingertips, I had altered the shot, and it was going to fall short. Everyone held their collective breath, transfixed and watching with us. The ball, suspended in the air, longer than usual.

When it finally descended on the rim, it missed the entire rim.

It did not touch any part of the rim and fell through the basket with an audible metal "swoosh." It was nothing but net. A perfect shot: she won.

It was the first, but not the last time I would lose to a girl in an athletic competition. It was humbling, but not in a way that diminishes a woman's value. It was humbling because it taught me and everyone watching never to overlook a woman.

They were not less than, nor were they weaker or somehow needing care. Women were perfectly capable and even better than men or boys. She beat me in every aspect of the competition. Losing to a woman changed my perspective entirely, and I started to see women and girls through a different, more equitable lens.

I always had, but this experience solidified my thought process for dispelling indoctrinated fallacies about my upbringing in Ecuador.

Ecuador, for all its beautiful culture and nature, did, unfortunately, propagate the typical stereotyping of women "belonging in the kitchen, taking care of their husband and children." This is a common generational occurrence in most Latin American countries and cultures. It is complete nonsense, and thankfully, new generations of badass women and open-minded men are creating the necessary change to begin the process of a more equitable relationship at all levels of society.

Mike had to pay up. The girl and her group of friends were laughing and congratulating her; my group was laughing as well, but they were laughing at me.

It did not matter I was one of, if not the best, basketball player in our group, I had just lost to a girl.

Like the immature little shit I was, I started to get embarrassed, and I could see Gina laughing at me. Seeing Gina laugh at my expense, turned my embarrassment into a simmering rage.

Chapter 26

I should have congratulated the young lady who beat me and moved on, but I was a complete idiot.

As I walked past their picnic area, they continued their celebration, and this pissed me off even further. I was looking for an excuse to be an asshole. I focused on the biggest guy in their group. He was standing with his back against a tree, one of his legs bent, and his foot resting against the tree. I became laser-focused on him.

The only thing I could see was his mouth opening and closing in mocking laughter. I took his laughter personally, and I walked right up to him, having to look up at him because he was easily at least six feet three inches tall. I said, "I dare you laugh again?"

He looked down at me, perplexed. His look quickly turned to one of pity, like he was thinking, "Really? Is this little guy for real?"

When I stood my ground while continuing to stare at him and dare him to laugh again, he realized I was not playing and took it as the challenge it was.

He took his weight off the tree and stood tall; he was fucking huge. My little man syndrome in full effect, would not allow me to find a way out of this mess by talking. I was committed and had to see it through.

He looked down at me as if I were inconsequential. He stared right into my eyes and slowly and purposefully grinned widely.

I was expecting it. He was underestimating me, and I took advantage of his mental error. I responded by hitting him with a lightning-fast and hard right hand to his jaw. He was not ready for it.

The surprise registered for a split second on his face, and he almost went down. He staggered backward and was able to maintain his balance by placing his hand on the ground, but I was immediately on him. I followed it up with a knee to his forehead as he was semi-crouched, and he went down.

My group of friends had slowly made their way over while this was all playing out. When I threw the first punch, it was like the starting gun for a race going off. A melee immediately ensued.

Mike and Dennis may have been one of the few people in attendance who knew I was about to act up because as soon as I hit the kid, they also swung at one of his friends. This caused a chain reaction involving boys and girls from both groups.

A massive fight at Paradise Park.

The sun had begun to set, and fighting scattered over the park grounds. Everywhere you looked, you could see kids engaged in a fistfight. There were two-versus-one and even three-versus-one skirmishes, but mostly, it was mano a mano.

People at the park, trying to enjoy family time, ran to their vehicles and were forced to flee the area. Police would arrive soon.

We began getting the best of them. Suddenly, out of nowhere, the guy Mike was engaged in a fight with was able to break free from Mike and pull out a gun.

Someone saw it and yelled "gun!"

Everyone froze. Everyone stopped fighting and looked around. The kid who had pulled out the gun had it aimed right at Mike.

As a singular group now, we all stopped fighting and condensed around Mike and the kid with the gun. A huge circle of people surrounded Mike, and this kid with the gun pointed right at his chest. His friends began pleading with him to put it down; everyone was scared.

Introducing a gun into any scenario is never a clever idea.

Mike, his adrenaline still pumping, walked right up to the gun. He put his arms straight out to his sides, like wings, and walked his chest into the gun barrel. Mike's moniker was "Crazy" and given to him for a reason.

He dared the kid to shoot him. He even verbalized the challenge, shouting, "Shoot me Nigga!"

As this standoff was taking place, I had quietly maneuvered behind the kid with the gun. There was a table with attached benches between us, and I had one foot on the bench, waiting for the right opportunity.

When Mike finally calmed down enough and stepped back away from the gun... I decided to act. I jumped on top of the picnic table and launched off the table into the air. I jumped as high and as far as I could. I was able to catch the kid with the gun by surprise and brought my right arm down hard on his right wrist and hand, which was holding the gun.

The gun fell out of his hand and onto the grass. Mike immediately picked up the gun, but the police were arriving in droves. Sirens were visible and audible as they raced to the park. Mike was on probation, so he dropped the gun and ran. Everyone else still lingered around, not knowing what to do. Who was going to run first? Who was going to take the gun?

I decided to pick up the gun. As soon as I had the gun in my hand, it was like I woke everyone up from a trance. Everyone took off, including my friends.

The police were starting to arrive and surround the park, but I could not shake the weird reaction of how everyone reacted when I picked up the gun. I had never shot anyone in my life.

I ran too, but I kept the gun on me. We ran to Dennis' house, blocks east of Paradise Park, and met there.

I did not feel comfortable holding onto the gun, and no one else wanted it. I ended up selling the gun a few months later to a gang member from California. They called him "Bruiser," and he had just moved into the area with his girlfriend Tina. I was happy to be rid of it.

CHAPTER 27

As I continued to fade away from any activity with 28th Street, I slowly continued to build my bond with Mike, Dennis, and the crew around my neighborhood. Gang violence in the valley continued to expand. The Rodney King riots in LA caused a domino effect of street-level protesting and violence in most urban areas.

Unbeknownst to me, during this time, Popeye from 18th Street, the kid who was part of the group who shot at us at Sonic, suffered a gunshot wound, which killed him.

I heard the story of what happened from multiple sources. Apparently, while partying at a 18th Street kickback, someone waked right up to him and shot him. Dead on the spot. Murdered.

The news of Popeye from 18th Street being shot dead, a somber reminder of the world I had entered. At the time, I didn't even know if someone had been arrested for his murder, or who had been involved. Rumors, started spreading almost immediately. I had seen him one time. Our interaction, a violent one. Now, he was dead. I felt bad for him and for his family, but I had no real attachment to him. He was a stranger who shared my street moniker, and had once tried to kill me. (I later learned it was someone from his own gang who killed him.)

Then, a rumor started floating around that it had been someone from 28th Street who shot him. Naturally, tensions between 18th Street and 28th Street grew exponentially.

Soon, the rumor somehow evolved that it was someone from our crew involved in the Sonic shooting who had killed him.

What?

The beef with 18th Street and 28th Street was scary. There was palpable tension on the streets, but it did not affect me because I was no longer actively involved.

I was careful about where I went and who I went with and lived in fear because 28th Street and 18th Street were actively at war. I was terrified; it was making me a target, and I had nothing to do with it. I had disengaged from 28th Street. But rumors have a tendency and the ability to take on a life of their own.

We were out on winter break, and I was going to Opportunity School due to the fight at Green Valley HS. Right before school started, Natalie hit me up out of nowhere.

She wanted to come over and "talk." I had not spoken to or seen Natalie in over a year. It was strange she had reached out, but I was curious, and like most boys my age, I was horny. "Talk" only meant one thing to me.

I walked to the main gate area of my apartment complex to wait for her, as I used to do when we dated. I could see past the desert and the Sam's Club parking lot from the front gate and watch her walk across Pecos Road toward me. I stood there, bundled up and staring at her condominium community, waiting to see her emerge on the sidewalk.

It was a frigid winter night. I had my Raiders jacket on and a Raiders beanie. I was freezing. After at least ten minutes of waiting for Natalie, I gave up on waiting. I was horny, but even the thought of sex was not going to keep me out there a moment longer. It was too cold.

I was getting ready to walk back to my apartment to call her when, from my periphery, I caught movement to my right. I turned my head and saw three cars with their lights off slowly rolling up to me on the opposite side of the street. The cars were full of vatos from 18th Street. I recognized Pitufo's green Buick Regal as the lead car.

On instinct, and out of an intense fear from everything going on between the two sets, I took off sprinting.

I was outside the gate and on the street side, so I had to run down the fence line until I reached the pedestrian gate. I ran through the gate at record speeds, slipping and sliding.

I heard car doors opening and slamming shut behind me. There was a thin layer of ice on the walkways linking the apartment buildings, and I slipped hard on one of them. Hard enough to slide off the path and into a small grass and dirt embankment. I rolled on the ground and lost momentum.

The fall allowed them to recover and the gap I had created narrowed significantly; I could hear their footsteps echoing off the buildings. It sounded like an out-of-tune snare drum, a terrifying sound that only motivated me to run faster. I could hear them yelling, "Gt him esse, get him! That's the twinkie!"

Hearing that frightened me to my core.

I have never been so scared or run so hard and so fast in my life. I knew I would be dead if they caught me. When your life hangs on the balance of your ability to outrun your prey, it drives home a terrifying perspective.

The stupid rumors and my gang involvement created a situation in which my life was going to be determined by how fast I could run. Thankfully, I was faster than most and had a head start, but it did not make any of it less terrifying.

I was running in between buildings and down pathways. Running and not really knowing where to go. I did not want to lead them to my house. As I was running past Ty-Buds apartment, which was on a corner I was trying to take a left on, a big strong hand snatched me by the hood of my jacket and violently pulled me backward off my feet; I fell hard on my butt, and looked back, afraid they finally caught me. Thankfully, and to my surprise, it was Ty-Bud. He continued to pull me into his apartment, and I assisted by crab-walking backward.

Ty-Bud had been driving into the complex as the chase had started on the street. He was waiting for me with his front door cracked open.

We both fell into his apartment in a sitting position on his carpet. He immediately looked at me and put his finger to his lips, motioning me to shut the fuck up, and not say a word. Trust me, I could barely catch my breath... I was not saying anything.

We remained sitting on the floor because the blinds on his sliding glass door leading to his balcony were open, so we maneuvered ourselves against his couch. His lights were off, and his girl and his baby girl were thankfully visiting family in Cali. Ty-Bud held a pistol in his right hand, which just made the entire situation so horrifyingly real.

We heard a dozen or more kids run around looking for me, their presence casting long shadows on the ceiling of his apartment as they ran past the streetlights, back and forth, searching for me.

They could not find me, and after what seemed like forever, we finally stopped hearing or seeing any signs of them.

Ty-bud whispered, "stay here, don't move," as he stood up and headed for the front door. He walked outside and checked the area to make sure they were gone. When he was satisfied it was safe he came back inside and said, "Lil homie, those esses want you dead. I had to leave LA over similar bullshit, don't get caught up."

He was on his way out, so he walked me out, dapped me up, and told me to keep my head on a swivel. Ty-Bud, an OG Crip from Hoover Street in Los Angeles, saved my life that night. I owe him a deep debt of gratitude. He risked his life to save a young kid he bought weed from. I never saw him again, but I will never forget him.

When I got home, my mom was crying.

The past year and a half, I had put unimaginable stress and anxiety on her. I knew she waited up for me to come home at night, and I can only imagine the kind of anxiety she must have felt. To see your son constantly beaten up, arrested, and make this deep, dark, and violent change must have been agonizingly difficult.

I know my dad shared in the stress as well, but he dealt with it by not dealing with it externally. He was always afraid of returning to alcohol, and I did not blame him.

My mom took the brunt of all the suffering I caused.

Through panicked tears, my mom told me four Hispanic kids dressed in all black had knocked on the door and asked for me by name. She said they were scary-looking and did not appear friendly. When she told them I was not home, one of them handed her my Raiders beanie, which I suddenly realized must have flown off my head while I was running. She said they handed her the beanie and told her, "Tell Jonny we are looking for him."

My mom demanded to know if I was in trouble. She wanted to know if those kids wanted to hurt me. I tried to talk my way out of it and minimize what had just happened, but I knew she did not believe a word I was saying. My dad stood quietly behind my mom, his emotions hidden behind his stern gaze. He did not say a word, but I knew his mind was churning.

I can only imagine the kind of guilt my dad may have been feeling. I suddenly felt so bad and ashamed for having disappointed my parents.

When I asked my mom to describe the kid she spoke to, she described Pitufo.

Three days later, there was a drive-by shooting in the building behind us. 18th Street shot up Lisa's house, a girl who hung out with 28th Street, and a place I used to frequent. They shot the wrong apartment, but I will never know for certain. I was obviously the target, thankfully no one was home at Lisa's when it happened, and there were no injuries.

The drive-by shooting was the last straw for my parents.

A week later, I was on a plane returning to Ecuador.

CHAPTER 28

Quito, Ecuador 1993

My parents arranged for me to live with my Aunt Maria (my mom's sister) and my Uncle Jay (an American friend of my dads who taught music at the international school in Quito, Academia Cotopaxi).

My uncles lived near Pomasqui, a small town located near the center of the earth, near the equatorial line dividing our planets' hemispheres.

Three of my uncles (Uncle Fausto, Uncle Fernando, and Uncle Miguel) and my Aunt Maria bought land in Pomasqui and built homes around a small avocado tree plantation.

Pomasqui was approximately forty minutes north of the capital city, Quito. My Uncle Jay and Aunt Maria set up my room in their basement. They built a beautiful home; it was their personal design, and thankfully, it included a large basement. The basement, designed for my uncle Jay to use as a music studio, was repurposed into a bedroom for me. Placed on their lap abruptly, they kindly made room for me.

The things you do for family; my Uncle Jay gave up his studio for me. I was lucky they opened their home and their hearts to me because I was going through a challenging time.

They put an old, stand-alone closet in the basement for me. The closet reminded me of the one described in The Chronicles of Narnia, which was a secret passage between worlds. This one did not offer any adventures into Narnia, but it did serve a dual purpose.

When I arrived, I learned I would not be returning to my old school, Academia Cotopaxi, with my old friends, which was hard for me to comprehend and accept. Instead, I attended Alliance Academy, a Mormon American School, which was also Cotopaxi's biggest rival.

I was not happy.

Arriving back in Ecuador brought back a myriad of memories for me. I had only been gone two years, but I had changed so much that I was having a tough time understanding who I was. Being back in Ecuador felt safe, like I could be a kid again, but my recent experiences deeply morphed my core makeup into a convoluted set of emotions, which had me confused and afraid.

Even though I associated and continue to associate Ecuador with the happiest times of my life, there was a darkness I kept at bay. It was recessed into the area of my mind where these dark thoughts go to hide. In the US, my trauma from my experiences allowed me to forget about my childhood trauma in Ecuador. But, now back in Ecuador, unburdened with the stressors of surviving the streets, my memories flooded my brain, and they became a relentless loop of emotional turmoil. Unfortunately, it was not something I could control.

I sat in the basement, feeling sorry for myself, missing my family, and contemplating my life before suddenly uprooting to the US and what it had become.

The earliest memories I can access are from around 1982, I must have been in first grade at Martin Cerere.

When I try to access memories prior to this time, I cannot do so—met with a very strange and scary sense of raw fear. My sister Denise has expressed a similar feeling. She has memories of a family friend doing something unspeakable. I know there is trauma I am repressing, but I am afraid to face it. The impending doom I feel when I have actively tried is just too terrifying to step into. At this point in my life, I do not even know if remembering would be useful.

As my young mind fissured with the inability to fully comprehend possible early childhood trauma, I pivoted to moments in my childhood which felt congruent and eased the panic beginning to set in. I sat alone in the basement and actively attempted to bring back memories of when I first stepped into a life I will never forget. A moment and a place which remain frozen in time, a unique and condensed environment which fostered the type of meaningful relationships people can only dream of. An educational institution so small, and so diverse; it forced a level of intimacy and community, usually only seen in close knit families. My memories slowly brought me back to my school, Academia Cotopaxi, but with all the warmth of comfort it brought, there was a darkness waiting to pierce the serenity I searched. Memories I actively repressed and worked hard to keep hidden in the deepest darkest parts of my temporal lobe. I fell fast asleep in the silence of the basement, remembering.

Chapter 29

Quito, Ecuador - 1984

Fourth grade at Cotopaxi started rough. I was in Ms. Hunsberger's class with my friends from last year. Ms. Hunsberger was tall and thin, with a short, round haircut. She wore glasses and always wore long dresses. My friends and I called her "Ms. Hamburger."

She was nice but stricter than Ms. Dee. She was also more demanding of her students. I was not going to make it academically with Ms. Hamburger. She did not care if my dad was her colleague or if English was my second language. It was clear from the start that she did not believe I belonged in her class.

Since arriving at Cotopaxi, I avoided the indignity and social suffering peeing my pants created. Thankfully, I was not forced to field questions about why my sweater was tied the wrong way, a tactic I had incorporated at Martin Cerere to hide my peed trousers.

It was a huge relief to have "grown out of it," but I continued to wet the bed at home nightly. My parents kept telling me it was normal and that I would eventually grow out of bed-wetting as well.

Not until I was an adult, with my own kids, and receiving therapy, did I begin to understand peeing every day at school was not normal and it was not something "you grew out of." I continued to wet the bed at night until I was 18 years old.

My academic problems, due to my lack of a firm grasp of the English language, continued to set me back in school. Halfway through fourth grade, they moved me into a permanent ESL class with my dad's close friend, Mr. Dibble.

It was sad to leave all my friends, but we shared recess and lunch times.

Mr. Dibble, my new teacher, looked like a hippie. He always had a tan because he rode his bike everywhere, which made his skin look a bit worn. He had light brown hair cut in the shape of a bowl and sported a thin athletic build.

Mr. Dibble became one of my dad's drinking friends at Cotopaxi, and he and my dad became close. Mr. Dibble was over at our house often and went out with my dad drinking daily. Mr. Dibble was also a Vietnam Veteran, and I am sure my dad and he bonded over their shared trauma.

Mr. Dibble was also a great teacher and a nice man. I began to quickly show academic progress. I was his favorite; Mr. Dibble had become a family friend of sorts, so it made sense he looked out for me and focused on my progress.

Being in ESL forced me to make new friends. I developed a close friendship with a kid from Israel named Dror, a girl from Venezuela named Paula, and as you already know, a kid from South Korea named Byung-Il Yoo. They were all new to the school and all struggled with English.

Paula became instantly popular. She was from Venezuela and fit the common stereotype of Venezuelan women; she was beautiful. All the boys in our grade liked her.

Dror, Byung, and I bonded over Mazinger (a Japanese anime), WWF Wrestling, and sports in general, while Paula slid in nicely with Fiona, Paulina, Monica, and Andrea.

I continued to feel like an outsider, an impostor, and kids sometimes went out of their way to remind me of it.

Comments about my clothes were a common reminder. While all the kids who played soccer used "Adidas or Mizuno," soccer cleat brands, I used "Kit Deportivo" cleats. Kit Deportivo was a local brand and the equivalent of a "Walmart" shoe purchase in the US.

My friends all acquired the new Sony Walkman's everyone loved in the 1980s or came back from vacation with a new Swatch

watch. The boys dressed in Guess and Lacoste, with sweaters draped over their shoulders in typical "preppy" fashion.

I did not have a Walkman; the clothes I wore were either used the year before or had been handed down to me by my cousins in Chicago. I certainly did not have a Swatch watch. Everyone had one, and everyone loved to show off their Swatch watches. It was annoying, and it also always left me feeling less than.

These small nuances made me feel out of place. I wanted those things, and I wanted so badly to fit into their reality, but I simply came from a separate set of circumstances—a realization that took me a long time to come to terms with.

The year rolled around effortlessly. My grasp of English was becoming stronger, and my ability to cope with my new reality was becoming more manageable. My friends were a tremendous help.

Chapter 30

While transitioning to Academia Cotopaxi, I developed my interest in skateboarding. It was an activity I could do alone, which is something I have always enjoyed.

My dad tried his best to be present and involved. At the time, he had started his Master's Degree program, taking courses at night, which unfortunately led to more opportunities for him to go out drinking.

My sister was not into the same things I enjoyed, my brother was too young, and my cousins were not always around anymore. From early on, I learned to use my imagination and play on my own.

This affinity for solitude manifested in running and endurance sports as I transitioned into adulthood. I find comfort in being alone and in suffering in silence. It is familiar.

In the spring of 1985, right before summer vacation arrived, my mom and dad moved us from our small apartment in Las Casas to an apartment within walking distance from our new school. The new apartment was on the corner of El Vengador y Mercurio, near the largest park in the city, Parque de la Carolina.

Right next to our new apartment was a large deserted lot with an unkept basketball court in the middle of the lot. It was designed to be a small neighborhood park, but the concrete basketball court was the only progress before abandoning the project. (I returned 35 years later to find the lot remained unchanged. A small childhood memory, frozen in time)

The absolute best part of moving, was my friend Dror lived a street up from us, and Byung about a 10-minute walk away. My friends from school were now also my neighborhood friends.

Dror loved to skate, too, and we strengthened our friendship over skateboarding. We rode our boards to school together and spent time skating around the neighborhood. After school and on weekends, we rode to the "Super-Maxi," a local chain grocery store with a location near our house. It was in a strip mall, and the entire mall was connected by an outdoor covered walkway. The walkway, built on a slight incline and connected by a series of stairs along the entire route; approximately eight flights of stairs, with four steps in each set.

We would begin at the top of the strip mall, near the arcade and "King Pollo," a local fast-food chicken joint. We would take turns leading and skating while jumping stairs all the way down.

Jumping the stairs was not easy, and the more we did it, the better we got. When we first started, we had problems landing any of the jumps or clearing all the steps, taking some gnarly falls in the process. Skinned knees and bruised body parts were common when we skated, but after hours of repetition, we were able to ollie over the stairs with ease.

The route ended at "Tropi-Burger," a local burger spot located right next to the west end of the strip mall and conveniently connected to the last set of stairs.

Dror and I always stopped for fries and a soda, and if we had enough money, we would get a burger too. The store owners and employees at the strip mall knew us, and we never got any pushback for skating. Skating at the venue was encouraged. An ice cream place called "Zanzibar" would often offer us free scoops of ice cream when the weather was hot. We jumped those stairs with such frequency that we became a fixture of the shopping environment.

I enjoyed cruising the neighborhood streets on my skateboard. There is an element of raw liberation I found in skateboarding. Moments of adrenaline and a focus on improving and mastering the art of controlling my body and the board simultaneously. Once you achieved the connection between the board and self, it was a feeling of exhilaration that left you yearning for more.

Skateboarding and its sub-culture would become a part of my adolescent identity.

Chapter 31

Three older Ecuadorian kids also skated in our neighborhood, and occasionally, they would stop and skate with us.

They were friendly, and they taught Dror and me new tricks. The older kids were good. Their names were Ignacio and Horacio. They were brothers, but they did not look alike at all. Horacio had long hair down to his shoulders. He was shorter and more athletic; Horacio was taller. He wore glasses, his hair was short, and he had a dark disposition.

Then, there was Mono (Monkey), a term used for individuals from the coast of Ecuador. I did not know it at the time, but the term was racist; oddly enough, it was also a term of endearment, and Mono introduced himself as such. Mono was short, with a typical skater cut, extremely athletic, and he was Black. He was a local skating legend. Mono was the best. Sometimes, they would skate with us in the street in front of my house for hours.

One night, before everyone went home, Mono pulled a Betamax tape out of his backpack and told Dror and me to watch it. He claimed we were now "The Bones Brigade Team" and said we would understand what it meant after we watched the movie.

Dror and I looked at the movie's title: "The Search for Animal Chin."

Dror spent the night at my house, and we watched the film. The Search for Animal Chin thrust Dror and me into a world we did not know existed. We learned about The Bones Brigade Team, Powell Peralta, and the best skaters in the world: Tony Hawk, Steve Caballero, Lance Mountain, Tommy Guerrero, and Mike McGill.

We fell in love with the entire subculture. We were now on our own mission, searching for the elusive "Animal Chin!"

Motivated by watching the film, Dror and I rolled a small launch ramp we had all built out to the street. Mono and the others had been teaching us how to launch off the ramp, and Dror and I spent all night trying to land new tricks.

Our Ecuadorian version of the Bones Brigade team came to life. For the rest of the summer, we skated every single day, all day. We street skated, ramp skated and spent any free time we could on the southeast corner of the Parque De La Carolina, where a large concrete skatepark was located.

The skatepark was free to anyone. There were no rules, and park employees were not monitoring or managing anything. It was also the only skatepark in the entire city, so it was always full of kids and parents. We shared the space with different platforms and levels of ability—our biggest rival for space were the kids with bikes. Bikes stayed on the north end of the park, where the ramps were taller and steeper; they also had control of the full pipe with a connecting bowl. Bikes dominated the park.

Little kids and "posers" inhabited the middle area of the skate park, where the ramps diminished in size and vert. This area included a large flat surface for beginners, and parents also congregated with their children. It was a chaotic situation, and you had to be aware of your surroundings; big collisions happened daily.

We, the skaters, had the entire south end of the park to ourselves.

The South end had a corner we could launch from (like the ramp we built, but made of concrete, steeper and taller). It had a small concrete half-pipe attached, which transitioned into a large quarter-pipe ramp with a small vertical wall.

Years later, I used the quarter-pipe ramp to land a high "method-air" trick, which won me the Championship in Quito.

It was all we needed, and we loved it. "Carolina" became my second home.

Chapter 32

Fifth grade was the last year we remained on the "baby side" of the school. Once we moved to sixth grade and Junior High School, we would rub shoulders with the cool High School kids. It was our final year of being "little kids."

Moving to sixth grade gave us access to the new computer lab. Cotopaxi had recently acquired the brand-new Apple Computers, the Apple Computers used in computer class, were all the rage. The screen was completely dark, with a green cursor pulsating to catch your attention. When you typed, there was a slight delay before your green letters appeared on the screen.

We mostly used them to play learning games, like "The Oregon Trail" and "Where in the World is Carmen San Diego?" Using a computer became a favorite activity for every student.

I had turned eleven years old and was in the sixth grade. I continued to skate and play basketball. Our Bones Brigade Skate Team remained intact, and we spent every afternoon after school at the skate park. Bones Brigade gained new members: Patrick, a good friend from Cotopaxi, and Dario, a surfer from Venezuela, whom we befriended at the skate park. We skated together daily.

My family was also doing better in terms of our quality of life. Working at Cotopaxi gave my dad a salary in American dollars, which elevated us on a socioeconomic level. My mom continued to work at USAID, and my dad continued his distance learning master's degree program provided after school at Cotopaxi. The master's program was sponsored and taught by the University of Alabama.

The stress of teaching, being a father and a husband, and now going to school at night took a toll on my dad. He began to drink on a nightly basis.

The biggest problem with my dad was residual, caused by my dad's trauma from Vietnam. As his drinking increased and became more frequent, he began to display an unfortunate tendency of volatility and unpredictable behavior.

To understand my dad and his deep trauma, you must understand his generation and his upbringing. Perspective is necessary.

While in Vietnam, he suffered a gunshot wound to the left calf—the round, a 7.62, fired from an AK-47. The wound left a long and visible scar running down the center of his calf, from just below the back of his knee to where the calf meets the ankle. The injury, initially treated in the field, created a gnarly scar on his leg, but it was his mind that suffered the worst damage.

Random scarring on his back was also visible due to wounds he suffered from shrapnel, and his skin displayed blotches of white skin caused by Agent Orange the United States used in Vietnam.

My dad suffered severe physical injuries while involved in one of the bloodiest, most savage battles of Vietnam, The Battle of Huey City.

War is not normal. It is an anomaly in a person's life for which no amount of training can prepare you. It is a savage primate awakening of carefully hidden DNA passed through ancestral feral barbarism, stored away, and activated to survive unexplainable horror. War fires up those neurotransmitters, causing something in your mind to shift permanently.

My dad, being only seventeen when exposed to war, his mind not fully developed with the necessary maturity to navigate the mental minefield; he did not properly cope.

A burden that healthcare professionals, at the time, were only beginning to understand. There was no specialized help for it. No actual resources. No one really cared or knew how to deal with the mental trauma caused by war.

My dad did not have the benefit of resources and treatments available today.

His remedy, to self-medicate with alcohol.

I do not blame him. My dad managed his trauma the best way he could. No one really understood his pain or his mental anguish. Imagine having to reach the hidden ability tucked in your brain somewhere, a coded gene that allows you to take a human life.

It is certainly not a current evolutionary trait we can access in regular twentieth-century life. To tap into it, it must rise to the surface under extreme conditions, usually conditions that present a life-or-death balance.

Anyone can access the ability to be violent, but having to cross the line repeatedly changes you.

Think about the break from norms and established reality you need to continually force yourself to make, creating a nihilistic mindset. It breaks men, and the journey to a level of normalcy is fraught with the kind of peaks and valleys that would exhaust expert mountaineers.

My dad numbed his memories and anxiety with alcohol. He drank himself into stupors.

His self-medication, unfortunately, grew increasingly toxic. Looking back, it was a steady progression of escalating incidents. He was crying out for help, but no one knew how to help him. It's such a sad de-evolution of such a good man—an unfair set of life circumstances.

Chapter 33

My dad's relationship with alcohol continued its downward spiral. Not only was my dad drinking daily after school, but he and a couple of other teachers began drinking during the day. Sometimes, during school hours.

Beatings at school soon followed. One is seared in my brain, again, not due to physical damage or trauma but due to the emotional burden attached to the circumstances.

On a weekend, my dad was out drinking late; he arrived home in his usual condition. He had been out at the bar with Mr. Jimenez (a Spanish teacher at Cotopaxi) and Mr. Capello, one of our neighbors who worked at the school.

I remember this night because my mom became unusually upset with him. One of the few times I witnessed her meek demeanor show some teeth.

I was in my room, listening to music, when I heard my dad come in. Everything seemed normal, or what was normal for us; my dad entered his bedroom, shut the door behind him, and usually, they went to bed.

This time, I overheard arguing. I could not make it out, so I quietly slipped out of my room and entered my sister's room next door. My sister's room was next door to my parents, who shared a wall. When I walked in, my sister was already nosy with her ear to the wall, and she shushed me by bringing her finger to her mouth. I took a place next to her on the wall and mimicked her by placing my ear on the wall.

My dad removed his clothes and left them on the floor to get into bed. My mom, as usual, picked them up and emptied his pockets before placing them in the laundry bag.

As she emptied his pants pockets, she found a condom. My mom was understandably very hurt and incredibly angry. They argued in the room, trying to keep their voices down, but my sister and I heard the entire exchange.

My dad slurred his words and denied doing anything wrong. He claimed it was just a joke, that Ramiro (Mr. Jimenez) placed it in his pocket as a joke.

My mom was not buying it, and we could hear the devastation in her voice as she cried softly. She must have cried herself to sleep; I am sure my dad passed out quickly, leaving her to suffer alone and in silence.

I slept with my sister that night.

I went to bed full of anger. I blamed Mr. Jimenez and Mr. Capello for my dad's actions.

Mr. Jimenez happened to be one of my teachers. When I entered his classroom on Monday morning, I felt red-hot rage—an intense anger slowly coming to a boil. I was directing all my frustrations and pent-up emotions at Mr. Jimenez, and I hated him for it. Instead of blaming my dad, I blamed Mr. Jimenez; it was all his fault.

The only sensible way I could produce, to express how mad I was, was to be as bad and as annoying as possible in his class.

I was in rare form that day. I started by breaking off the erasers from all my pencils and throwing them at Mr. Jimenez when his back turned. I was throwing them hard and with bad intentions. Aiming for his big dumb head. When I missed, the erasers bounced forcefully off the chalkboard with a loud "whack!" Mr. Jimenez turned beet red and moved me from the back of the class to the front row. He admonished me for my behavior and warned me he would send me to the principal's office if I continued.

I did not care.

After he placed me in the front row, I waited a couple of minutes and began shooting spitballs at him.

I used an empty pen shell to shoot them and made them extra wet and extra soggy. I started shooting them at his back. He was wearing a sports coat and could not feel them, but they were sticking to his coat, and it was funny. The kids started to laugh. He was clueless. He kept turning around, trying to catch what was happening, but it only made it funnier. I loved it.

Finally, I shot a big juicy spitball right to the back of his head. It landed with an audible wet "smack!" I did not even try to hide the fact it had been me. I held onto the empty pen casing and stared at him with contempt.

He sent me to the Dean's office to see Mr. Burniske.

When I arrived at Mr. Burniske's office, my anger and aggression left my body all at once. My anger melted out of me during the walk to his office. The only emotions left were exhaustion and sadness.

Mr. Burniske was a friend of my dad's. He was a kind man and easy to talk to. He played basketball with my dad twice a week, so he knew me well.

I burst into tears the second I sat on one of the chairs in front of his desk. I explained what I overheard at home and told him I hated Mr. Jimenez and how I blamed Mr. Jimenez for the entire thing.

Mr. Burniske listened patiently without interrupting me. Then, he calmly talked to me and reassured me that my parents would be okay. He asked me not to overreact or think terrible things about my dad.

He calmed me down, and I stopped crying. Once I had composed myself, he sent me to see the principal, Mr. McCann.

I sat with Mr. McCann for the remainder of the period and into the next one. He listened to my story and, like Mr. Burniske, assured me everything would be okay.

When my dad arrived, I stepped out of the office to wait while Mr. McCann and my dad spoke. Approximately twenty minutes later, my dad emerged and, without even looking at me, gruffly said, "Come with me," over his shoulder as he walked by me.

I half walked; half jogged to keep up with him on our way to his classroom.

His classroom had relocated to a better and bigger one above the elementary school playground. The new ESL department consisted of four classrooms. We walked up the wooden steps to the second level and made a right; his classroom was the first one on the right. It was empty.

He held the door open for me and stood at the threshold, waiting for me to walk in first. I walked in and heard him close the door behind me.

I slowly turned to face him, and as I completed my half-turn, I was greeted by my dad taking a hard and aggressive step forward and shoving me hard with both hands directly on my chest. The power from the shove lifted my feet off the ground and sent me crashing against his metal desk.

He then started to "talk to me," which was more of a barely controlled, vexed whisper. He was struggling to keep himself together, and his anger was palpable. He said, "How could you tell Burniske what happened at home?" "What happens at home is no one's business, and now you have embarrassed me in front of the entire school!"

He followed his barely controlled admonishment with a swift and hard punch to my stomach, which crumpled me. The strike took the air right out of my lungs. He took more swings, hitting me on my back, ribs, and shoulder, but the impacts felt unusually powerful. His anger was evident in the pain he was delivering.

Alcohol, clearly oozing out of his pores and heavy on his breath. I was still trying to catch my breath from the first blow and lying on my side, his desk behind me. I had my eyes closed. I did not want to look. I had learned to close my eyes because remembering my dad's features when he was in a drunken rage corrupted my mind from the man I knew him to be. His worst moments were not a reflection of his life or his love. I did not want those mental polaroids.

I lay there, cringing in the darkness behind my lids and expecting a second wave of pain. Instead, I heard his footsteps recede; the door opened and then closed. I opened my eyes. I was alone.

I stood up, sore in the places he had struck me. Tears were streaming down my cheeks, but I was not actively crying. I heard kids laughing in the playground below me; I gingerly walked to the window and looked down.

Elementary kids were having recess. I watched as they slid down a slide, walked over rubber tires, and jumped off them onto the grass. They played tag and tetherball or congregated with the teacher on duty. I watched from my perch and took it all in. It was only a few years ago that I had been doing the same thing on the same playground, but now, it felt like a lifetime ago.

As I watched, my dad walked by the playground, away from me on the concrete pathway and towards the front of the school. His usual gait and Marine like walk, were not present. He was walking slowly, pensive-like, and his body sagged. His shoulders were slumped, and his gaze was fixated on the ground. I watched him walk away diminished, and I knew he felt bad for what had just happened; I started crying.

I was crying hard, alone in his empty classroom; I openly sobbed. I loved him so much, and all I could think about was how I had disappointed him and caused problems for him at school. I just wanted to be good and make him proud so he could get better.

I watched the kids play by the window until the bell rang. It was the final bell, and the school day was over. I picked up my book bag off the floor, wiped my face with my shirt, and walked out of the classroom. I walked into the empty playground where kids had been playing moments ago. I walked to the front of the school and picked up my skateboard from the guard shack. No one checked on me. No one knew. As I exited the front gate, I walked through crowds of teachers, parents, and kids.

My dad was on gate duty and talking to a group of kids out front, just outside the gate. I walked by them all, unnoticed and kept going. I did not ride my board home, I walked. I felt alone.

As I walked home, dejected and sore, I realized home was not where I needed to be. I felt ashamed of having embarrassed my dad and, in the process, my mom. My weak emotional immaturity caused a domino effect of problems, which now involved my entire family.

I could not go home. I went to my one safe place, my place of emotional refuge. I put my board on the street and started skating to Fiona's house.

Chapter 34

Over the years, Fiona became one of my closest friends, and I became dependent on her. I spent so much time with her that I developed feelings for her. Fiona was sisterly, even maternal, and a caring friend to everyone, but she had a distinct way of calming my mind and helping me solve all my problems.

The feelings I developed were not reciprocated, and even though it crushed me, I was happy to have built such a close and strong friendship with her. When most girls would get annoyed at unwanted attention, Fiona embraced it and helped me channel my feelings into a meaningful and lasting friendship.

She always treated me kindly, was always available to listen, and had the right temperament to calm me down when I was in turmoil. There was no one I trusted more with my problems than Fiona.

When hanging out with Fiona, most of the time was spent on the seventh floor of her massive house. The seventh floor was the top floor, which was designated for her and her sister Vanessa. The entire floor, about three times the size of our family's entire apartment, was a virtual play area. It had its own T.V., with Betamax and VHS, and was decorated with comfortable couches and large floor pillows. The layout included a ping-pong table, toys, and an ample collection of board games.

I have been to impressive houses in my lifetime, but Fiona's house was unique in its design and architecture. It is my favorite house of all time.

As I rode my skateboard to her house, I used the ride to calm my mind and to consider the eventful and exhausting day. Sometimes, Fiona would look out for me, watching from her parent's private elevated yard, and she always seemed genuinely happy to see me. I loved spending time with her.

Fiona was of British and Peruvian descent. Her dad was an executive at Lloyds Bank in Ecuador, and they were very wealthy. Fiona was uniquely empathetic, non-judgmental, accepting, and an awesome human. She was the one person I told everything to. I could share all my problems with her, and she did her best to help me navigate them. We would often sit in her room, or one floor up (on the seventh floor) of her house, and talk for hours, Madonna usually playing in the background.

On this visit, Fiona noticed I was more troubled than usual. So, in typical Fiona fashion, she pulled out an old school tape recorder and took me down to her room.

We sat underneath her open window, and she stuck a blank tape into the recorder. She immediately took my mind off my problems by engaging me in an impromptu live interview.

It worked. She successfully redirected my attention, and we talked into the tape recorder about nothing and everything.

Fiona kept the tape, and years later, when we were entering midlife, she mailed it to me. I could not believe the tape was still in existence after so many years.

When I played the tape, it felt surreal. I was overcome with emotion as our voices brought the past to life. I was transported back to the moment, sitting under her window, Madonna playing in the background.

My mom picked me up from Fiona's and took me home. The entire way home, we did not talk about what happened. We rode in silence. When we arrived, my dad was sleeping, and I was relieved. I was emotionally exhausted.

The next day, my dad apologized. I felt such strong respect, love, and empathy for my dad that forgiving him was easy and natural. I felt bad for him and just wanted to help him. I begged him to please stop drinking.

He promised me he would and told me it was his New Year's resolution.

Chapter 35

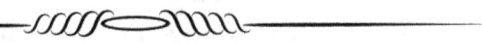

My dad tried to change. The beatings became less frequent, except for a notable one.

Before Christmas arrived, I found a U.S. $50 bill in my dad's dresser. I stole it. It is important to understand how much 50 dollars was worth in 1988, especially in Ecuador, where $1 U.S. dollar was worth approximately $3000 Ecuadorian Sucres. I took those 50 dollars and went to "El Caracol" (The Snail), a mall near Parque de la Carolina designed to look like an actual snail.

I spent the money on gifts for Fiona. If I remember correctly, I bought her a large teddy bear, a box of chocolates, and flowers. The salespeople one hundred percent took advantage of me, and I used the entire $50 on items I could have obtained for $3.

I was excited to be able to express myself to Fiona through gifts.

I took a cab to Fiona's house and was giddy about presenting her with the gifts. A small part of me was hoping she would love them, and like in a movie, suddenly and unexpectedly, she would express her love for me. Happily, ever after.

The Disney ending, which I built up in my mind, did not happen.

She met me downstairs to open the front gate. I awkwardly handed her the gifts as she stared at me in disbelief. She was confused. She did not smile shyly or express any positive vibes; she did not suddenly throw her arms over me, announcing her hidden crush, and her face went from inquisitive to concerned to mad in a matter of seconds.

She was processing everything, then her face turned stern and serious, and she stared into my eyes. She was not happy with me or with her gifts either.

She immediately started telling me how my parents showed up at her house. My dad figured out I took the money, and knowing how close Fiona and I were and that it was Christmas... it was probably where I was headed.

Fiona told me my parents were annoyed with her over my actions, and the entire exchange made her uncomfortable.

Not the way this interaction had played out in my mind.

I don't know if they tried to take the gifts back or not; my memory is hazy about what happened with the gifts. What I do remember is what happened when I got home.

I went straight into my room and put my INXS record on. I played the music loudly, trying to drown out my mom and dad's argument. I knew they were arguing about the money, about my actions, and about the fact that the money was more than likely gone and unrecoverable. I heard the argument intensifying as my dad attempted to walk to my room.

I could hear my mom and sister crying and yelling: "No, John, please don't!" "No, Dad, please just leave him alone!"

The door to my room flung open forcefully. I had been lying on my bed, and I jumped up fearfully. Knowing what was coming.

My dad stood on the threshold of my door, breathing hard, clearly drunk, and half-carrying both my mom and my sister as they continued to try to stop him. Each attached to one of his arms. He shrugged them off as if they had been nothing more than toddlers.

He crossed the room to my bedside in one long and intimidating step. He stood directly in front of me, staring down at me menacingly, the alcohol from his breath soaking my senses. There was no talking; he reached out with his right hand and wrapped his bear-like paw around my throat. He spun me around, my back now turned to my mom and my sister, and he proceeded to lift me off the floor while choking me and simultaneously walking me against the wall.

I hit the wall hard, both my hands clutching at his right hand, trying desperately to break his grip. He used the wall to apply more forward pressure on my throat. He was still only using his right hand and pushing my mom and sister away with his left.

I started to feel the world closing in around me, losing consciousness. I could feel myself slowly slipping into darkness.

Suddenly, my dad let me go. I was standing directly in front of him; in one swift and impossibly quick motion, he punched me with his right hand right in the mouth. I had a split second of registering and recognizing the blow coming and turned my head and body low and to the left, trying to duck or slip the punch. I failed. I took the force of the blow on the right side of my jaw. This time, I succumbed to the darkness and fell fast asleep. Knocked out.

I woke up to my mom sitting next to me on my bed. We were alone in my room. She was weeping softly while gently holding my left hand in her own. I looked at my mom and felt a mixture of emotions. Her pain, her tenderness, her attempt at trying to protect me, her disappointment in what I had done, but more than anything, I felt a deep strength in her love for all of us.

A quiet determination to see our family through the worst of times. At that moment, I realized my mom was much more than I ever realized. She was the steady foundation that kept our family from crumbling. She was our safety line and the one person we could always count on, all of us. Without her quiet strength and devotion to us, we would never have survived our challenges.

My love and respect for her took on an entirely new meaning. I saw her in a way that switched my perspective of her. Where I once saw a meek and controlled woman, I now understood the force of nature she truly was. She was unbreakable, and everything she did or endured was from a place of deep love for her family.

CHAPTER 36

Religion is woven into the fabric and national identity of most Third-World countries. It provides an illusion of hope where otherwise none exists.

My mom and my grandma weaponized religion.

The ultimate psychological controlling mechanism known to man, is fear-based theism.

I bought into religion in a big way; I did not have a choice. I was indoctrinated into its beliefs from early on. The fear of the devil and hell a present and a constant reminder not to veer off the Christian path or suffer in eternal agonizing pain.

Of course, you could repent to a random priest who would absolve you of all your sins. In penitence, pray ten Hail Mary's, and God will forgive you.

What a joke.

It is a historical manipulation of epic proportions—a swindle so powerful that nations went to war over it.

I never liked going to mass, and they dragged me every Sunday. Church was the most boring place on earth. The only place I hated more was a trip to the dentist.

I was forced to pray every night before going to bed and every morning when I woke up. I was made to feel fear and guilt for anything I "might" do or even think of doing wrong.

Anyone in Ecuador who lived life outside the religious norms and expectations was judged privately, vilified, and demonized. If you were not Catholic, you were a bad person.

My grandma, Mercedes Terán Guerra, and my mom constantly reaffirmed the worst aspects of religion. They would tell us "bedtime" scary stories, like how my great uncle encountered the devil and fought him off in his barn.

My grandma told us how my uncle committed a sin (the sin was whatever fit anything we may have done that day) and how, while he was walking home from work late at night, he saw the devil.

The devil manifested to him in the form of a black dog with red eyes. According to my grandma, no matter where he turned or how fast he ran, the dog always remained visible, watching him menacingly. When he finally got home, he thought he was safe and began preparing dinner. While cooking dinner, he heard something in the barn. He went out to inspect the noise, and according to the tale, a demon attacked him.

Of course, during the battle, he asked God for forgiveness and was able to fight off the demon. As proof, he had large claw-like injuries on his back.

Theist fear-based stories were common. She repeatedly told well-known local legends like "La Mano Negra" (The Black Hand) and "El Carro Ronco" (The Hoarse Car).

These kinds of religious fear-mongering techniques, used with the intention of manipulating children into "good behavior," caused me to suffer from extreme anxiety into adulthood.

I was impressionable, gullible, and trusting of adults; I believed all of it.

La Mano Negra caused me to have an unhealthy, extreme fear of the dark.

La Mano Negra presented to us as "The Devil's Hand." They told us it would appear in the dark, materializing right out of the street or out of a wall. The hand was immense, bigger than a human, dark and hairy. They told us Mano Negra snatched kids, and they disappeared forever, taken to hell for being bad.

To say the tale traumatized me is an understatement.

These theist-based tools caused me to be in a constant state of fear. Anytime I did something "wrong" or "unchristian-like," it caused me to believe the devil, at night, would pull my feet, pulling me under my bed and into hell.

To this day, I continue to tuck my feet under the blanket because it was something I did to cope with the fear as a child.

These fears, implanted in my mind as a child and constantly reinforced as a manipulation tool, remained rooted in my psyche until my late twenties. I could not shake them. It was so ingrained into my identity that I could not apply basic logic to them.

My mom used fear and religion to manipulate my behavior, never understanding the psychological damage it caused me.

> In her defense, my mom did not know any better because this is exactly how she grew up and explains so much about her.

My mother and my sister continue to be fervent believers in Catholicism, and my mom continues to use religion arbitrarily in attempts to control emotions, influence decisions, and overall insert her ideology over our personal views. Sadly, it is a generational and institutionalized mentality she will never be able to shed.

Even though I complained about it, and it affected me, I know it all comes from a place of love and care. In her mind, she is doing her duty to God and deeply believes in prayer and religion.

My path away from theist beliefs caused daily friction between us and has become a source of deep sadness for my mom.

Regardless of our differences, my mom is the common denominator in our characteristics related to kindness and empathy. My mom wears her heart on her sleeve and has always made every decision for her family firmly rooted in love and her interpretation of what is right. My mom is my version of what an angel would be if they existed.

Kindness personified.

My dad was a bit more complex. He was also raised Catholic and participated in the church from an early age. When I was a kid, my memories of my dad were of a man who played along to get along. He did not go to church with us, and I never saw him or heard him praying, but he claimed to be religious when the situation required it.

The times my dad beat me were always preceded by heavy drinking and the surfacing of his untreated PTSD. Anytime I suffered a beating from my dad, it was almost routine for him to find me in my room and apologize.

His apologies were sincere and heartfelt. The agony and guilt he felt were genuine, and I could see it in his eyes. It made me unbelievably sad, and his pain was evident. Any suffering I experienced paled in comparison to what I could feel my dad going through. His eyes always searched mine for a hint, indicating I understood. I could feel the remorse emanating from him, trying to will me into full comprehension. An unseen battle raging in his heart and mind.

I understood him and never took any of the episodes personally. I never felt like there was anything to forgive, only to understand. Religion was a tool I utilized to forgive my dad. I prayed for him every night.

Chapter 37

On New Year's Eve 1988, I was a teenager and too cool to participate in dressing up and begging for money, which is part of a unique set of traditions Ecuadorians use to celebrate New Year's.

My mom's family celebrated with us, and my good friend Scruggs also came over. There was food and loud music, and the party was in full effect. Inside and outside of my house, family, friends, and neighbors commingled. My uncles brought a box full of fireworks to set off at midnight, and the box was placed on the sidewalk right in front of my house.

At around 11:45 p.m., everyone congregated outside near the empty lot next to my house. They were preparing the fireworks, and everyone was excited.

A beautiful Finnish girl named Anna had recently arrived and moved down the street from us. Anna was tall for a girl, a little taller than me. She had long, toned legs, full lips, and gorgeous long blonde hair. She was also an excellent basketball player, and we instantly bonded over our shared love for the Chicago Bulls and Michael Jordan.

Anna even had the first Jordan shoes to come out, the Jordan One's. I was so jealous.

Anna attended Cotopaxi as well, and she and I developed an instant connection. She was confident and experienced in expressing herself. She was not shy about her feelings and had no patience for shy little boys like me.

I was timid and scared, especially around girls. Anna's confident nature terrified me. I was naive, with little to no experience interacting intimately with a girl. The most I had ever done with a girl before meeting Anna was hold hands and dance with my ex-girlfriend, Jennifer.

While we waited for the fireworks to be set up and the new year to come around, Anna, Scruggs, and I were hanging by the entrance to the empty lot next to my house and standing away from everyone else.

Anna held my hand and gently pulled me toward an abandoned building next to the lot. She wanted to kiss. I was such a dumb little baby and initially resisted because I was scared. I had never kissed a girl before.

Anna was undeterred.

She pulled me into the building, and even though I was terrified, I wanted to kiss her as well, so my resistance was subdued by my curiosity. We walked up to the terrace on the third floor overlooking our entire street; it was a magnificent view because the building was on the corner, and we could look both ways down both streets. We were looking over the side, watching the party below us, when Anna grabbed my face with her hands, made me look at her, and kissed me.

It was my first kiss. I am sure I was terrible, but the moment was like magic. I did not know what to do, but it was okay because Anna was the one in control. We kissed for a while, and I loved every second of it. Having such a special and beautiful girl be my very first kiss had me walking on clouds.

When Anna was ready, we stopped. She looked at me, smiled, grabbed my hand, and, like a lost little baby, guided me back outside to the lot. I know I must have had a shit-eating grin plastered on my face.

We returned and stood by the entrance to the empty lot with Scruggs. It was a familiar place for us; she and I began our friendship playing basketball in the lot. I was still floating above the ground and felt like the luckiest boy in the world. I was in love.

We stood watching as a new year ushered in. My uncles were beginning the fireworks display. Suddenly, as one of my uncles started to light one of the fireworks, a piece from the burning fuse dislodged and landed on the box of fireworks. The box instantly caught on fire, engulfing the entire box with flames.

Fireworks started flying in every direction. A cacophony of lights and sounds mixed with smoke assaulted all our senses. Streaks of colors flew across the sky in every direction. The whistles and explosions were an endless assault on our ears.

The night turned into an uncontrolled pyrotechnic nightmare. Everyone ran away, seeking cover. Some laughed and enjoyed the erroneous yet dangerous display; others scared and cowered behind cars and walls. Anna, Scruggs, and I retreated into the lot and watched safely from behind a concrete pillar.

Out of the corner of my eye, I caught someone on the ground making an odd movement. The individual was near the sidewalk directly in front of my house.

I turned my full attention towards the person on the ground and looked closely. It was my dad.

On instinct, I left the protection the pillar was offering us and approached him as the fireworks continued but subsided.

The thick smoke, which made it hard to see, was slowly dissipating. I could hear my dad yelling something unintelligible and was frightened by it. I approached carefully, unsure of what was wrong and not knowing how to help him.

He was on the street, next to the sidewalk, rolling around on the ground with his hands covering his ears and yelling from deep in his lungs a raw and terrifying, "Take Cover! Take Cover!"

Watching my dad in such a vulnerable state broke me. All my shared trauma with him; his drinking, his guilt, his suffering… It all played out in an emotional erosion for everyone to witness.

During the fireworks accident, my dad was mentally transported back to Vietnam. None of us fully understood what it was like for my dad. The terror on his face, the pleading intensity in his voice, the reality he was reliving; a violent juxtaposition seared in my mind and my heart.

Watching my dad at that moment brought me the kind of comprehension one wishes never to reach. It was painful and heartbreaking. I stared at him, confused and frozen with uncertainty.

My mom suddenly appeared out of the mist and was by his side, gently getting him to stop rolling around and yelling, whispering something to him only he could hear.

My mom slowly brought him back to reality and calmed him. My mom helped him sit up, and the look on his face was confused. He was visibly trembling, and tears ran down his face freely. My uncles assisted my mom in helping him up, and my mom took him inside. Everyone stood around in stunned silence, solemnly processing what had just occurred.

The party was over. Happy New Year.

Chapter 38

The relationship between my dad and I grew stronger. He organized a group of students, including my close friends, to play flag football every Saturday at Cotopaxi. I played a little on Tuesday and Thursday nights when he played basketball with his friends.

The most meaningful development, which later became a major therapeutic, Zen-like part of my life, was my introduction to distance running. Occasionally, I joined him on his morning runs at Carolina, if I woke up early enough. Those early morning jogs became a silent bonding between father and son.

The air at dawn in Ecuador was always cold, crisp, and damp. Our breath, visible as we exhaled, and the cadence of our strides pounding the sidewalk... the only conversation we needed.

The silence was loud and full of emotion. Each mile connected our energy, and the pounding of our hearts healed us from all our shared trauma. Running became symbolic for me in so many ways and for so many reasons.

My dad continued to drink, but his propensity for violence slowly, but not fully, evaporated. The changes in my dad created positive familial and social ones as well. My sister and I started to perform better in school, and our social life expanded in healthy ways. Our family was making steady and positive progress as a unit. We crawled out of the fire together, and we were slowly beginning to heal.

Unfortunately, my good friend Dror, my Bones Brigade teammate, and my partner in the elusive search for Animal Chin, moved back to Israel. I missed him, and skating was not the same without him.

I continued to skate daily, but the joy of sharing it with Dror diminished it. Jumping the stairs at Super-Maxi, something Dror and I did daily, was no longer fun. Scruggs was not biking as much anymore, and Patrick lived too far to join me, so most days after school, I skated by myself.

Ignacio, Horacio, and Mono, the original Ecuadorian Bones Brigade team, broke up. Unfortunately, Ignacio and Horacio started abusing drugs, and skating was not a priority for them anymore. Mono went back to Guayaquil (the second largest city in Ecuador on the Pacific coast), where he was originally from, and the only remaining member of our skate-or-die Bones Brigade skate squad was me.

Skating remained a huge part of my life and my identity. I grew to idolize Tony Hawk, and even though home life was much better, I preferred to be at the skatepark. Even now, as an adult, when I meditate, my mind goes to the skatepark in Carolina, to the empty concrete waves, the sun shining warmly, and the only sound... the wheels of my board as they smoothly roll up and down the concrete embankments, in endless serenity.

Chapter 39

1989 is in the running for being one of the worst years of my life.

One great thing about 1989, before I delve into how sucky it turned out to be; was my dad completely stopped beating me. He occasionally spanked me, when I deserved it, but his drunk Vietnam fueled beatings, ended.

The first indication 1989 was going to be bad, came in the beginning of the school year.

Teen boys, in general, are lacking in anything resembling an actual thought process. It's all testosterone, impulsiveness and a whole lot of stupid. We "invented" a game on the pull-up bars at school. The object of the game was to grab the bar as if you were about to do a pull-up but remain hanging. Then your friends begin to push you from behind as you swing back and forth. With each push, you gain speed and momentum. To win, all you needed to do, was reach the highest point of the swing, and jump off.

Genius! What could go wrong?

Strict rules were established, of course. You couldn't push too hard, you could choose two people to push you, and once the person on the bars, yelled, "Stop!" No more pushing was aloud.

It was lunch time, and I was up next on the bars. I chose Patricio and Paul to push me. I was close with both of them and trusted them to be careful.

My good friend Mario was in the crowd watching, Mario was a known prankster, and never skipped an opportunity to create a laugh. If he wasn't spitting into his hands and patting down the sides of his hair with his saliva… he was playing a joke on someone. Mario was our very own version of a funny Ricky Martin.

Patricio and Paul slowly and gently pushed me as I hung from the bar. I gained more and more altitude with each shove. As my momentum gained, I started getting nervous and was about to yell out, "Stop!"

When… Mario, in an attempt to be funny, used the opportunity to get behind me, joining Patricio and Paul, and gave me one final and hard shove.

The combined force of their collective final push was enough to propel me high into the air, causing me to lose my grip at the apex of my ascent. I flew off the bars, legs and arms flailing wildly. As I felt myself nearing the ground, I instinctively placed my hands out and slightly behind me, attempting to absorb the impact. I landed with a hard thud on the grass. My hands landed first and then my butt, but my hands and arms took the brunt of the impact.

I knew something was wrong, but I sat there, somewhat dazed and confused. I was in shock, but at the time I didn't understand what was happening. Everyone was standing in a tight circle around me. Some of my classmates covering their eyes and turning around, some with mouths open in disbelief, and some unable to look away, and turning pale with a worried look on their face. All of them staring right at me.

I was in a state of total confusion; I heard someone yell out, "Oh my God, look at his wrist!"

I was still sitting on the grass, exactly the way I landed. Legs splayed out and separated in front of me, leaning on my hands which were placed behind me. I slowly brought my right wrist into my field of view and could see nothing wrong with it. Before I could even register relief, someone yelled out, "The other one!"

I started to bring my left wrist into view, and when I was able to look at it, I almost fainted.

My left hand was completely limp and dangling awkwardly, as if attached to my arm only by my skin. Both bones connecting my wrist to my hand, obviously broken. The broken bones, visible protrusions pushing against my skin, barely contained and stretching my skin in an abnormal manner.

It was a gruesome visual.

I yelled! Not from pain, because I wasn't feeling any yet, but because the sight of my arm scared the shit out of me. Everyone's reaction to the fall did not help to alleviate my fear, it compounded it. Watching my hand hang, unable to control or move my fingers, was terrifying!

Suddenly, my dad was at my side, "Jonny Boy, what happened? Are you ok?" He picked me up in his strong embrace and carried me to the nurse's office. I was crying now, but still from the gruesome visual and the fear it invoked, I was not feeling any pain yet.

We arrived at the nurse's office with a crowd of kids and faculty trailing us.

The school nurse, a nice caring lady, could not hide her deer in the headlights look as she saw my hand. If a look could talk, she would have been screaming, "Oh shit!"

My dad sat me down on a chair, and she nervously tried to assess the damage, but even through the shock of the moment, I could tell she was not prepared to deal with this kind of an injury.

She conducted a quick examination of my wrist, turned towards my dad, and said, "I think they are just dislocated."

She asked my dad to hold me tight, while she tried to place my obviously broken bones back into place! I think my dad was so nervous and stressed out, he wasn't thinking clearly, because he went with it.

The nurse grabbed my limp hand with one of hers, and then used her other hand to grab my forearm, just above the injury. She pulled and pushed, in an attempt to set my bones.

I felt the pressure of the broken bones as she tried to unsuccessfully push them down into my arm. The pain I felt in that moment assaulted all my nerve endings and senses. It was one of the worst feelings of pain I have ever experienced and hard to put into words. It was agonizing, and as expected… I passed out.

As I came to, my dad was carrying me from the nurse's office, across the campus, and out the front gates; he hailed the first cab he saw. He got into the back seat of the cab still cradling me in his arms, and told the driver to drive fast to Hospital Metropolitano (the best hospital in the city).

My dad held me for the entire ride, draping his sweater over my arm, and comforting me with encouraging words I don't remember. Keeping my injured arm as immobile as possible. The tenderness he looked at me with, causing an existential understanding of a father's love for a son.

The cab ride was important for me. Rare moments of emotional vulnerability displayed by my dad left an indelible imprint in my memory.

During the ride, he petted my hair, and kissed me on the forehead repeatedly. He was worried, and I was in pain.

The hard shell he engulfed himself with his entire life, crumbling freely and unapologetically, showing his soft loving nature. Emotions he usually hid, due to generational complexities, and traumatic events, faded. His demons temporarily at bay, and the only persona flowing through him; a loving and caring father.

I suffered a compound fracture, passed out from the pain of an attempted "resetting" of my bones and had to endure an impossibly long cab ride through 3rd world traffic; the moment with my dad, was one of the most meaningful, paternal memories I have and hold close to my heart.

When we arrived at the hospital, my dad refused to leave my side. He remained holding my hand until I entered the operating room. I was operated on at Metropolitano by Dr. Guerra. He was able to place my bones back without using screws or pins. I had a compound fracture on both my radius, and ulna bones, and was in a cast for six months.

The injury gave me permanent wrist problems. I don't have equal strength or range of motion in my left wrist and am unable to touch my thumb to my pinky.

Gracias Mario

CHAPTER 40

At the beginning of the 1990 school year, my ninth-grade year, two brothers from Argentina arrived at the school; I will call them the "S" brothers. One of them, Javier, became my classmate; his older brother, Luis, was a Junior in High School. They were short and displayed the Napoleon complex commonly associated with insecure individuals. Both smart asses, bullies, and prone to prey on those they felt were beneath them.

Javier was funny and shorter than Luis, and he kept his negative characteristics in check. We became friends, but our friendship was not built on normal values but more out of convenience. Javier became close with Fiona, so naturally, I had to spend time with him. He did grow on me and, with time, became likable.

His older brother Luis, on the other hand, was a jerk and a troublemaker. You would expect people with unusual or uncommon physical appearances to be more empathetic and sensitive to others who may share similar or perceived traits.

Not these brothers. In ways, they were both a rare breed of bully. They used mean-spirited words in preemptive verbal attacks to deflect the narrative and take attention away from them. It was a clever tactic.

They did not physically intimidate anyone because their stature prevented it, but they were rude and mean. They hid personal insults and slights behind "jokes," masking distasteful behavior behind manufactured laughter. They both shared this characteristic, but Luis was consistently persistent.

Luis turned out to play a key role in the trajectory of our entire family's future.

Cotopaxi was known for hosting fun, creative, and inclusive events. Every year, different festivals held at the campus: cultural festivals, food festivals, science festivals, music festivals... you name it, Cotopaxi had it. The festivals were always fun, filled with a plethora of activities for both adults and kids.

The entire campus was usually utilized for festivals. Every section of the school offered a separate set of entertainment possibilities. There was always live music, multiple food options, carnival games, and of course... alcohol for the adults.

In 1990, during my ninth grade at Cotopaxi, the school held a huge International Food Festival. All my friends and their families attended. Attendees included diplomats and their families from multiple Embassies, students and teachers from other American Schools, and the who's who of the local wealthy class system.

Everyone always looked forward to the festivals; hanging out with friends and running around the school freely with little to no rules was a rare opportunity.

During the Cotopaxi 1990 International Food Festival, I was having fun. I spent time with friends, eating food, playing games, watching live music, etc. The entire festival was a blur of laughter and good vibes. As the day started to turn into night, with the sun setting, parents started to gather their kids to head home.

My entire family was at the festival. My sister Denise, who is three years older than me, was with her group of friends and was too cool to interact with me. My little brother Kevin, who is five years younger, was just a little guy running around with his own friends, doing little kid things. I occasionally saw him running by, having the time of his life.

My mom left the festival as other families began to disperse, wanting to get home before the rest of us. I had seen my dad sporadically during the festival but had not seen him for hours; I suspected he was drinking with his friends in one of the classrooms, which was the norm at school functions.

In today's updated social and professional expectations, teachers drinking in a classroom during a school-sponsored event would be illegal and deeply frowned upon. Back then, for educators and parents to co-mingle and consume alcohol at an event with kids around was commonplace and just part of the culture.

As the campus slowly emptied of people, I was conversing with friends by the outdoor basketball court, sitting at a picnic table discussing basketball. It was not unusual for my dad to be one of the last people to leave. He was in possession of the school's master keys and trusted with locking things up during events like the festival.

I was in a heated debate with Scruggs and Jeremy about Michael Jordan and Magic Johnson when, out of my periphery, I saw my uncle Jay, my sister, and my brother walking quickly toward me. Their body language and my Uncle Jay's sad look made me instantly nervous. I knew something was wrong.

My uncle Jay was the head of the music department at Cotopaxi. He stopped short of the basketball court and beckoned me with his hand to join him. The sick feeling I already had in my stomach intensified. As I bid Scruggs and Jeremy farewell, I slowly and fearfully walked over to my family. When I arrived in front of my uncle, he said, "I have to take you guys home." The tone in his voice and his stern face were enough for me to follow silently.

When we arrived home, my mom was waiting by the door, crying. We walked into the house, confused and anxious. My mom stepped outside with my uncle, and we eavesdropped from the window.

My sister told me what she knew: Luis had engaged in an incident with our dad. She heard Luis had become disrespectful and something bad had happened, but she did not know any additional or specific details.

My mom and uncle's conversation filled in my sister's fragmented story of what occurred.

My dad grabbed Luis aggressively by one of his arms, causing an injury. One of Luis's parents was at the festival, and a confrontation ensued. My dad was in trouble.

When the full story came out, it was embarrassing. My dad made a mistake, but context is important.

My dad had a well-known drinking problem, which created the environment for the narrative of the incident focused solely on his behavior. My dad was wrong, and I will not excuse his actions, but in my experience, the gray areas are where the core of the truth lies.

I received multiple versions of what transpired from various sources. Sources present during the incident or with direct knowledge. The following is the closest interpretation of what may have happened:

My dad volunteered to work and supervise during school-sponsored functions. When he finished with his assigned duties, he usually met with his co-workers in someone's classroom, where they drank beers and hung out. It was not unusual for parents and faculty to walk in and out of these get-togethers during events.

During this festival, they chose Mr. Dibble's classroom. The door to the classroom was kept open, a common occurrence, and people freely walked in and out, including students.

One of the teachers drinking with my dad, and a good friend of my dad's, was Mr. Szweda.

Luis saw the teachers in the classroom and entered the classroom to interact with them.

From everything I heard, Luis started a friendly and funny banter with the teachers. The friendly exchange became serious as Luis became disrespectful, and the interaction became negatively charged.

Luis focused his verbal abuse on Mr. Szweda for no apparent reason. Mr. Szweda, known as a kind, intellectual man, was considered an easy target by Luis, compensating for his insecurities.

Everyone loved Mr. Szweda. He was tall and thin, with bright red hair and a full bright red beard to match. He wore glasses, and his suits were usually mismatched and too big for him. He was the visual definition of what people would categorize as nerdy but a cool nerdy with a unique flair.

Mr. Szweda was beloved by the students and faculty; he exuded kindness and compassion.

Luis continued hurling unwarranted insults at Mr. Szweda, calling him "Gay" and a "Faggot," among other denigrating comments. His remarks were repulsive, and the banter stopped being funny or playful to everyone.

Before I continue, keep in mind that most kids at Cotopaxi come from extremely wealthy and important families—well-connected families that exerted considerable influence in Ecuador. Teaching jobs at schools like Cotopaxi were highly coveted. Teachers received a salary in US dollars, and the job was instrumental to their quality of life overseas.

So, while the teachers attempted to control and reprimand Luis for his behavior, they were too afraid to physically remove him. Luis was out of control and enjoying the malicious nature of the exchanges he was creating. He relished his perceived status and power over Cotopaxi employees. All the teachers, too afraid to lose their jobs, just enabled his behavior. Luis was incessant until my dad decided he had heard enough.

While Luis continued his undeterred disrespect, my dad silently watched it unfold and brooded. When my dad reached the limit of his patience, he stood up and menacingly told and directed Luis by pointing at the door, telling him to leave the classroom immediately.

Luis, in typical rich, spoiled, and bully fashion... refused.

At Luis' refusal, my dad began to step aggressively around the table and move towards him; Luis hurled verbal insults at my dad, and then, in an act so unexpected and vile, Luis spit at him.

Please take a moment to consider the kind of perceived narcissistic superiority someone like Luis needs to have learned or developed to think spitting at a grown man, or anyone was ok.

Luis treated Cotopaxi teachers as peasants, servants he could bend to his will. He showed no respect, and this behavior was obviously reinforced, allowing him to treat people menially. On this day, Luis chose wrong. He crossed the wrong line with the wrong person. His callous and offensive disrespect was about to come to an abrupt halt.

As soon as Luis spit at my dad, my dad instinctively rushed at Luis aggressively. Luis, eyes wide in fear and surprise, not expecting any actual consequences, let out a pathetic yelp and took off running.

Luis took off sprinting towards the front gate of the school, crying and calling for help, my dad hot on his heels.

My dad caught Luis by one of his arms as they neared the front gate to the school. Luis was in a state of terror and being combative, trying to pull away and kick at my dad.

My dad struggled to restrain Luis and, in the process, twisted his arm to gain control and compliance. I don't know if my dad was intentionally trying to hurt Luis; my guess is he was not, but his intentions didn't matter; he hurt a kid, and regardless of the circumstances, he was wrong.

Allegedly, the twisting of the arm to control Luis injured his arm. They claimed my dad had broken his arm.

My dad lost his job over the incident. The school, to their credit (with a huge influence from Mr. McCann, the High School Principal) found a clinic in Boston, MS., specializing in Vietnam Veteran's with Post Traumatic Stress Disorder (PTSD).

Cotopaxi facilitated and paid for my dad to get treatment at the clinic. My dad was gone for approximately six months, getting the necessary mental health treatment to help him cope with his experience in Vietnam.

Upon his return, he found himself out of a job. Ecuador is a small place, and Quito is even more condensed, and he was unable to find work at any other international school. The incident with Luis was a major factor.

Unable to find a job, suffering from professional and personal embarrassment, and needing a fresh start, my dad decided our only alternative was to move to the United States.

A place I had only visited once, to Florida, to visit my Aunt Mo (my dad's sister).

My parents had to sell everything, leaving us with only the clothing items with which we could travel. They did not have work lined up or a place to move into. Our lack of options left us with only one option: move to Chicago, Illinois, to my grandma Sullivan's house on the west side of Chicago.

My grandma Sullivan lived alone in a one-bedroom house the size of a standard two-car garage. There were five of us, plus my grandma, in this tiny house.

Welcome to America.

Chapter 41

1990 - Chicago, IL

Arriving in Chicago was a disruptive culture shock for all of us but intimately visceral for my sister and me. We had just spent 15 years (the first 15 years of my life) in Ecuador, a third-world country. All we knew were the lives we had to abruptly leave, and as a family, we were unprepared for the challenges a city like Chicago would mercilessly thrust at us.

My dad and mom found jobs quickly. My dad was a teacher at a school, and my mom went back to work for Mars Chocolate Factory, where she met my dad almost 19 years ago.

My little brother Kevin was the only family member who seamlessly assimilated to the drastic change. He was young, only nine years old, and it took him little time or effort to integrate into the American culture.

My parents spent a considerable amount of money to send my brother Kevin and me to private Catholic Schools. I went to St. Patrick's High School, located in the northwest area of the city, and my brother went to St. Francis Borgia, located on the west side and a block away from my grandma's house.

They invested in private education, mainly to prevent us from attending public schools in Chicago. They thought we were unprepared for the social pressures and challenges a public school in a big city would bring.

They were not wrong.

We only spent one year in Chicago, and I stayed to myself. I was not foreign to bullying, but I was not expecting the kind of mean-spirited, physical bullying I experienced in Chicago.

I spoke almost perfect English, but I did have an accent. Spending the first fifteen years of your life in South America, with Spanish being your first language, will do that. My accent caused me problems at school. Private Catholic schools in Chicago are separated by gender and attended by a mostly white student body.

At school, the students mocked my accent, called me racist names, and at times pushed or shouldered me in the hallways. Sometimes, the shoves caused my belongings to drop on the floor. The big city environment and the culture shock I was experiencing forced me to withdraw into a cocoon; I was scared. I became shy, and my confidence and self-esteem suffered; socially, I became awkward.

While in Chicago, my love for all Chicago sports only intensified. There was a park a block away from my grandma's house, Hiawatha Park, and I spent every moment I could there playing basketball. It was mostly young adults who played at the park; they played rough and took the game seriously.

My time on the blacktop at Hiawatha assisted in my knowledge and skills of the game and exponentially elevated my growth in the sport. I continued to improve and slowly gained a reputation on the court for being a talented player.

I went from being picked last or not picked at all during pick-up games to always being picked on a team. It felt great.

On weekdays, I was at the park as soon as I came home from school, and on weekends, I spent every waking moment at Hiawatha... usually remaining until the basketball court lights shut off.

To this day, I regret not trying out for the basketball team at St. Patrick's HS, but my dad facilitated soccer to be my focus.

My dad had grown up with the athletic director at St. Patrick's, and when they spoke, he told him I was a good soccer player. They asked me to try out for the freshman team. (I had to repeat ninth grade because English continued to be an issue for me, especially grammatically.) After ten minutes of playing with the freshmen, I moved to the varsity team.

I excelled athletically at St. Pat's, but it did not help me socially. I played soccer with the varsity team and football with the junior varsity, so the few friendships I made were with upperclassmen. I was a freshman at school and had zero connections with any of my freshman classmates.

The bullying at school continued. In Ecuador, I did not face any exposure to any racially motivated hate or behavior. It was not a part of our lives. Never brought up or discussed. I had little to no experience with racism. So, when students at St. Pat's insulted me, I did not understand what the insult was and only recognized it as an insult by their tone and the mocking laughter that usually followed.

With the help of my cousins, I slowly started to identify the racist terms slung my way.

I learned my mom was experiencing similar interactions at work, mostly due to her being an immigrant (she was not a US citizen yet) and for speaking English with a heavy and noticeable accent.

Derogatory and racist slurs were made toward her, and she was having a rough time adjusting. Our house was small, so even when my parents tried to keep conversations private, we could usually overhear it. My mom was suffering. I began to empathize with my mom in a big way and felt bad for her. She missed Ecuador, and she missed her family. Moving to Chicago was difficult for her.

At school, when kids found out I had recently moved from Ecuador, the first reaction was usually confusion because I looked white and did not look like a "foreigner."

Classmates in Chicago did not know where Ecuador was located. Once, during Catholicism class, when the teacher asked me about life in Ecuador, a kid asked me, "Do you guys live in the jungle? On trees?"

The sad part, he was not joking.

When a group of kids at St. Patrick's noted my accent, which until moving to Chicago, I never even knew I had, they started to call me "beaner." This group of kids wore cowboy boots and cowboy belts with large cowboy-themed metal belt buckles. When school finished for the day, they would put on their cowboy hats, which they kept in their lockers.

There was one kid in the group who was particularly cruel. I do not remember his name, but he was big and fat, and I remember him looking older than us. He had noticeable facial hair and projected a mean disposition.

He was mean for no reason, and one of his cruel tendencies was to slap the books out of student's hands as they walked past him in the hallway. He mostly did it to the nerds, the vulnerable, and the marginalized.

The few times he got me, he always followed it with, "You little beaner," as he walked away with his friends laughing.

It was annoying, and all the kids who were victims of his bullying hated him. We tried to avoid him in the hallways, but it was not always possible. He would leave a wake of kids on hands and knees, picking up books and papers off the floor. Their laughter and the clicking of their cowboy boots echoing off the walls left a residual and infinite shame as they walked away triumphantly… their laughter slowly fading with distance.

Chapter 42

Basketball at Hiawatha became a second home, and I was slowly gaining my confidence back. My cousins were also a tremendous help. My cousins, Mike, Jason, and Joey, lived close to our house with my dad's sister and my aunt, Patty Ann. My cousins started trying to hang out with me, and Jason and Joey began coming to the park. Once they recognized I was decent at basketball, our relationship solidified.

All my cousins played sports and took athletics seriously. They played football and basketball at their schools and were known in the area as being athletically gifted. Being athletically gifted was typical of all my family from Chicago.

With my cousin's presence, basketball at Hiawatha opened a new circle of friends for me. Other kids congregated at the park, usually sitting around and talking, so I never had a reason to speak to them. My cousins knew these kids, and they introduced me. Soon after basketball, I walked over to Oleander Street, my cousin's street, and hung out there with a group of kids.

Oleander was a popular street, full of kids my age. Every weekend, they participated in an activity. They played whiffleball, street football, tag, or just hung out on one of the porches and talked. My cousins were instrumental in creating a small group of kids I could call friends. It was helpful in getting me through the constant cultural shift I experienced daily.

Slowly, I started to feel more like myself, and my confidence grew; socially, I began to step out of my shell. Bridget, a nice girl from Oleander (my cousin's neighbor), was an important outlet I started to tap into.

Bridget was always kind and thoughtful. She was always curious about my life in Ecuador, and every time she saw me, she greeted me with a genuine smile. In retrospect, I connected with Bridget so well because she shared Fiona's best qualities. She made me feel welcome, cared for, and comfortable. Bridget became a lifeline in a sea of uncertainty.

At school, my confidence and social awkwardness started to recede as well. The bullies continued to target those they felt were weak and vulnerable, and I was beginning to lose my patience with them.

I castigated myself for having to reroute my path around the school to avoid them, arriving late for class on multiple occasions. Once, I even hid in a bathroom stall to stay clear of them. I did not like how intentionally avoiding them made me feel. There was something intimately distasteful about it. I knew a confrontation was imminent, but I was afraid.

The confrontation presented itself unexpectedly on a rainy and cold afternoon. I remember it being rainy and cold because I had to walk multiple blocks after taking the city bus to arrive at St. Pat's, and I was cold, wet, miserable, and in a foul mood.

Before I delve into what happened, a little backstory is necessary.

In Ecuador, I took three years of Shotokan Karate. The school was two blocks from our house, giving me something to do other than skating. I did not go every day and was not fully committed, but I did progress to a green belt. Earning a green belt does not really amount to anything. Karate is not the best martial arts to practice, but the one advantage it gave me was basic knowledge of angles, kicking ability, and basic fighting fundamentals.

So, continuing...

I knew a confrontation would occur. The mood I was in that day contributed to what happened next.

A period finished, and I began making my way to my next class, walking up a set of stairs. As I trudged upward, still generally pissed off, I could hear the bullies above me as they slapped books out of student's hands and as they ran down the stairs toward me.

They were predictably laughing and behaving like total pricks. Hearing the chaos developing above me made me even angrier. The hard tapping of their dumb cowboy boots as they made their way down the stairs annoyed me to my limits.

I was ready.

As we neared each other on the stairwell, and they were moments from turning the corner and being face to face with me, the bravery and anger I had been feeling drained right out of me. Instead, they were replaced by fear and the urge to avoid them. Fight or flight mode was in full throttle—flight, trying to overpower any bit of courage I had mustered.

The stairway was filled with kids going to class. There was no available bathroom stall or connecting hallway, so there was nowhere to run or hide.

Suddenly, they rounded the corner and made their way down the stairs towards me, presumably still laughing at one of the students they had just terrorized. The fat bully was leading the pack, walking down the stairs in his Z-Cavaricci pants, panting and sweating. We locked eyes, and he gave me a menacing scowl as we passed each other.

I remained on the inside, near the guardrails, forcing them to walk by on the outside, hugging the wall. I quickly shielded my books by transferring them from my left hand to my right hand and away from their reach.

As I made my move, shielding my belongings, his friends all made the instigating "Ooooh!"

This clearly annoyed Pig (which is what I will call him because he looked like one), and as we passed each other, Pig tried to turn and come up from behind me, attempting to knock my books out of my hand from behind.

I sensed his posse pause and turned my head slightly, just in time to see him turning towards me on the stairs. Even though I was terrified, my mindset was clear, I was going to fight.

As he tried to knock my books out of my hand from behind, I turned towards him, using my left hand for support on the handrail, and side-kicked him with my right leg. The kick landed forcefully right in the middle of his ugly face.

I caught him by surprise, and he was unbalanced on the stairs. His awkward positioning caused him to get a little air as he fell backwards. He bypassed the final three stairs suspended in the air and landed unceremoniously, with a loud thud, flat on his back on the landing below him.

As cool as it was and as cool as it felt, the kick was total luck. He was standing two stairs below me, trying to reach my books, and stretched out unbalanced. As I turned towards him in a quick and unexpected motion, Pig shrunk back in surprise, caught in the act. The kick was really a waist-high kick, but due to our placement on the stairs, it connected with his face.

The only thing preventing him from significant injury and me from being in major trouble was the large backpack he wore on his back. Thankfully, his backpack took the brunt of the impact as he landed on the floor. His winter jacket was rolled into it, and he bounced off the floor and hit his head on the wall.

The bully was stunned, and his friends were equally so; every student on the stairway froze in place, me included.

My kick gave him a bloody nose, and he became discombobulated from my swift and violent action; he did not try to get up and continue to fight. Thank God.

I looked at each of his friends (three of them) carefully, making sure the fight was over for them as well; it was clear it was. Then, I casually turned around and continued up the stairs.

It was by far one of the coolest moments of my teen life. It felt electric. The adrenaline filled my body and nerves like a constant low-voltage electric shock.

The bullies never bothered me again. The kick must have been a memorable visual because everyone talked about it. As I walked around school, kids pointed at me and whispered. One of the "nerdy" kids, Greg (who had become my only friend at St. Pat's), thanked me for it. He had been a frequent target and was happy someone stood up to them.

As a bullied kid who always felt out of place and less than, this was a moment I daydreamed about daily. I could not believe I had gone through with it. I was on a high over it.

The high ended quickly. I arrived home that evening, still feeling good about myself. I was the last one home, and as I walked in, I was met by my entire family, clearly waiting for me to arrive. They were all patiently seated at the kitchen table and stared at me.

My dad looked up at me with a smile on his face and announced, "Good news, Jonny Boy, we are moving to Las Vegas!"

Yay, another move, another school. It could not be worse than Chicago.

CHAPTER 43

Quito, Ecuador - 1993

I woke up startled, confused about where I was, and shaken by how real the memories had been in my dream.

For a moment, I sat and reflected on what I had been through since we first left Ecuador in 1990. My experiences left me feeling like I had lived an entire lifetime in someone else's body.

I was emotionally exhausted. Almost three years later, finding myself in the basement of my aunt and uncle's house was a disorienting and confusing reminder of what my life had become.

Day had turned into night, and the darkness was stifling. We were in the middle of nowhere, and the land where my uncles built their homes had no streetlights. The moon's ambient light, the only reassuring glow, allowed me to make out the objects in the room. I did not have a watch, and there were no cellphones, so I did not know what time it was, but it was quiet, so I imagined it was late.

I immediately turned on the lamp next to my bed, fear of the dark and the devil giving me instant and extreme anxiety. The basement, built with a thin line of windows running along the edges of the wall, was located just below the ceiling. So, if someone walked by, I could see their feet. I could also see the shadows from the avocado trees and hear the wind blowing through them, causing leaves to rustle and other strange noises I could not identify. I was terrified.

When I speak of the unhealthy fear I had of the dark and the devil, it was a very real and paralyzing fear for me.

I had to pee, but the bathroom was upstairs in the main part of the house. It would require walking up the stairs in the dark, which was already a no for me.

It would require me to navigate through a house I barely knew, attempting to find the bathroom. I could already imagine every weird and scary sound, every unfamiliar shadow in the night... I imagined the devil slowly stalking me, mocking me with La Mano Negra around every corner.

Nope.

I was not going to walk to the bathroom; it was just not happening.

Here I was, a gang member who had been in multiple fistfights, shot at, and beaten with a bat... too scared to go upstairs to take a pee. Afraid of the dark.

It was equally demoralizing and humiliating. I could not help it. My psychological fear of the devil and the dark had a firm grasp on the part of my brain that dealt with logic. I was deathly afraid of both.

I looked at the Narnia closet and decided it would have to be my bathroom.

So, I walked over to it, opened it, and removed everything from the bottom. I then proceeded to pee inside the closet. It was the first time, but not the last time I used the Narnia closet as my toilet. I am not proud of it.

I left the lamp on, put a dark shirt over it, and went to bed.

My time back in Ecuador was a blur. My Uncle Jay, Aunt Maria, and cousins were everything you would expect from a kind, loving, and supportive family. They were patient and helpful and did their absolute best to help me assimilate into their home, their family, and my new school.

Alliance Academy, my new school, was of little importance to me or my life. I went to school but did zero work; I did not care. I was not paying attention and was putting in no effort academically.

I was homesick, and even though I loved my family in Ecuador, it was different being away from my mom, my dad, my brother, and my sister. Their absence, something I took for granted, caused me to appreciate and value my family in a renewed manner. Being away from them started to become unbearable, and I was not managing it very well.

While I was in Ecuador, my parents moved out of the apartment complex in Las Vegas and moved to Boulder City, a small town approximately thirty minutes south of Las Vegas. My mom had joined a "Mom's Against Gangs" group and was learning how to cope and help me with my problems. Moving to Boulder City, in their mind, was far enough away to keep me out of trouble.

So, they moved and settled in. My grandma Sullivan moved from Chicago and moved in with us as well. Once they settled in and everything was in order, my parents flew me back to the US.

I spent over six months in Ecuador, with little to no communication with my old Cotopaxi friends. As I reflect on that time now, I cannot put my finger on why that happened. It is possible that my changes were so severe and off-putting that I simply did not fit in anymore. Regardless, the distance with people I cared for made my time back in Ecuador lonely and confusing.

A condition for my return home was made clear: I had to stop any relationships or friendships with gang members. That was an easy yes for me. That part of my life was receding long before they sent me back to Ecuador.

I returned home in the summer of 1993 to a sweltering but familiar heat. Boulder City was quaint and quiet, and it was nice. I was happy to be home.

CHAPTER 44

I spent the summer of 1993 hanging out at home with my family. No one knew I was back, and I felt safe for the first time in almost two years.

August rolled around, and I was preparing to start my fifth High School.

There was little to no gang activity in Boulder City, and on my first day, the principal gave me a warning.

The principal took out a file, laid it on his desk, and proceeded to highlight my worst moments at Green Valley High School. He was clear in letting me know he knew I was gang-affiliated, for which he had zero tolerance.

He explained that if there was even a whiff of gang talk or fighting involving me, he would act swiftly and remove me from the school. He told me this was my chance to start over—a clean slate.

I responded by thanking him and assured him he would have no problems with me. He stood up, and we shook hands.

At Boulder City High School, I bonded quickly with two football players: a short but very muscular Black boy named Mark, who went by "Lil Man," and a huge six-foot-four white kid called Paulie. Lil Man had connections to Las Vegas and to gangs, so we clicked right away.

For about three months, everything went well. I had a good relationship with my new friends, went to parties, and even had a girlfriend. Her name was Heather, and she was a Hispanic skater chic. Life was good.

My relationship with my parents was also improving. We had established a tense but mutual trust, and I was putting effort into my education. My little bro Kevin was excelling in Boulder City. He was doing great in school and became a star baseball player for the school team.

Overall, the move to Boulder City started in a positive way, giving us all hope.

I was settling in Boulder City. I got a job at the local McDonald's and did my best to avoid any trouble.

Sometimes, trouble comes looking for you.

I had an incident at school, which almost turned into a fistfight. Two large kids called me out at the school and challenged me to a fight in the hallway as we were between classes. The hallways were empty; everyone was already in class, and it was only them and I.

I did not want to fight or be involved in anything which could get me thrown out. I was doing well and trying hard to stay on the right track.

The two kids who challenged me were both large humans, so not only was I trying to avoid trouble, but these guys were also intimidating. Thankfully, as they became more aggressive, and defending myself my only choice; a teacher came around the corner and made us all go to class.

My friend Paul knew both kids who challenged me. That afternoon, after school… we ran into them at the convenience store. Paul spoke to them and told them I was his friend. He asked us to squash our problems, and we did. I shook hands with them, and the beef was over.

The next day, a student aid pulled me out of my first-period class and told me to report to the principal's office. I knew something was wrong when my dad and the principal both greeted me.

The principal explained he heard I almost engaged in a fight with two other students. He asked if it was true, and I admitted to it, confused because nothing had happened. He asked me to give him the names of the other kids. I could not do that. I did not know their names, but I would not have snitched on them even if I did.

He reminded me of our initial conversation when I arrived at the school and asked if I recalled it. I replied in the affirmative, and he reminded me of his zero tolerance for gang activity or any suspicious behavior from me. He placed me on an immediate suspension pending a review.

My dad drove me home, and to my surprise, he supported me. He told me he was proud of the changes I had made. He noted the effort I was applying to my schoolwork and expressed his understanding of why I felt like I had to defend myself.

He said, "No matter what happens moving forward, I know you tried, and I hope you continue to do so. I am proud of you Jonny Boy."

His words, tone, and support resonated with me in a way that made me happy. My dad's pride in me and understanding made everything okay. It gave me hope and left me smiling.

CHAPTER 45

Summer 1993 - 18 Years Old

I was expelled from Boulder City High School.

An example of the system failing. Zero-tolerance policies leave no room for discretion and treat students in a bland system of subjective rights and wrongs. They forget a child's fundamental propensity to make mistakes, rob them of their individualism, narrow their curiosity to fit a square box, and prevent them from learning and adjusting.

My only choice, to continue my education at Opportunity School. Opportunity School is reserved for troubled youth, kids unable to cope in normal school environments. A school for the impulsive and maladjusted, troublemakers and habitual truants.

My final year in high school would be at Horizon South High School, my sixth and final school in my scholastic career.

Horizon South consisted of five portable classrooms, which were moved into the desert behind Vo-Tech High School (now SECTA) and fenced in to separate us from the regular kids.

The fence was strange; it did not make sense because we had to walk into the main Vo-Tech campus to use the restroom and for lunchtime, but whatever optics helped parents agree to allow us "bad kids" back there worked.

The summer of 1993 was supposed to be my first summer out of High School. But since I had to repeat ninth grade in Chicago, I still had a year left. All my friends in Ecuador had graduated and were beginning their college journeys. Fiona was going to a school in New York, Paulina to an American college in Ecuador, Steven to Maryland, etc. I still had a year of high school to endure.

My parents and I had built trust. Being away from each other for six months was traumatic for all of us, and we found a way to become closer. Communication, something we were never good at, was something we were all working on.

On weekends, my parents allowed me to borrow their car to visit my friends in Vegas. They gave me leeway, and I did not want to disappoint them.

I spent the summer hanging out on Pearl Street with Mike, Dennis, Gina, Melissa, Jenetti, and the rest of the usual suspects.

Gina and I started talking again since I had been back, but she was back and forth from North Las Vegas, more committed to her gang life than anything else. I could tell she did not feel the same way about me anymore, which emotionally crushed me all over again. I still loved her, but she had clearly moved on.

Dennis and I got closer, and I started staying at his house. Dennis, his mom Regina, and his brother Sal lived alone in a house, and they welcomed me to stay with them. My parents were okay with me spending time at Dennis', because they spoke to his mom on a regular basis and were aware of my whereabouts and activities. Dennis was Mike's next-door neighbor; we were always together and became inseparable.

I knew running into Gina could and would alert my old friends and enemies of my return to Las Vegas. It was a risk I took. We talked about it at length, and she promised me she would not tell anyone I was back. I believed her. We were not on great terms but remained friendly and cared for each other.

While hanging out on Pearl Street one night, Dennis pulled up in his low-rider Regal and wanted to take us to visit new girlfriends he had made. They lived in Villa Knolls, the same apartment/condominiums Natalie and Hasson lived in.

Mike, Dennis, and I drove to these girl's house. We pulled up in front of the building and got out of the car. Dennis walked through the door without knocking, and Mike and I followed.

The first thing I noticed was two Hispanic girls sitting on a couch watching TV. One of them was cute, with a noticeable scar on her face, but the other one was an absolute beauty—a head-turner.

I immediately noticed fresh burn wounds on her. They were bright red and keloid out. She had wounds on both her forearms and her left leg. Later, she also showed us one on her stomach. Her name was Dacia, and to avoid awkward questions, she told us what had happened to her.

Dacia moved to Las Vegas as soon as she could. Her parents divorced, and their inability to coexist made it hard for her to be around them. She traveled to Farmington, New Mexico, often. Farmington was where both sides of her family lived. Her dad had moved to Phoenix with her brothers, so she liked to visit her mom and other family members.

She was dating an older boy named Ronnie. Ronnie, as Dacia described him, was a kind and creative individual. He loved to play the guitar and loved the Eagles. One of Ronnie's friends, Freddy, who was even older, owned a Jeep Wrangler and provided a ride for Dacia and Ronnie on their way to Farmington.

On their way to Farmington, Freddy drove the Wrangler with the top off. Ronnie was in the passenger's seat, and Dacia squeezed in the middle, sitting on the center console. None of them used seatbelts. Freddy had been drinking and either fell asleep or miscalculated a turn because he was drunk; he ended up running into a guardrail at a deep curve on the highway.

When they slammed into the guardrail, Ronnie's right arm was outside the vehicle from the inertia. The impact with the guardrail severed his arm from his body. Causing a fatal wound.

As Freddy tried to overcorrect, he flipped the Jeep, sending all of them flying out of the car. Dacia and Freddy slid on the pavement with enough force and speed that their clothing disintegrated, causing third-degree road burns and other injuries to both their bodies.

They stopped approximately one hundred feet from the Jeep. During the rollover, Ronnie tried to hang onto the car near the turned-over Jeep.

Dacia, who was suffering from extreme shock, was not feeling pain. It was dark, and the highway did not have streetlights. Dacia wandered up the road, trying to find Ronnie. She found his severed arm first, picked it up, and continued looking for him. When she found him, Ronnie was barely clinging to life. He had lost a lot of blood. Dacia lay down next to him on the side of the road, holding his hand before she, too, lost consciousness. Ronnie was airlifted from the scene, but sadly, Ronnie lost his life.

Dacia spent a whole year in and out of the hospital recovering from her injuries and was still recovering from her wounds when we met her. She was a fighter.

The fresh, red keloid burns on her body could not distract from the natural beauty she was. She wore no make-up and had long brown hair. Her features were perfect. Nice large brown eyes with a green tint, a small nose, and nice lips. To top it off, she also had a beautiful athletic body. If you could see past the wounds, she had a phenomenal butt and toned legs with a flat and toned stomach to match. She was perfect.

The biggest and most impressive trait about Dacia, which just drew you into her orbit, was her genuine smile and kind nature. She had just been through a horrible, traumatizing experience, an experience that cost her someone she loved and almost cost her own life in the process, but you would never know by being around her.

No one could say she was suffering. She smiled and was full of fun and genuine positive energy. Nothing was slowing her down. She was incredibly special, and that was clear to anyone who met her.

I became instantly attracted to her. Her self-confidence was also intensely alluring. She was a beautiful girl with very visible and very gruesome wounds on her body, and she did not care to cover them up. She exuded a silent resilience that forced you to see past her injuries. She was incredible. I was fascinated and in complete awe of this uniquely wonderful girl.

Dennis brought me out of my daydream and introduced us to her cousin, Mandy. They had both recently moved from Farmington, New Mexico, to live with their aunt Cindy in Las Vegas.

Dennis ran into them while visiting Hasson at Villa Knolls and befriended them. He had started coming around to hang out with them and told no one about them until now.

Dennis made it clear on the way over that he was trying to get with Dacia. I could understand why. As much as I connected with her, I could not make a move. Dennis called dibs on Dacia, and I was going to respect it.

Plus, while hanging out with them, I learned she was dating her older boyfriend in New Mexico. It was Freddy, the driver of the car in her accident. Locked up and in county jail, but she talked to him every day and called him her boyfriend.

Going to hang out with Dacia and Mandy became a thing. They also started going around Pearl Street and just became part of our group of friends.

Dacia had a job and a car, so she was in and out doing her own thing but did spend time with us. She was also friends with Yolanda (Yoyo from 18th Street), and she had a thing for Yoyo's brother Robert.

Dacia knew and understood my history with 18th Street. She was not a gang member but did hang out with Yoyo sometimes. I trusted her not to say anything.

Dacia and I became close. We enjoyed each other's company and had much in common. She was quickly becoming my best friend.

Dacia would talk to me about her boyfriend Freddy, Robert, and Dennis, and I would talk to her about Gina. We started telling each other our most intimate secrets, and soon, we became our most trusted confidants.

Dacia broke up with Freddy that summer, and Dennis moved in quickly. Dacia and Dennis started to date. This became difficult for me because Dacia and I had become so close, and my feelings for her had grown.

I was still living with Dennis; she was always at his house, hanging out in his room. I did not know how to feel about it. Dennis and I were like brothers, so the feelings that were emerging were difficult to maneuver.

Gina and I continued to talk, but her presence around the group receded considerably. She spent her time in North Las Vegas.

With the school year fast approaching and doing nothing all summer, I listened to my parents and decided to get a job.

Dennis and I both applied and got a job at Cinnabon at the Boulevard Mall.

CHAPTER 46

The situation with Dacia was wearing on me. We continued to talk every day and tell each other all our personal problems, but I could tell something was brewing underneath. I know she could feel it as well.

We held our gazes longer than we should have, and we always found excuses to be together. If a trip to the store needed to happen, Dacia and I went. Someone needs a food run from having the munchies—no problem, Dacia and I made all the runs. While we left what we were feeling unspoken, we both knew it would eventually become a problem.

There were times we caught ourselves staring at each other, and both of us would look away shyly with a smile. It was a tricky situation. Dennis and I had become close. I was living with him at his house, and I put on pause any feelings developing with Dacia. It was not something we were willing to explore. We never talked about it—we just avoided it.

School started, and I was back home in Boulder City. My mom and dad dropped me off at school on their way to work and picked me up on the way home. My senior year of high school was upon me; I just needed to make it to graduation. I was there.

On my first day at Horizon South HS, I met our hall monitor, Ms. Betty. Ms. Betty was an OG (Original Gangster), a former gang member; her kids were all gang members. She took zero attitude from anyone.

Ms. Betty was a middle-aged Black woman with braided hair and the longest nails I had ever seen on a human. She could only hold objects using weird angles. Betty and I hit it off immediately. She took me to see Mr. Robinson. Mr. Robinson was the Dean of our problem school. His main job, though, was as an Alderman for the City of North Las Vegas.

Mr. Robinson reminded me of "Principal Joe" from the movie "Lean on Me," played by Morgan Freeman. Mr. Robinson looked nothing like him; he was bald on the top, with hair on the sides, and he looked more like Mr. Jefferson. Mr. Robinson had a no-nonsense demeanor, which demanded your attention and respect. He wore a well-trimmed mustache and dressed in nice conservative suits.

What made him most like Principal Joe was his memory. He knew every kid and their stories. He knew the names of your siblings, and he knew if you had done well or misbehaved. He had his ear all over the school, and he would find out if you had done something. So, he usually already knew the answer when he asked you something.

Between him and Betty, they did their best and cared for the problem children at Horizon South HS. Betty always looked out for me. She realized I was in way over my head and I did not have the street savvy and confidence that most kids growing up in gangs displayed. She saw me for who I really was—an impostor trying to survive.

CHAPTER 47

Senior year started to fly by. At school, a small group of friends developed out of necessity. Drifter from 28th Street also attended Horizon South, and we attached ourselves to the West Coast Bloods (WCB).

I did not have a choice; if I ignored Drifter and the truce with WCB, I would find myself alone, unprotected, and a target for all gangs at the school.

The West Coast Bloods leader at Vo-Tech and the shot caller for our group was a tall and skinny young Black man who wore a large afro, and they called him "Ho-Killa."

Vo-Tech, the school Horizon South shared space with, was full of Crips and 18th Streeters, who had also formed an alliance. So now, we were involved with their beef as well.

Drifter had a falling out with Gordo and his crew, so he was cool about lying low. He asked me to keep his whereabouts to myself, which worked out perfectly because I needed the same thing from him.

Plus, we were the only two 28th Street Raskals at the school. I was not openly gangbanging, but I also could not ignore it. Drifter was there, and half of Vo-Tech was 18th Street. I had already seen Pitufo cruise by after school and knew he was looking for me.

During my final year in high school, my parents moved back to Las Vegas. They bought a nice house on Cisco Lane, and for a while, everything was right in the world.

I was managing to stay out of problems. My sister was still in college but had gotten pregnant. My little brother Kevin was doing well and getting ready to start high school. Unfortunately, his baseball career ended during a Junior High game while he was sliding into second base. His foot got stuck on the edge of the base, and he broke his ankle. He suffered a compound fracture to his ankle, and he could not play after the injury.

After his surgery, he was prescribed Oxycodone, and later, when his pain became a chronic issue, he was prescribed OxyContin. We did not know it then, but the drug would play a devastating and leading role in the trajectory of my little brother's life.

Dacia and I continued to talk every day and see each other as much as possible. On the weekends, I stayed with Dennis, and if I skipped school, Dacia usually picked me up, and we would spend time together.

Dennis and I had maintained our jobs at Cinnabon on the weekends. Cinnabon was one of the best jobs I have ever had.

Our team leader at Cinnabon was a young Black man named Sam. Most nights, the three of us worked the same shift.

Sam was an aspiring comedian and a huge fan of Martin Lawrence, so he would practice his jokes on us and just clown us the entire shift.

I do not remember a time we were not laughing aloud. I am sure customers thought we were all high or being weird, but it was just Sam having us bent over and in tears from laughing so hard.

Dacia usually picked us up from work. I finished my duties early one night and walked out to the car. Dennis was still inside and had about another 30 minutes of cleaning.

I got in the car and Dacia was looking gorgeous. She smiled at me, and it melted my heart. We started to talk, and I began to tell her the multiple numbers I had pulled from girls while working. She did not believe me, so I pulled them out and showed them to her. She laughed and asked, "You think you are a pimp or something?" I looked at her and jokingly said, "Damn right I am; I could pimp you, too, if I wanted to."

I expected her to laugh or hit me playfully, but to my surprise, she stared into my eyes and turned away shyly.

What?

I did not know how to react or what to do. Her reaction caught me off guard. So, like an idiot, I quietly asked, "I can, can't I?"

Dacia did not reply; she just turned to look at me, and we both leaned in at the same time and kissed.

It was wrong, and we should not have done it, but the danger associated with the act only made the kiss more exhilarating and special.

We kissed slowly and tenderly but kept looking away every few seconds to make sure her boyfriend and my friend was not coming.

We kissed for about thirty seconds, and neither wanted the kiss to stop. It felt right.

Finally, we stopped, and I jumped into the back seat. Minutes later, Dennis walked out, and Dacia drove us all home.

There was obvious sexual tension between Dacia and me, but we never acted on it, and we never actually talked about what happened. We just let it hang in the universe to see what would happen next.

Chapter 48

By the spring of 1994, my parents separated. My dad told my mom he fell in love with one of his students at an adult ESL class he was teaching. My mom, brother Kevin, sister Denise, and her newborn son, my nephew, Juan Andres, moved back to Ecuador.

I remained to finish high school, but I stayed at Dennis' house or bounced from couch to couch on weekends. I did not care to be home.

At school and on the streets, things were getting very tense. Gang violence was at an all-time high. Shootings and stabbings were commonplace. Not a day went by without multiple violent incidents.

A big melee happened at Vo-Tech. It began between Ho-Killa from WCB and a crip from Rolling 60's. The fight caused everyone in the lunchroom to start fighting—at least fifty kids fighting in the Vo-Tech lunchroom. The fight was so big and out of control that LVMPD responded to break it up. They had to use the large canister of pepper spray reserved for riots to get participants to stop. Multiple arrests were made.

I had been beaten up badly during the melee. Two crips blind-sided me and beat me up until Betty stopped them, and she whisked me away.

To this day, I do not know why Betty and Mr. Robinson looked out for me the way they did. It seemed intentional, and I could feel an investment for my well-being.

I never asked them or my dad, but a part of me believes they knew my dad; somehow, my dad's influence, or even via a personal request, caused Betty and Mr. Robinson to look out for me and to help me graduate.

CHAPTER 49

Dennis and his family treated me like one of their own. So, it was no big deal for me to show up unannounced and enter the house without alerting anyone.

I was downstairs in the kitchen, looking for snacks, when the house phone rang. Regina and Sal were gone because her car was not in the garage, and Sal was not pestering me about something. I figured Dennis was sleeping, so I picked up the phone and said, "Hello?"

It was Dacia. She had called from Arizona, where she was still on Spring Break. She told me she was having a wonderful time visiting with her brothers and then told me, "I have to tell you something, but you can't say anything to anyone."

I said, "Ok," now very curious about what she had to say. She made me promise, which I did. I sat on one of the kitchen chairs, ready to hear whatever she told me.

She just came out and said it. She explained that she had attended a party in Arizona and hooked up with one of her brothers' friends while at the party.

"What should I do?" She asked me.

We did not know this, but Dennis woke up when he heard the phone ringing. He picked up shortly after I picked up the phone and started listening to our conversation. We were oblivious.

I did not know what to say or how to respond. A part of me was happy because cheating on Dennis meant she was not committed to their relationship, giving me the possibility of a chance. A part of me was also jealous because my feelings for Dacia were only growing stronger every day, and imagining her with someone else hurt.

So, I told her, "You should just tell him the truth."

Dacia's response was, "Are you crazy? If I tell him about this, I might as well tell him about us."

There was a moment of stunned silence as if we were all simultaneously catching our collective breath without realizing we were all connected.

At this moment, I heard the phone upstairs crash against the wall, and Dacia and I realized Dennis had been listening to it the entire time. I heard him walk to his room and slam the door shut.

Dacia and I quietly said goodbye, and I left the house.

CHAPTER 50

Dacia and Dennis broke up. About a week later, I took Dacia out on a date. I was back at home staying with my dad, and after we went out to eat, she came home with me.

I can still remember what she was wearing. She had white shorts on with black dots on them and a black tank top with a sheer black blouse over it. She looked out of this world beautiful, and I felt like the luckiest guy in the world.

When we arrived at my house, my dad was already sleeping. We stayed in the living room watching TV and decided to put on a movie. I grabbed pillows and a blanket from my bedroom, and we lay on the floor to watch a movie.

I cannot tell you what movie we were supposed to watch, because as soon as we were both lying on the floor, we began to kiss. It felt like the first time, but more intimate and connected.

Our hands were all over each other, cautiously probing. Slowly, our clothes started to come off, and each removal elicited an opportunity to explore areas of our bodies. I slowly traced her burn scars with my fingers. I found her scars sexy and told her. She smiled and laid down, pulling me down with her.

I had only experienced sex like this with one other person, and it scared me we were having such an emotional connection on our first time.

Our bodies did all the talking. It was a beautiful and sensual experience. We connected on a level that made the sex feel different. Our energies were synchronized, and movements orchestrated in a hypnotic rhythm. When finished, we walked to my room and had sex two more times before falling asleep.

Dacia knew I was still in love with Gina; it was not something I hid from her, but my feelings for Dacia were growing quickly. The emotions I felt were rooted in friendship first, which made the transition into romance special.

Dacia and I started dating. Our relationship and feelings progressed faster than either of us expected. We planned to move in together, which was a huge step in our commitment to each other.

We both worked, but Dacia had two jobs: one at Walmart and another at a call center on Flamingo. When we had enough saved up, we found an apartment.

The money from our jobs was barely enough to get by, but her friend Tina left her boyfriend, Bruiser, and needed a place to go, so we took her and her son in as roommates. It worked for all of us.

We found a two-bedroom apartment on the corner of Tropicana and Spencer, near the UNLV Campus. We moved in, and soon after, I bought my first car: a dark grey Honda Civic, a stick shift.

The night I bought the car, Dacia and Tina invited friends over to the apartment for a kick-back: Mike, Glenn, Willow, Mandy, and Mandy's sister, Tisha. Tisha had just moved to Las Vegas from New Mexico and was also living with their aunt Cindy.

Cindy was the nicest woman you could meet. She always greeted you with warmth and a smile and was always willing to help with anything. She treated all of Dacia's friends like her own kids. The only problem with Cindy was her addiction to meth, which, unfortunately, she introduced to all her nieces. Cindy and her boyfriend Phillip introduced meth to Dacia and her cousins.

Dacia and Tisha, in particular, began to use it heavily. Tisha was only fourteen years old at the time.

I arrived that night with my brand-new Honda Civic, and everyone came out of the apartment to have a look at it. Everyone loved it. This was the first car I was able to buy on my own.

Mike, Glenn, Matt, and Ryan got into the car and asked me to take them to the store for drinks. On the way to the store, Mike tells me, "I'm going to do a beer run, bro; it's perfect because you don't even have plates on your car; we will be in and out; that way, we have alcohol to drink tonight." I reluctantly agreed. Fuck it.

We pulled up to the 7-Eleven, and I parked on the east side of the store. I backed the car against the wall, ready to take off if needed. They all got out and entered the store; a couple of minutes later, all four came sprinting out with liquor in their hands, and the cashier chasing them with a bat.

They sprinted to my car and jumped in. As I was making my way out of the parking lot and about to make a left onto Spencer Road, an undercover METRO police officer lit us up with his light and sirens. He had parked on the West side of the store, and none of us saw him.

He watched the beer run and was on us quickly. In the few seconds it took me to decide, I made the wrong choice. I knew Mike was on probation, so I decided to try to outrun the police.

I sped straight past Spencer and into an apartment complex. I drove through the narrow streets at a high rate of speed, hitting speed bumps fast enough to make our heads hit the top of the car. I made a random right turn, not knowing where we were headed, and we found ourselves at a dead end, with covered parking flanking both our left and right sides.

The police officer in his undercover car pulled up and blocked the end of the street, trapping us. To make things worse, a random, helpful Samaritan who observed the beer run and the short chase decided to get involved and pulled his big white truck next to the police officer's car, leaving us little room to move through. It was not a good situation.

I turned the car around, and we now faced each other. We did not know what to do. We were in a stand-off, and we had no visible avenue for escape. We were all afraid and extremely nervous. The possibility of going to jail was enough of a motivator for me to continue making bad choices.

Mike turned his head, put his seat belt on, looked at me, and said, "Fuck it!"

I saw a sliver of room behind the white truck. It would require getting up on the curve with two wheels and maneuvering through the covered parking area, but it was doable. I told them to hang on.

I hit the gas and maneuvered the small Civic through empty parking spaces and onto the sidewalk, barely missing the back end of the white truck. I looked over and saw the driver scowling at me and the police officer running back into his car.

We landed on the street, and I took off. We were still in the apartment complex but finally reached Tropicana Avenue. The pursuit was on.

The undercover police officer and the white truck were hot on our heels, traveling west on Tropicana. I was driving in and out of traffic. We heard the sirens of regular patrol units arriving, then saw them in the opposite lane, traveling towards us and going east.

I looked through my rearview and saw them all making a U-turn. We were speeding down the left lane, cars pulling over to the side of the road; I saw a small break in the median, and because there was no oncoming traffic, I decided to make the turn.

It caught everyone by surprise. I made a hard left turn, using my hand break to perform the maneuver, and followed it with an immediate hard right turn. Now, we were driving the wrong way on Tropicana Avenue.

The undercover and the patrol cars were unable to make the turn and remained on the opposite side of the median, waiting for a break to get to us. I saw one of the patrol cars slow in my rearview and watched as he started to drive over the median slowly.

I dodged oncoming cars, horns blaring, and cars skidding to a stop or pulling over.

Mike yelled, "Turn left, turn left!"

I did; I turned left into a random neighborhood, passed random streets, and turned left again. We could not see the police officers behind us anymore, but we could hear them, and they were close.

To our left was a long wall, the perimeter wall of a housing complex, and to our right, a bunch of small neighborhoods ending in cul-de-sacs.

Mike saw an opportunity in one of them and directed me to turn right. We could hear the police officers somewhere close behind us. I drove to the house he had pointed out, with its garage door open.

I gently pulled the car into the garage, shutting the engine off and allowing it to roll forward on neutral. Mike got out of the front seat, quietly went over, and manually shut the garage. As the garage shut, we could see the lights of a police cruiser driving by.

We sat in a stranger's garage, listening as METRO tried to find us. They brought out the ghetto bird, and we could hear the helicopter searching. We sat in complete silence, just breathing. We were all terrified because running from the police the way we had would have landed us all in jail for a lengthy sentence. We had endangered drivers on the road and the police, which was a poor choice.

A little over an hour had passed when we finally stopped hearing police activity. We waited another thirty minutes after that to be sure. When we felt comfortable enough to risk leaving, Mike opened the garage. We pushed the car out of the garage and slowly drove home, taking the back streets—all of us on full alert.

When we finally made it back to my apartment, we were able to relax and laugh about the whole thing. What a crazy epic beer run—one for the books. My driving exploits on that night live on to this day, and we always talk about it whenever we meet up.

Spun up from the adrenaline and from having outsmarted the police officers. We partied all night and got drunk and high.

Partying at our apartment became a weekend event. I was living on my own now, making my own decisions and doing whatever I wanted—living life and having fun.

Not long after moving in together, Dacia told me she was pregnant, and everything came to a screeching halt.

We would not realize it until later, but it was the best thing that could have happened to either of us. At the time, though, we were both terrified.

Chapter 51

Dacia was supposed to be on the pill but had forgotten to take it for days. I did not know how to feel when she broke the news to me. It was not something I expected or considered in the realm of possibilities.

Prior to getting the news, Dacia and I were both on destructive paths.

Dacia, along with her cousin Tisha, began to abuse meth heavily. The ease of obtaining it from their aunt Cindy and Uncle Philip caused a pattern of familial enablement. Dacia and Tisha were both spiraling out of control.

They were using the drug daily and multiple times a day. Before Dacia became pregnant, she was down to around ninety-two pounds—rail thin and unhealthy from abusing methamphetamine. Tisha was following the same road map.

On the other hand, I continued to make bad decisions. My family's separation continued to trouble me, and I was looking in the wrong places for answers. I began to steal cars and get involved with other petty crimes.

I was barely twenty. I was still not entirely over Gina and was young, dumb, and naive. I was not ready for any of it.

We decided the right thing to do was drive to my house and tell my dad. We needed guidance. The one thing Dacia and I have always done, is to communicate openly and often about our feelings.

On the drive to my dad's house, I became increasingly apathetic. Internally, I was blaming Dacia for all of it. How could she just forget to take the pill? I was being selfish and deflecting any responsibility. I was not supporting her the way she deserved. She was just as scared and confused as I was. I was being an asshole.

We arrived at my dad's house, and the garage was open. My dad was expecting us. We parked on the driveway and walked inside through the garage.

As we walked inside, my dad was in the kitchen making coffee. He was in a great mood because we were visiting. A part of me instantly felt guilty for not having come over to spend more time with him.

He asked us to sit, and we all sat at the kitchen table. I am sure he could sense something was off, and he sat down and said, "Tell me what happened. What is going on?"

Dacia and I looked at each other nervously, and I said, "Dad, Dacia is pregnant."

My dad sat quietly, sipping his coffee and looking at us. We were both looking down at the table, embarrassed and ashamed.

My dad allowed the silence to simmer, making sure we understood how serious this news was and how profoundly important our next decisions would be. When he finally spoke, my reaction to what he said was something I deeply regret to this day.

He said, "Ok, I will need to let your mom know, and Dacia, you will need to tell your parents, but the right thing to do is for you guys to get married."

"No!" Instantly blurted out of my stupid mouth. I looked over at Dacia; she was quietly sobbing while staring at the table. I felt like such a piece of shit.

My dad looked at me sternly and stated, "You will fulfill your responsibility and be a man."

I got up from the chair and walked outside. I needed air; I needed to run away.

My dad came outside through the garage and stood beside me as we searched the empty street for answers. The empty street provided no answers, we left my dad's in solemn awkward silence; both of us deeply lost in our own thoughts.

My dad abruptly woke us up early the following morning by knocking on our bedroom door loudly. Tina, our roommate, had let him in. He said, "Jonathan, put your clothes on and come out of the room." I was annoyed but obliged.

When ready. I walked out of the room, and my dad led me outside. We stood in the alleyway between the apartment buildings and with a soft, calming tone, said, "Jonny Boy, you have managed to fuck up your life in a big way. Headed to prison or the grave. I will not let you do that. I know this must feel like too much to handle. You feel overwhelmed and stressed about the uncertainty, but I need you to trust me. I will help you, but it is going to require drastic changes on your part. You need to become a man, and you need to do it in a hurry. You are going to be a dad; let that sink in. Now, do you trust me?"

I nodded and looked up at him. He said, "Good, now jump in the truck with me."

I got in the truck with my dad, and he started to drive. I asked where we were going, and he responded, "To the Marine Corps Recruiting Station."

I started to panic and reminded my dad I still had a pending criminal case in court, and he told me not to worry about it.

I sat silently the rest of the way there, thinking of how I could get out of this. I was scared. Memories of my childhood again presented themselves with clarity, and I considered the possibilities.

Will the Marines make me violent the way my dad had been? I was afraid of becoming the worst version of my dad. Was the Marines the answer? I was so confused. I just had to go along for the ride. I was dumb, and I knew it too. I made dumb, impulsive decisions, and it was time to trust my dad.

As usual, I had little control over what was happening in my life, and things were once again moving fast. But as the drive wore on, I slowly realized that I justified all my failures with excuses, always blaming someone else. I did have control, and I had made a series of bad choices that brought me to this point.

Instead of being responsible at the moment and exerting full control over my future, I chose to be reactive and accept the limited options I had in front of me now—no more excuses. Dacia and our baby needed me.

We arrived, and we exited his truck together. We walked into the Marine Recruiting Station, and I sat on a couch while my dad talked to the recruiter, explaining everything.

They both walked over to me, and the recruiter extended his hand and introduced himself as Sergeant Monet. They had me take the ASVAP test without delay. When I was done (I did not score well on the test), I signed an "open contract" and was scheduled to leave for the area MEPS in Phoenix, Arizona, in two days. Everything was happening at warp speed.

I had to fill out a bunch of waiver forms for my criminal history, drug use, tattoos, and pending criminal charges, but I was told not to worry.

My dad drove me back to my apartment, and I was still confused about what had just happened. Somehow, we went to tell my dad Dacia was pregnant, and I signed up to become a Marine. It was comical.

I was not expecting this outcome. It was not even a consideration. My mind was spinning, and I felt pushed and pulled in directions I had no intention of going.

When I entered the apartment, Dacia was waiting for me. She asked me what happened, and I sat down and told her. She was surprised, but I think a part of her was happy and relieved. To her credit, as soon as she learned she was pregnant, Dacia gave up all drugs and never again touched them -ever.

Becoming a mother was the most precious gift Dacia could receive. She was such a beautiful person inside, and I knew she would become the most amazing mother to our kids.

She supported me in joining the Marines and was by my side until the day I left for San Diego to start Marine Corps Bootcamp. Dacia always supported me and always has. She has always displayed an unwavering loyalty, which, on occasions, I may not have deserved. But her love for me and our family has always been something she puts above anything else.

No matter what it is. No matter how her family may judge her, Dacia has always sought empathy, facts, and the ability to listen to objective reasoning.

She has never failed me. Sadly, I cannot say the same, but her flawless characteristics only made my love for her stronger—a love rooted in a deep respect for the strong and capable woman she was and is.

Chapter 52

Before I fully understood the magnitude of signing on the dotted line, I shipped off to Marine Corps Boot Camp in San Diego, California. A young know-it-all punk, gangbanger, with a kid on the way.

I was not prepared for what was to come—a life-altering experience and a transition I initially resisted.

The Marines completely broke me down, exposing all my insecurities and fears and squeezing every aspect of my personality out of me.

By the time the first phase of Marine Corps bootcamp finished, I had no true sense of who I was anymore—deeply immersed in the Marine Corps culture. The Marines are known and extremely adept at creating empty vessels during training. They then repurpose those young, impressionable human shells and fill them with the kind of indoctrination that creates men unwilling to accept defeat and with an unhealthy and unrealistic perspective of their own capabilities.

They picked up all my broken pieces and molded me into a deadly and capable fighting machine—war fodder, or, as commonly referred to by other branches of service… "crayon eaters."

I excelled in Marine Corps Bootcamp, scoring perfect scores on all the fitness exams. I was an advanced swimmer and a qualified expert with the M16-A2 rifle. With discipline and purpose, without distractions, I performed well above average.

Marines are the fiercest fighting force in the US Military. They train in small squad elements and fire teams. They can attack from the air, land, or sea. Due to their superior training and fitness,

Marines are considered fearsome warriors and are usually the first conventional fighting force sent into any war or danger area.

Marines are known for having the most demanding physical requirements. Their training is twice as long as that of any other military branch, and it is focused on infantry tactics. Marines are, without question, the fittest and most capable conventional small force the US Military can deploy.

I excelled in boot camp and was twice put in leadership positions. I relished the daily dose of discipline applied with pain and suffering. It almost felt like my entire life had been a trial for this very moment.

When I saw weakness from anyone in our Company and/or Platoon, I instinctively helped. When a fellow Marine was having a tough time with a run or with a hump, I was one of the first ones to be by their side providing quiet motivation and support. This selfless behavior caused the Drill Instructors to believe I had leadership potential.

But the reality is rooted in selfishness and fear. Those moments were grounded in a carefully constructed façade. When a fellow Marine broke from the physical and mental demands of Marine Corps training, Internally, I exhaled in weak satisfaction it was not me who broke first. I would manipulate the moment, pretending to care and offer help and motivation, only to slow down and catch a break for myself. I was no leader.

Marines' fear of failure resonates in a deeper, more profound interpretation. Failure has a very real and permanent finality to it. Fear of failure is a looming and alarming presence because the failure of one Marine meant we all failed. Failure of any sort is always met with the consequences of physical pain and pushing one's body to the limits of its perceived capabilities.

Penitence for failure of one, paid by all. But regurgitation was an essential fuel to the soil of one's personal growth.

Throwing up from exertion and then finding the will to continue is what made you a Marine.

So, when I helped others, I helped myself in the process. When I assisted in ensuring no one in my Platoon failed, it was out of fear of suffering the consequences. Marine Corps training was a daily exercise in mental and physical fortitude. Marines provide a structural foundation built to contain the impulsive, raw energy of young men like me, often directed in unhealthy ways. It saved my life.

To this day, the self-discipline the Marines instilled in me continues to be a constant characteristic of my life. A warrior's ethos guides my need to remain in peak physical condition, creating a powerful sense of duty and honor, shifting my core makeup, and altering my sense of self. This drastic change felt like a rebirth.

Chapter 53

April 2000 - 25 years old

As I turned the corner onto Maryland Parkway to head to Danny's apartment, my gut was overreacting, or so I thought. It was just nervous energy, but I could not shake the feeling that kept building, mentally screaming at me to turn around.

I ignored my gut feeling, which was a mistake. Always go with your raw intuition.

As I pulled into Danny's apartment complex, I was startled by how long I had been in my head. I was moving through the city as a responsible driver, but I was so lost in my thoughts that I could not remember the details of the trip.

Strange, how our brains can function simultaneously in a conscious and unconscious state. Feeling perplexed by my experience, I carefully parked near his building and noted Mike's car parked nearby.

The strange hypnotic experience on the drive was replaced by excitement to see my friend.

I was not particularly happy about seeing Danny.

I knocked on Danny's door and looked around nervously, hoping no one would recognize me. After so many years, I was still scared of the bounty of sorts 18th Street had put on my life. I knew it was silly to think anyone would remember me or even think the same people were still around, but the fear closed in on me nonetheless. I knocked on Danny's apartment door with urgency.

Danny finally opened the door; I entered quickly, in my mind, dodging a bullet I knew was coming. I pushed past his open arms as we exchanged pleasantries. With my foot, I pushed the door shut, and Danny looked at me like I was crazy.

I saw Mike with Earnest sitting on the couch. They stood up, and we greeted each other warmly. Mike introduced Earnest to me, and he and I talked about the Marines.

Mike, who had been listening to Earnest and I talk, interrupted and then excitedly relayed the plans for the evening.

He prepared a small reunion at a local bar he frequented. He invited old friends to meet us and to celebrate my birthday. Mike, hyped up about the get-together, was ready to have a fun time. His mood was infectious. Mike always demonstrated a special social skill in reading a room and making it his own. He was a gifted shit-talker but did it in a funny, non-threatening way. He was quick-witted and timely with quips and comebacks. You could always find somebody laughing near him.

Mike was dark-skinned, darker than most. His mom, Ruby, had immigrated from Jamaica and ended up in Las Vegas. When Mike smiled, his jagged white toothy grin and large, friendly eyes were impossible to miss. Anyone at the receiving end of Mike's grin unconsciously smiled in return. He was always full of positive energy.

Before departing for the bar, Danny pulled Mike and me to the side, took us into his bedroom away from everyone else, and pulled out two guns from his closet. One was a semi-automatic .380 pistol, and the other a .38 caliber revolver.

He was trying to show off and appear "hard," something we were all unfortunately too familiar with, as it related to Danny—his immature attitude and showing off for no reason, a mentality Mike and I left behind.

The interaction was strange, unprovoked, and in direct conflict with our state of mind and energy.

Danny relayed some troubling news about his dad before showing off his weapons. Danny claimed his dad was currently in the hospital, dying from an illness. It was not something we were expecting to hear. Upon arriving at his apartment, his friendly demeanor did not indicate anything troubling in his life. This dark sadness came out of nowhere, but we understood.

We expressed our sincere sympathy and suggested that he sit out the night. We all felt the right thing to do was for him to spend time with his dad. We told him to be with his family, expressing our sincere understanding.

Danny refused.

As teenagers, Danny had earned a reputation for being aggressive and impulsive. He was an instigator, and for those who didn't personally know him, his appearance was intimidating.

He had a bald head, an athletic build, and a menacing outer intensity that emitted a propensity for violence. To those of us who knew him, we understood it was mostly all for show. Danny did act tough and conduct himself with confident bravado, but usually, this was on display only when his homies were present and when he knew it would not be a one-on-one scenario.

He was a typical bully; he found bravery in numbers and used the reputation of others to create a fake aura of machismo. I had personally seen him punk out of fighting on multiple occasions. Danny and I were never close, but he and Mike had grown up together, so I begrudgingly accepted him into our circle.

We calmly asked Danny to put the guns away. None of us cared about the posturing we found cool as teenagers; Danny obviously failing to mature at a similar pace.

I explained I could not be associated with any illegal behavior now that I was in Law Enforcement and asked him to please put the guns away. Mike did the same, asking him not to cause any problems and to get his head right.

Danny promised us he would behave, and I saw him put the guns away in his closet. Before walking out of his apartment and departing for the bar, Mike asked Sara to please page him with any news on Danny's dad. She seemed confused but replied with a barely audible "Okay."

CHAPTER 54

We arrived at the bar and were greeted by multiple smiling familiar faces.

People were drinking and reminiscing, which is exactly what you would expect from a small reunion of a small group of friends. It was a fun atmosphere, with people dancing, playing pool, and overall enjoying themselves. There was no drama.

I sat at the bar, talking to Jayme, Mike, and Melissa. As we discussed something, Mike received a page. He excused himself to use the payphone, and when he returned, he looked upset.

Sitting back down, he said, "Sara just paged me. I called her back, and she told me she had spoken to Danny's dad. He is at home, not the hospital, and nothing is wrong with him."

The conflicting information confused us. As we discussed why Danny would feel the need to lie about something so serious, a sudden rise of angry voices rose above the music and our own conversations. It caused us to pause and turn in our chairs to look. We half-stood on our stools, straining to see past a sea of people. Through the crowd, I caught a glimpse of Danny sucker punching a stranger. The stranger he punched happened to be at the bar with a large group of friends.

Chaos ensued.

The punch Danny threw, created a chain reaction of violence. The violence was instant, and dangerous. Pool sticks swung as weapons, bottles and glass ware thrown with malice and complete strangers engaging in fist fights.

Bodies everywhere, people fighting in all available real estate. There was no controlling the size of the fight.

Police were on the way; I could hear the faint wail of the sirens drawing nearer in the distance. I made my way through the sea of bodies and found Mike. He was throwing someone over the bar, and I pulled him away as he sent a poor soul flying headfirst into liquor bottles. I let him know the police were on the way. Mike was a felon, and instantly understood it was time to go.

I yelled out, "Police," and people started to scatter.

Mike and I ran to my car in the parking lot. He was livid. He was drunk and justifiably upset because it was a bar he frequented with his wife. Mike was heated. He let me know he felt disrespected by Danny's actions. He felt slighted; he had specifically asked Danny not to act out. His frustration and anger palpable. Danny's fabricated pity party about his dad being ill just compounded Mike's frustrations. The more he stewed on it, the angrier he got.

Since Mike had parked at Danny's apartment, we headed back there. The ride was eerily silent. We did not even play music; we just sat in silence. When we arrived, Danny was standing shirtless outside his open front door.

As we walked up, Danny smiled and started to boast about how he had "fucked someone up!"

Mike cut him off with a sharp "fuck you, Danny!" Mike immediately let Danny know how he felt as he walked towards him.

As Mike berated him, Danny became defensive; he walked into his apartment, talking shit back to Mike over his shoulder. Telling him, "You are acting like a bitch!" The argument continued as we entered Danny's apartment.

By the time I closed the door and said hi to Sara and Earnest, Mike had called Danny out to a fistfight.

Mike started approaching Danny aggressively; both were drunk and talking shit to each other. I intervened before a fistfight could start.

I could sense Danny was scared. We all knew Danny would lose the fight if we allowed it to play out, and Danny knew it too.

Fear evident in his eyes, and the tone in his voice softened as he realized Mike might be for real. Even though Mike was moving on from this type of behavior, he did have a reputation as a tough and feared street fighter.

Mike was an imposing figure. A dark Black man of Jamaican descent, he stood six feet two inches tall, weighed over two hundred pounds, and was built like the track star he was, full of sinewy muscle. Mike was solid and athletic, no one really wanted to willingly engage him in a fight, least of all Danny.

I placed myself between them, facing Mike and turning my back to Danny. I was holding Mike back by putting my hands directly on his shoulders.

I easily controlled Mike, which was odd because he was much bigger than me. I quickly realized he was mostly putting on a show, trying to prove a point to Danny. If Mike wanted to get by me, he could have muscled his way past me; standing 5'9, and at the time weighing 170 lbs., I would have been a mere nuance if he was determined. I calmed down a bit and was hopeful this would all end peacefully.

Mike was only applying minimal pressure with his body as I continued to stand between them. He wasn't actively trying to get by me. It was all optics, he was not seriously considering fighting Danny.

Danny's girlfriend Sara was yelling at Mike and Danny to stop. Earnest stood just outside the kitchen area, watching the drama in disbelief. Mike and Danny continued to talk shit. During one of the exchanges, Mike called him out on his history of cowardly and immature behavior.

Mike started to provide examples of times Danny had punked out of fighting. Airing his cowardly behavior in front of his pregnant girlfriend and putting Danny in a proverbial corner.

Danny did not have a ready reply for it, and his silence was a bit unnerving.

I looked up at Mike and could tell they were staring at each other. I felt Mike tense up, and then Mike started to remove his shirt. He was ready to fight now. The energy in the room changed instantly—the posturing Mike was doing, suddenly real.

He felt challenged by Danny, and the room became charged with violent tension. I closed my distance with Mike and tried to hold him lower around his waist, thinking that if I had to, I could grasp my hands behind his back and take him down to control him. His entire body was tense and sweaty, and his muscles were hard and flexed, the light shining off them making him look intensely menacing. I started to try to talk him down, "Mike...," I started to say.

Bang!

The loud bang startled me, an explosion right next to my left ear, causing a loud and painful ringing in my ear and temporarily disorienting me. Mike's body disengaged from where I had a hold of him. His body flung backwards emphatically by an unknown force, and he fell with a heavy thud on the floor. He did not get back up or say anything. He did not react. He just lay there, looking up at us.

I looked at Mike on the floor and slowly turned to look at Danny. I was confused, my brain foggy, and unwilling to accept what had just happened.

Danny was standing to my left and in complete shock. His arms were down by his sides, and the .38 caliber revolver he showed us earlier was clutched in his left hand. He was staring at Mike in disbelief.

As the shot rang out, and everyone tried unsuccessfully to process what happened, I must have subconsciously taken a step or two away from Danny and now found myself by the couch. Danny also retreated and took steps away from Mike, keeping himself in line with me.

As the haziness and initial shock faded, the weight of the events brought reality crashing down.

I fully understood my predicament. I realized running was not a survivable option; standing in place waiting for Danny to decide witnesses were not a good thing to have, was also not an option.

Danny's attention, luckily, remained fixated on Mike, trance-like. He was bladed, the right side of his body exposed to me, while he faced Mike, holding the weapon in his left hand.

Mike started to make strange noises; I noted he may have suffered a sucking chest wound because his breaths were wheezing and wet. I was becoming increasingly worried for Mike. I knew from my time in the Marines, a sucking chest wound requires quick treatment. Mike was dying. I decided to make a move, to try to catch Danny by surprise.

I slowly shifted my weight and angled myself to drive through the small corridor-like path between the table and the couch. I moved with painstakingly slow movements, inch by inch, doing my best not to arouse any suspicion from Danny and avoid sudden movements that his peripheral vision could detect.

My body was on fire; I was sore, sweating profusely, and my muscles started cramping. If I was going to act, it had to happen soon.

I stared at Danny, his focus still on Mike. I decided to go for it. It was now or never. I started to sidestep to get through the gap between the table and couch, but before I could even plant my foot, Danny, with surprising speed, switched the revolver from his left hand to his right and brought the gun up.

My momentum propelled me forward as I tried to fully stop. Unable to come to a complete stop, I took a halted and awkward step towards him. I found myself staring at the revolver just inches from my face. Not good.

To top it off, I froze in a semi-crouch, unbalanced with my right foot in front of my left, and my body turned awkwardly, putting me at a complete and total disadvantage.

He calmly turned his head to look directly at me and said, "Don't even think about it, Jonny."

My focus slowly shifted from the bore of the revolver. I found and met Danny's eyes. Nothing separated us, and I became trapped between the couch and the table. His eyes were red and unfocused.

There was a haze or fog in them, which I found frightening. He was in another plane of existence, not attached to the moment's reality.

The look in his eye caused the blood in my body to cool. I felt my heart drop and thought to myself, "This is how I die."

My kids and my wife quickly flashed in my mind, acknowledging what could soon be the greatest loss of my short life.

Danny appeared to stare straight through me, not seeing me. He licked his lips, sweat pouring down the side of his face. He looked manic.

His icy stare, coupled with the shock of the moment, sent a chill of fear through my entire body; a chill felt deep into my bones.

I reached a level of fear and desperation that is hard to put into words. When life is seconds from ending, there is no filter on what comes out of your mouth. Survival overrides logic or any actionable plan you think you have.

I began to plead with him. Trying desperately to extend my life in any way possible… "Danny, please do not shoot me, bro. I have kids." He did not respond. Just stared.

I begged him to let me take care of Mike, asking him just to run before the police arrived. "Danny, just go, bro. The police will be here soon. You need to leave and let me take care of Mike!" I begged in exasperation. He did not even blink.

He was lost in whatever mental space his choices took him to. His obvious disconnect with reality caused my chest to tighten with fear. My breath came in rapid, panicked, short bursts.

This was my end. I could not believe it.

The difficult acceptance of my impending doom caused me to disconnect from everything around me slowly.

I looked into Danny's eyes, trying to find hope. I stopped trying to reason with him. The rest of the room melted away into darkness. I no longer saw Mike on the ground in my peripheral vision. I could not see Sara or Earnest standing in the kitchen. I could not hear anything but the rapid beating of my heart and the short burst of breaths I was taking.

The only thing my mind could process as I waited to die was Danny and me. My reality narrowed; Danny and the gun became my universe.

It was a tense stand-off, and I was incapable of doing anything to help myself. I was immobile from my lack of options and frozen in place with fear.

The sweat running down Danny's face started to drip into his mouth. I noticed him licking his lips, using his upper teeth in a menacing manner as he bit his bottom lip and slightly thrust the gun forward.

He was seconds away from shooting me. I could feel his decision in his posture, and the air in the room seemed to stop circulating. He was committed. Everything went deathly silent; the air was sucked out of the room.

It was only me and him. I held my breath.

I honed in on the gun and his trigger finger. I watched intently for any movement that would mean the end of my existence. Suddenly, I felt a strange calmness flood through me as I noticed he started to apply pressure on the trigger.

Then, Sara screamed!

Sara finally came out of her shock, took in the scene in front of her, and emitted a blood-curdling scream.

A long and powerful burst of air escaping her lungs, the kind you can only achieve when truly panicked and in a moment of extreme stress and fear.

Her scream... saved my life.

I was still staring at the trigger, but the scream startled me and brought me crashing out of whatever my brain concocted to prepare me to die.

I desperately looked into Danny's eyes again, and this time, he blinked.

Danny blinked again; it looked like he was coming out of a trance. Whatever mental breakdown he was experiencing was fading. Confusion etched on his face, he looked at me as if seeing me for the first time. He looked around with intense perplexity, took in the room, and slowly, the magnitude of his actions came crashing down on him.

I noticed it because his body deflated. His head hung, his shoulders slumped, and all the menacing energy he had been emitting sucked right out of him.

He looked back at me, the revolver still pointed at my face. He said, "I'm going to leave," but it was more like a request than a statement. I nodded. He walked away slowly past Mike, still pointing the revolver at me, and then ran out of the front door into the cold and dark night.

Chapter 55

As Danny exited the apartment, I yelled at Sara to call 911. She was still in shock and had to tell her three times before she started to make the call. I immediately knelt next to Mike and my Marine Corps training took over, I was also still in shock, but repetition and training, override the shock of the moment and you act in a robot-like manner, reverting to the training you had for situations like these. I began to examine Mike carefully, assessing his injuries and checking on his vitals every few minutes. I was not sure, but the lack of an exit wound, and his short, wet struggle for breaths; along with his pulse being dangerously low, gave me the impression his right lung had collapsed. His lung was filling with blood, which is why with each breath he took, blood started to pool around his mouth.

I acted on pure instinct borne from training. I placed Mike on his left side in the recovery position. If his left lung was collapsing, the blood would now start to travel down to his right side, gravity providing some necessary relief for Mike.

It worked. His pulse started to slowly rise, but not by much, unfortunately his breathing was not improving. He was critical. He was also going into shock, which could prove fatal. Earnest was standing by me, waiting to assist with anything. I asked him to grab two pillows and a blanket. Earnest understood what I wanted to do, he was also reverting to his training. He put the pillows under Mikes legs, elevating them above his heart, and covered Mike in the blanket, trying to keep his body warm. This would hopefully prevent him from going into shock.

EMTs arrived with the police and immediately started emergency services on Mike; the last visual I had of him as they rolled him out on the gurney was of a medic performing chest compressions and someone pumping oxygen into Mike from a hand pump.

Las Vegas METRO interviewed all of us, and we had to provide written statements, but they let us all go. They told us they took Mike to University Medical Center (UMC), the only Trauma One Hospital in Las Vegas, and I headed there as soon as they released us.

When I arrived, Mike's mom, Ruby, his sister Leslie, and his wife, Nora, were already there. Others began trickling in after me, but it was all kind of a blur.

Ruby was a no-nonsense Jamaican woman who was always warm and kind and carried herself in a way that demanded respect. She was intimidating, and I was always scared of her, but when we saw each other, she crumbled into my arms. I had to use all my strength to hold her up and could not understand anything she was trying to say. Her thick Jamaican accent and her uncontrollable sobbing prevented me from understanding a single word.

But, I understood her pain and fear clearly, in the way her body physically responded to the incident. Words were not necessary. Ruby was experiencing intense sadness and anxiety.

I could see Leslie, Mike's older sister, leaning against a vending machine, tears streaming down her cheeks. Her head down, she stared at the floor. Nora came over and helped me with Ruby. We helped her to a bench and sat her down. We consoled her until other family members arrived and took our place.

Nora and I walked outside, and she told me what she knew. Mike was in surgery; they did not know if he would make it, and the prognosis was bad. Mike could die.

The emergency room doctor treating Mike, told Nora, and later also told Mike; the basic life-saving actions Earnest and I took in those critical moments before EMS arrived, likely saved Mike's life.

A couple of hours later, it was time for me to leave. The sun was rising, and I had to drive back to Ely, Nevada, where I would have to report this incident to my superiors. I was not looking forward to it.

Ely, Nevada, is located approximately four hours north of Las Vegas in White Pine County. It is a sad mining town of approximately five thousand people.

Mining, as most people would imagine, was actually not the major employer in Ely. Ely, due to its small size and rural location, had been chosen to receive a state prison; approximately 20 minutes north of town. The prison, known as Ely State Prison or (ESP), was the only maximum-security prison in the entire state of Nevada. It housed Nevada's death row unit, and its prisoners were the most violent and volatile criminals in the state of Nevada.

Ely State Prison was my first job in law enforcement; it began a path I could never have expected after leaving the Marines. What a wild set of circumstances: becoming a gang member, committing crimes, and being involved in a form of violence for the majority of my life… to ending up working in a place where I could have ended up in myself. In a prison.

A complete role reversal.

Chapter 56

I arrived in Ely in April of 1999. Initially moving on my own, while Dacia waited with the kids in Las Vegas. By the time my family followed me up there, we had created three amazing children. Jordan, our oldest boy, born in 1995; Gabriella or Gabby, our oldest girl born in 1996, and Alicia our youngest daughter, born in 1998.

Ely was my first jaunt into small town living. Ely, like most places, has defining qualities which make it special. Ely is tiny, nestled in a valley, which brings freezing temperatures in the winter and amazing weather in the summer. Ely is known for a couple of western historical sites; the Ghost Train of Old Ely, a working steam engine left over from 1906, and the historic Hotel Nevada and Gambling Hall in downtown Ely, which opened in 1929 and remains in operation today.

Ely is quaint, sometimes even serene, with decent people, living a simple life. Unfortunately, Ely also fits the common stereotypes associated with small town living.

When I arrived in Ely for the first time and drove around the town trying to find the motel; I could not shake the bad vibes I felt every time I saw a confederate flag proudly displayed.

They were everywhere. Vehicles had them, homes and businesses displayed them, and in the twenty minutes it took me to find the motel, I had seen so many of them, I began to feel uncomfortable.

Rebel flags represent only one thing. When you strip away their tarnished and disgusting historical place in our nation's history, they become exposed for what they truly are… A representation of people who fought a civil war to keep slavery legal. It means nothing else.

It is a representation of racist views. To say otherwise, is wrong, irresponsible, and promoting revisionist history.

I checked into the motel, parked my car, and entered an old but clean room. I put my things down on the bed and sat on the edge of the bed, thinking. This was a big move for our young family.

My family trusted me. I would be uprooting them from Las Vegas, where they enjoyed their grandparents and cousins and extended family; to bring them to a small town, a little racist, to support me as I followed my dreams.

When I left the Marines, I applied to law enforcement positions, and Ely State Prison, from the Nevada Department of Corrections, was the first to offer me an opportunity.

I accepted, but if I could have predicted what would happen while working there; I would have stayed as far away from Ely, Nevada, as I could.

Chapter 57

April 2000 - 25 years old

As I drove towards Ely after leaving Mike at the hospital, a sick feeling in my stomach consistently grew worse with each passing mile. I did not want to report the incident; my experience at Ely State Prison (ESP) had not begun well, and reporting my involvement with what could end up being a homicide would just add fuel to the fire.

I was stressed, so I used my Blackberry to call "Clem," Clem was a Correctional Officer at ESP; his full name was Kevin Clemons, but he preferred "Clem." Clem was the only Black officer, not only at the prison but in the entire town of Ely.

He was an imposing figure, a former United States Air Force Military Police Officer, standing at just over six feet seven inches tall, with an athletic build and a commanding presence. Clem and I had struck up a friendship early on, both of us immediately recognizing the common lingo and swag attached to familiarity on the streets.

Clem answered the phone, and I began to tell him everything that had just transpired. Clem listened calmly, asked questions only when he needed clarification, and took time to process the information before responding.

Clem and Mike had recently met when we and our significant others all got together on a weekend and went out to drink at a karaoke bar in Las Vegas. Clem and Mike got along from the start, and we had a fun time.

So, Clem knew Mike and was familiar with our past life, which is why he took his time giving me advice on what to do. When he did finally give me his advice, he coldly and calmly said, "Don't tell those motherfuckers anything."

I continued my drive to Ely in silence, fully reflecting on what I had been through there, the mistakes I had made, and how I had grown to hate the job and the town.

Ely has a rich racial history. Ely is historically known as a "sundown" town. This meant any Native Americans, or non-white people, had to be outside the town city limits by sundown, or else...

The persecuted were from the Shoshone tribe, with its reservation only a forty-five-minute drive from Ely, but it also included any person of color.

As I noted when first arriving in town, the sentiment was alive and well, with Confederate flags proudly displayed from cars, businesses, and homes.

The most disturbing aspect of the comfort of its love for the confederacy was the number of Correctional Officers who freely and confidently displayed the confederate flag on their pick-up trucks and clothing.

I thought about all of this as I continued my drive towards Ely. I called Dacia from the hospital and explained everything to her. Dacia was sad, crying, and worried about Mike but relieved I was ok. I could not wait to get home to see my beautiful wife and kids.

I conducted the last portion of the drive in silence. I had to think. I turned the radio off and contemplated how I had fucked up from the very beginning. My naive interpretation of the world put me into a losing battle before I ever stepped foot into the prison.

CHAPTER 58

May 1999 - Ely State Prison Police Academy

My peers in my academy class voted me the class leader. To work in any Law Enforcement capacity, you must attend and pass a Police Academy.

I was in my early twenties, and I was young and dumb. I entered my new role with a mindset that my gang experience would prove invaluable. I could use my past experiences to assist and become an asset to the institution.

Part of the hiring process included disclosing my past, which included my gang activity.

I was happy ESP gave me an opportunity, especially after the negative reactions I received from Las Vegas METRO, all due to my gang involvement.

ESP saw potential, and even being aware of my background, to include my past gang involvement, related crimes and connections; they took a chance and gave me an opportunity. I was grateful and supremely motivated to prove their decision, had been the right one.

While my class and I were still in the Academy, and before releasing us into the institution, word had already filtered: Sullivan is not white; he is a Latino, he speaks Spanish fluently, and he is a former gang member.

The release of my personal information into the institution, instantly created a hostile work environment for me. When the Police Academy concluded, and I was finally able to enter the prison and begin working, I was excited, and ready to make a difference. The illusions I had created in my mind of becoming an asset and furthering my career, took an unexpected punch in the gut, which I was wholly unprepared for, and drastically set the ambit for my experience at ESP.

When we finished our training, we had a graduation ceremony. My family: my dad, my mom (who had returned to the US to be with my dad again), Dacia, and my kids drove up from Las Vegas for the ceremony.

I have always been an empath, and after the class chose me as the leader, I was responsible for giving the graduation speech.

When I wrote my speech, I wanted to speak from the heart and amplify issues I thought were important.

I have never felt particularly embarrassed or lacking in confidence when speaking about my vulnerabilities or world views, but after the speech I gave… It had me reconsidering it.

Personal information, is sometimes best kept to yourself. I learned a hard lesson in knowing your audience, and the kind of judgmental backlash, which can manifest into real work-related consequences. When arriving in Ely I was half-way done with my Criminal Justice Degree, and had already developed world views from the education I had obtained, and continued to receive. After the Marines, I did not lack in confidence. The opposite in fact, and willingly spoke about my vulnerabilities, about areas of my life I lacked education and experience in, and about my opinions and world views. After my graduation speech, the kind of vitriol I received from fellow officers, seriously had me reconsidering how I communicate and the platforms from which I choose to communicate from.

My speech involved praising my classmates and instructors and included the expected talk about how our future was beginning, blah, blah, blah.

I also spoke of my past and articulated how I could have been an inmate at ESP. It was important to me for people to recognize the humanity in a person who could have ended up as an inmate and was just lucky not to have been.

I spoke about our duty as Correctional Officers, which included not dispensing cruel or unusual punishment.

Reminding everyone of the importance of safeguarding everyone's constitutional rights. Focusing on the 8th amendment and driving the point home to the entire audience; my past could have easily placed me in ESP as an inmate. It was a visual and verbal representation of a reality many in the small town of Ely, did not comprehend. But I tried. My efforts, fell on deaf ears, and only caused me problems.

I thought it was important for my audience to process the value of how uncontrollable circumstances in a person's life could result in situational behavior, others may never have to experience.

Police are always quick to point out how their life and death decisions play out in split-second moments and reactions, rooted in a level of high stress and anxiety, which is fair and true.

Would be criminals, specifically, juveniles; in limited ways, sometimes fit the split-second moments of life altering decisions, subjectively similar to those of police officers. Obviously, the comparisons are objectively contrasted by our laws and social behavior, but when bridging my unique life experiences, rooted in both perspectives; I find a level of comprehension which aligns. When considering juvenile crime and including all the labels, economic and educational factors, environmental conditions in the home and community, and allowing for the government to view an offender as a child; in a very complex way, it aligns. I know it does, because I lived it.

My graduation speech immediately traveled through the prison gossip line, and not in a pleasant or supportive way. Judgment had already taken place before I stepped into the institution for work. Co-workers distrusted me, disliked me, and branded me. I never had a chance.

Officers Huston and Officer Till went out of their way to show their disdain for me.

Other officers shared their sentiments, but some were more careful about displaying those views.

At the very first shift brief I ever attended at ESP, Officer Till and Officer Huston, who I did not know at all, happened to be in attendance. They worked my scheduled shift, and we were all in the briefing room together. I did not know who they were, but I learned very quickly.

As I walked into the briefing room, where we gathered our daily assignments and intel, Till, and Huston stood beside one another by the entry door. In coordination, both feigned sneezing simultaneously and clearly said, "Spic" masked in a fake sneeze. It would not be the last time they feigned a sneeze while insulting me with racial slurs. It happened a handful of times.

I saw the other officers, including the Associate Warden, who was leading the brief that morning, try to hide smiles and suppress laughter. The insult, obviously directed at me, immediately eroded any excitement I may have had about starting my new job. I was left only in a state of rage, defensive anger, and distrust of everyone.

I took stock of both Till and Huston, as men usually do. Measuring both men up, imagining how I would fare in a physical fight against them.

Till was a tall, corn-fed type of white boy. Broad-shouldered, with a long blonde mullet which reached past his shoulders and down his back. Till had a big head and a look of permanent confusion etched on his face. Till always had Tobacco chew in his mouth, and his skin was always red, as if he had a permanent sunburn. Till stood approximately six feet two inches tall but was out of shape with a big beer belly protruding from his uniform. I was confident I could beat him easily.

Huston was shorter, even a little shorter than me. He stood around five feet eight inches tall; he wore cowboy boots to work and had a mouthful of tobacco chew. Huston always wore the same baseball cap. An ESP baseball cap, which appeared to have never been washed, as it was always coated in white scrapings of dried sweat. Huston thought himself and alpha of sorts. This was primarily due to his perceived superiority over inmates. He carried himself in what I recognized immediately as manufactured confidence, hiding his true nature.

Huston had a bushy mustache and sported a nice beer belly of his own.

They used empty soda bottles to continuously spit their nasty habit into the bottle. I already hated them. They instantly reminded me of the racist bully cowboys I encountered in Chicago.

My very first assignment out of the Academy was Death Row. Ely State Prison is separated down the middle by the gym, the prison industry, and receiving buildings, causing a near-straight line to cut down the center of the prison.

Lining the inner fence area on each side of the center line of buildings; rested the inmate housing units. Both sides, separated from the center buildings, by a large yard. The buildings were designed in the exact same architecture. Both sides, left or right, looked exactly the same; but the difference, was in the type of inmates they housed.

Walking into the prison, to the right was the Protective Custody (PC) yard and the PC unit, Unit 1. PC housed inmates who had acquired gambling debts, received death threats, and snitches. But, they were in the minority in the unit one population. The majority of offenders in protective custody, where the bane of human existence, the scourge of humanity. Child sex offenders and killers. The regular inmates, detested them, and called them "chomos," a play on the words, child molesters. They required protection, because at any prison in America, there is a green light to murder any and all child molesters and killers. Street justice, I agree with.

Attached to Unit 1 on the PC yard was Unit 2. The entire building was "the hole" or housing for inmates who got into trouble or inmates not allowed into the general population (GP) due to their violent behavior.

The final building in the PC yard was split in half. Unit 3 had additional cells assigned for the hole, and the attached building was unit 4, which was reserved solely for Death Row.

As I entered the hallway connecting both units, I was assaulted by the smell of institutional soap. Inmates wash everything with the soap provided to them by the state. If fortunate enough, inmates could receive money from their families or loved ones, which they could use at the inmate store. But even with better smells available, nothing overpowered the facility more than the state inmate soap. Inmates used it to wash their clothes, their cells, and themselves. Inmate soap overpowered any other smell.

I walked into the "Bubble" of unit 4, the control room for Death Row. Three officers were already in the bubble. One of the senior officers, Officer Johnson, a bald, kind man, took me under his wing. He began to explain the various buttons on the board. He took his time and repeated things multiple times to make sure I was retaining the information.

After I got a crash course on the bubble's duties, the senior officer in the bubble asked us to start heading out to the sally port (a series of security doors that require one side to be completely shut before the other one can open) and to get ready for tier time.

Tier time is allowed only in general population work units and death row. Inmates must earn their way up to these units (apart from death row) to receive free time on the tier and in the big yard. The tier is the communal area outside the cells, which allows for exercising, table games such as chess, and general interaction with other inmates.

As we walked into the Sally Port, I heard all the cell doors opening, and I could see all the Death Row inmates step out of their cells and onto the tier.

Death Row Inmates are usually the best-behaved inmates because they have the most to lose. Death Row inmates go through multiple and lengthy appeals processes, which could reverse their case and, at a minimum, give them life in prison.

It was in their best interest to show good behavior, adapt to incarcerated life, and stay out of trouble. Death Row did not have access to the big yard but did have access to the small concrete side yards attached to every unit at ESP. In these yards, death row inmates were the only inmates in the entire institution who had weights.

The unit side yards all came equipped with the same allowable activities, a basketball hoop, and a handball court. The basketball hoop and handball court shared the same wall. Since Death Row Inmates at ESP were the only inmates allowed weights, they resembled people you would expect to see featured in muscle magazines and ripped in a way that only multiple workouts a day can create. They were intimidating and menacing.

I was scared, terrified. These inmates, accused serial killers, were walking around Johnson and me freely as we patrolled the tier. It was such a surreal moment and experience, knowing these men had committed violent acts, causing at least one person's death and as many as thirty of them walking amongst us.

My imagination started to cause me to panic. It almost felt like being inside a cage full of predators, like lions or tigers. This caused me to behave strangely and act in a super hyper-alert state. I was constantly looking around, waiting for an attack at any moment.

I was fortunate to have Officer Johnson as my training officer. He noticed my anxiety and calmly walked me through the job. He treated everyone with respect and dignity, and inmates responded with equal behavior.

Johnson was one of the few officers who was not there to judge anyone for their crimes. He explained that his life revolved around living with them for ten, twelve, or sometimes sixteen hours a day, and he found that treating them the way he would want to be made his job easier.

It was not our job to make anything intentionally difficult for them. His philosophy had kept him safe for years, and he felt confident that if there were ever times when inmates rioted or became violent, he would be safe simply for doing his job without extra-judicious behavior. Johnson treated everyone firmly, fairly, and consistently, which was the actual motto for officer behavior; he exemplified it. Unfortunately, that is not how the majority of the staff behaved.

CHAPTER 59

Ely State Prison - 2001

I started my second year at ESP and became complacent. My past created a strange dichotomy, placing me in tricky situations, situations where I considered, even if it was for only a second, engaging in criminal conduct.

Clem and I knew most officers at ESP hated us and in the town of Ely in general. Clem, being the only Black person in town and at ESP, took awful abuse from the citizens in Ely.

Clem lived at the edge of town; he rented a small house at the end of Main Street. He had a small, gated yard, and he usually traveled to Las Vegas on his days off.

The citizens in Ely, when they found the location of his home, decided Clem's front yard was a good place to dump their trash.

So, when he returned from Las Vegas every weekend, he would find other people's trash thrown on his front steps and lawn. A significant amount, too, multiple people defiling his home. Deliberate disrespect and an attempt to intimidate.

He reported the incidents to the local Sheriff's office, but no resolution ever came of it. Clem was so angry and disturbed by the racism in Ely he began waiting in his home with his firearms ready, thinking at any moment, things would escalate. They would not catch him slipping.

Clem was actively looking for work to take him out of Ely. I did not blame him.

The problems with Officers Till and Huston continued to metastasize. I provided unintended fuel for their prejudices and anger to simmer slowly to a boil.

I was working on intake, which required the help of multiple officers because it was the day when new inmates arrived at ESP.

As inmates exited the bus, we conducted inmate body searches and private property searches, a tedious and disgusting process. It is imperative to do an excellent job on the searches because missing weapons or drugs could result in the loss of life. So, the inmates waited in line as officers took turns searching.

After about an hour of searching, a Hispanic inmate arrived at my workspace and placed his hands directly on the wall, and facing away from me. He was following directions and took his clothes off. As soon as his shirt came off, my heart dropped.

I knew this person. "28 St" tattooed on his back and "Orco" on the back of his neck. Shit!

Orco turned his head and smiled sheepishly. I appreciated that he was too savvy to let anyone know we knew each other. He gave me a slight nod, which I returned, and continued the intake process.

I was trying to remain calm and indifferent but having this secret past relationship with this criminal... made me feel guilty. It felt like everyone in the room had just observed our very nuanced interaction.

I could feel officers staring at me in disgust. I started to panic. What do I do now? Do I report this? What is he going to expect from me? I turned my head slowly, expecting disappointed stares, but to my relief, nobody had noticed. Orco moved along with the other inmates, never looking back or saying anything.

I still had "28 St" tattooed on my left hand and "Sur 13" on my right hand. It wouldn't take long for someone to make the connection. I watched as Orco walked away, carrying his yellow tub with all his possessions, and felt bad for him. A harsh and real reminder, which had me imagining, was me walking along with leg shackles on, carrying a bright yellow tub with all my possessions.

I did not see Orco again for months. Prior to Orco arriving at ESP, I had to deal with the questions my visible hand tattoos created. There were multiple Hispanic prison gangs at ESP, and I recognized Hispanic gang members from the streets. Street affiliation or loyalty meant zero in prison.

If you were Hispanic, you either belonged to Mi Raza Unida (MRU) or the Mexican Mafia (La M). There were multiple smaller offshoots, but those were the two major ones. There was a war happening in prisons across the US between these two prison gangs and the control of the drug trade.

I lost count of the times inmates questioned my tattoos and affiliation. The reactions were consistent; first, they would ask with an attitude, thinking I was a weird white boy trying to claim a gang.

Then, their dismissive attitude would turn into curiosity at my mastery of the Spanish Language. Things would slowly digress from there; once they understood I was really a Latino and I was a former gang member, they would always, and I mean always… try to compromise me into smuggling in something for them. Always.

Getting compromised was drilled into us at the academy from day one and specially drilled into me by Sergeant Booker because of my past gang affiliation. He took extra time to help me understand how difficult the situation could get for me. He stressed reporting any and every interaction.

The problem was, if I had reported every time an inmate tried to compromise me, I would have had to report daily.

Instead, I opted not to report and to dissuade inmates by simply telling them the truth.

After the first few interactions, I had my speech rehearsed. I explained that I had kids, joined the Marines, and changed my life. I was clear: I would not risk my family's future for anyone. Period.

The inmates had one of two reactions. They either understood or respected it. "Or, in particular, if they had known me or heard about me on the outside; their reactions were never positive ones. I received verbal threats of future physical harm and sometimes even death.

I was young, cocky, and supremely confident. Which was a mistake, a mistake which could have cost me my life.

Over time, I was able to form relationships with staff and inmates (you see them every day; it is impossible not to form a working relationship). However, I began to become complacent in my professional expectations and behavior with inmates.

There was a senior corrections officer who may still work at ESP. He was young and down to earth. To protect his identity, I will call him Chico. There is a possibility he may still work at the institution.

Chico and I became friends and found we shared things in common. By the time I arrived, he had been at ESP for about eight years, so he knew inmates intimately.

Chico introduced me to the game of handball. Each unit at ESP has a bubble (control room) and a gun rail (a window located above the small concrete yard where an officer posted with a rifle and shotgun). The senior officer also had a set of master keys so he or she could bypass the electronic locks.

One night, while working overtime in his unit, Chico said, "When the esses from cell sixteen come out to the yard, I am going to step out with them. Do not be a snitch!"

I did not know what he was talking about. We were in unit five, on the opposite side of the institution, and the first unit an inmate arrives at when they finish their time in the hole. Housed in the hole meant no big yard freedom, no roommates, controlled movements with officers only, unable to receive visits, and only one hour of yard time per day, on their own, in the small unit side yard.

The side yard was a small concrete yard available in every unit. While housed in the hole, inmates spent twenty-three hours of the day in their cells.

Unit five was meant to ease them back into normal prison life. In unit five, inmates could have a cellmate, and cellmates were allowed in the small yard together. All the small yards were the same (apart from death row, which had weights). The best way I can describe the attached unit's small yards is that they are triangles trying to be squares. Every small yard had a basketball hoop attached to the wall and a white line painted across the wall for handball.

Handball was huge at ESP. Inmates had tournaments and could get competitive. When we opened the small yard in unit five for two Hispanic inmates to come out, I saw Chico walk out with them.

I was on the gun rail looking down at them. Chico joked about shooting the inmates if they tried anything, but he simply took off his work belt, placed it on the corner (inmates knew not even to get close to it), took off his work shirt, and casually started to play handball with them.

I loved it. I kept hearing "changa!" I had heard changa daily, all inmates used the term, but I did not know what it meant. So, I yelled down and asked Chico, "What does changa mean?"

"Game point," he yelled back.

He finished the game, came back into the bubble, and relieved me. Out of breath, and between sucking down water, he said, "Your turn."

I took his keys and climbed off the gun post. I opened the security doors and found myself with two older Hispanic males, both smiling at me and waiting for me to play.

I took off my belt and work shirt and stood awkwardly, waiting for them to initiate. They already knew I spoke Spanish, so they just started introducing themselves. They were both from a small gang, a sub-set created in Mexican prisons, known as the Border Brothers (BB), and they hated both MRU and La M. Border Brothers, who were mostly illegals, did not speak English well, and banded together out of necessity in US prisons.

I spent the next two hours learning how to play handball. It was the most entertaining shift of work I had ever had. Chico introduced me to a whole new world within the prison.

These handball and basketball relationships grew, and word amongst the inmates spread. Everyone knew I was "okay," like Chico and the inmates treated me with respect and kindness.

I searched for overtime to work with Chico in his unit, and we got to the point where we were both down there playing against inmates with no one in the bubble and no one on the gun. We were just out there having fun—no gun coverage, the master keys available, and no one supervising the bubble.

We began wagering "daddy pushups" when we played against inmates, which I learned at ESP, and I have continued to use in my daily life when competing for friendly wagers with friends and family.

But our actions and behavior were dangerous and, for the lack of better words, extremely stupid.

Thankfully, no one ever took advantage of our irresponsible behavior, and no incidents or injuries happened from our complete lack of professionalism.

Chapter 60

April 2000 - Ely, Nevada

I pulled into our house's driveway and shut the engine off. I sat in my car contemplating and further processing. I called Nora to check on Mike. She did not have good news. Mike was still in surgery, over five hours in now.

I looked down at my pants and my shirt, covered in Mike's blood, and suddenly hit with a wave of nausea and emotions. I sat in the car and quietly cried, hoping Mike would pull through.

Dacia opened the back door, which came out directly onto the driveway, and she stood there, holding Alicia in one hand, our newborn Nico in the other, and Jordan and Gabby visible by her legs.

I paused to consider the visual and admire the force of nature Dacia was.

Dacia managed to be a mom to four young children, tend to the house, and prepare meals for all of us. If she had to go anywhere, all four kids went with her. I did not understand where she found the energy or how she always stayed so calm, but nurturing and being a mother was something Dacia did with amazing efficiency and grace. She was fueled by the purest love known to humanity and in our known universe... the love a mother has for her children.

Dacia was the best mother our children could have had. These moments always reminded me to respect Dacia properly and to make sure I expressed my sincere love and appreciation for her sacrifices. I was an incredibly lucky man.

I got out of the car, and the kids ran down the steps towards me. The blood was already dried up, but I took my shirt off anyway and hugged all three in a great big hug (Nico was a newborn, so Dacia held on to him); I picked them all up and dropped them on the grass next to the driveway, and we began to play wrestle, Nala, our dog (a lab mix) came over to play with us as well. Nala was visibly pregnant, which was a bit of a surprise.

After we put the kids to bed, Dacia and I talked about what happened. We waited another hour and called Nora back to get an update. Mike was out of surgery but on a ventilator and in the intensive care unit.

The prognosis was still up in the air. He suffered internal organ damage, including a severed spine. If Mike survived, being paralyzed would become his new normal.

Dacia and I sat quietly on our couch, both lost in our thoughts. The new implications caused us to contemplate what life would look like for Mike if he survived.

We fell asleep on the couch. When we woke up, three of the kids were lying on the floor below us on the carpet, their heads resting on Nala.

I paused and tried to take in every detail, creating a mental Polaroid of my family as they slept peacefully. These types of moments are rare, and I often wonder if other people share them.

I understood one thing: the cosmic connection with a child is incomprehensible. The emotional attachment is unable to be described with words. We share energy, an unbending and unbreakable connection. We are the dust and particles of the stars, bonding and combining each other's energies in a way that creates shared growth and a constant pulsation of love... validating our attached existence.

I checked on my "Flaco boy," my nickname for Nico, and left the rest of the family asleep where they were. I took a shower and got ready for work. As I was walking out of the door, I saw Dacia had moved off the couch and onto the carpet to lay and hold the kids. I walked out feeling lucky and with a smile on my face, thinking about stars and the universe...

With four kids, we decided a minivan was the only way to go, so I got into our minivan and started the drive to ESP. Ely State Prison is nestled deep in a valley north of the town of Ely. It is approximately twelve miles north, and there is only one road to access the institution: Lackawanna Road.

I drove down Lackawanna Road, thinking about how I would report the shooting and my involvement. I decided to go to the only other Latino at ESP, Sergeant Garcia, for guidance.

Sergeant Garcia was close to retirement. He was short and sported a sizable belly from too many beers. Sgt. Garcia oversaw the inmate kitchen; he supervised all the inmates and civilian staff who worked in the industrial-sized kitchen. Every time I saw him, I pictured an old Mexican cowboy, pulling his pants up every five seconds with a sombrero and a bottle of tequila. He looked like he belonged to an old Western movie. He was a character and always had a new joke to share. He was also helpful and trustworthy, and he looked out for me.

I arrived at ESP, parked the van, and walked through the various sally ports and security checkpoints necessary to gain access. I was early, so I went straight to the kitchen to find Sgt. Garcia in his office. I walked in and closed the door. He could tell I was not there to fuck around, so he said, "Que hiciste pinche cabron?" (What did you do fucking asshole?)

I sat down in the lone chair in front of his desk and told him everything. He listened and shook his head repeatedly. When done, he stood up and said, "Come with me."

I followed him to the administration building. Before we entered, he said, "We are going to go inside and tell Lt. Liverani. You technically did not do anything wrong; you were just at the wrong place at the wrong time. Liverani likes you, so let us see what he says."

Lt. Liverani did like me. He was a huge man, standing at least six feet three inches tall and weighing in, and I am guessing here, around four hundred pounds. He was rotund. I do not know why he liked me, but he did. He was always nice to me and treated me fairly. I was following Sgt. Garcia's lead, so I just went with it. We walked into Lt. Liverani's office and told him everything.

He seemed to think the same as Sgt. Garcia, I did not commit a crime and was guilty of being in the wrong place at the wrong time. The only problem they foresaw was my friendship with Mike, who was a felon who had served time for attempted murder as a juvenile.

Lt. Liverani told me not to worry about it. I did the right thing by reporting it, and nothing should come of it. He told me not to talk about it with anyone. I shook his hand, and then Sgt. Garcia walked me halfway to my unit before he bid me farewell, and we both went to work.

I walked to unit six, my assigned unit for the day, feeling better about my decision. I felt lighter and no longer crushed by the fear of losing my job from my involvement in Mike's shooting.

CHAPTER 61

I worked a double that night. I finished my shift in unit six and walked to unit five with Chico. We got down with handball all night. I had been stressed, but as the day was winding down, I felt everything would be okay.

After we were relieved, Chico and I walked out to the parking lot, and he left in his truck. I walked over to the van and immediately noticed it was keyed. There was a blatant and long grind along our van's entire driver's side. I had just finished working sixteen hours, and I was exhausted. I had to be back in the morning, so I decided to wait until the next day and report it. I drove home, too tired to be mad about it.

As I drove into the parking lot the next day, I parked my car as close to the gatehouse as possible. Once inside the institution, I went in for a briefing and was told I would work unit two with Officer Till. This was odd because, usually, we did not get paired. I waited for everyone to leave and reported the damage to my car to the desk sergeant. Could I prove it occurred in the parking lot? Did I have pictures of my vehicle before the alleged damage?

Obviously, I did not have any of it, and his reaction to my report only pissed me off.

I stayed on the tier all day. It is common for officers to hang in the bubble together, especially in units like the hole, where no movement or activity is allowed on the tier. I did not want to be in the bubble with Till, so I stayed on the tier, doing my job and staying busy.

Inmates housed in the hole have zero ability to do anything. If they are out of toilet paper, we must provide them with a roll. If they are out of soap, we must provide them with soap. If they want to shower, handcuffs must be placed first, taken to the shower, secured in the shower, and then released.

While serving time in the hole, privileges like a TV are not allowed, and they only have one hour a day in the small yard on their own. The food is transported from the kitchen to them in carts, and then officers deliver the food via the food slot of their cell door.

At ESP, officers went out of their way to piss off the inmates. They took an immature sort of deranged joy and pleasure in delaying things inmates needed or wanted.

Sometimes, they intentionally refuse to help the inmate and leave it for the next shift to deal with. These officers would delay showers, phone calls, toiletries, and even food. I want to say behavior like it was the exception, but it was more like the norm.

Today, I was making sure all the inmates had their basic needs. I went to every door and asked if anyone needed anything. Multiple inmates needed showers, claiming they had not been able to shower in days. I needed Tills' permission to shower inmates. He controlled the cell doors from the bubble, so I asked the inmate to press the intercom button and ask Till if he could shower. The inmate pressed the button repeatedly, but Till ignored it.

Inside the bubble, when an inmate presses the intercom button, a light blinks on top of the button assigned to his cell door, followed by a beeping sound, which only stops after you press the intercom or silence the alert.

I walked over to the bubble and one of the windows. I asked Till if he could see the inmate trying to reach him. He said, "Yeah, I see it; I'm busy." He was not busy; he was doing jack-shit.

I returned to the inmate, apologized, and told him I would keep trying.

At lunchtime, the food carts arrived, pushed by inmate workers from the kitchen, and supervising the inmates was none other than Officer Huston.

I could not believe my luck or lack thereof, the two most openly racist officers collaborating with me. The officer they detested the most.

I think their hatred for me was not only because I was Hispanic and a former gang member but because I looked white. I was supposed to be one of them. It bothered them, to their core, that my worldviews were in stark contrast to their own.

Huston and the worker inmates pushed the cart inside the tier, and then Huston walked into the bubble with Till. The two inmates who helped to push the cart asked me if it was okay if we started getting trays out and preparing the meals to serve them. I said, "Yes."

As soon as they began opening the hot boxes, Huston walked over to the closest bubble window and yelled, "What do you think you are doing?

I told him we were getting everything ready to deliver the chow, but he replied, "Put it all back. We won't have time to serve it before count time; it will have to wait until after count!"

There are three times during the day when an institutional count takes place. Counting is meant to account for all inmates. The midday count was still forty minutes from officially starting. We had ample time; they were just being dickheads. Soon, we could all hear country music playing loudly from the bubble and see Till and Huston talking and laughing inside.

I sat on one of the tables on the tier with the two inmate kitchen workers, and we chopped it up until count time. When the institutional count time arrived, I walked by every cell door and saw a living, breathing person in every cell. I finished my count and gave Till the numbers.

The inmates in the unit were banging on the doors and yelling - pissed off. They saw the food cart come in and knew chow had arrived with enough time before counting to feed them; now, their food would be cold.

They were not happy about it. As soon as the all-clear came over the intercom, I started to feed the inmates. Huston and Till did not even bother to step out and help. They sat in the bubble, country music on blast and visibly laughing.

As I was picking up empty trays and cleaning up, Till tried to reach me, but it was loud, and I could not hear him. I was on the second level, when I heard Till over the unit intercom. Using the unit intercom, meant everyone in the unit heard what he said. He stated, "Hey, inmate in green, come down here."

He was referring to me. Our uniforms were green, and he and Huston were laughing inside the bubble, disrespecting me and making me look like an ass.

I walked over to the window, visibly pissed off. I could hear them laughing inside. Huston came to the window and said, "Hey, good job cleaning up all the mess; now take the two inmates and the cart and escort them back to the kitchen. I will wait here with Till until you get back."

This motherfucker now wanted me to do his job. I was livid, but a part of me did not mind; it would get me away from them, and I would intentionally slow-play coming back. I might even sit with Sgt. Garcia and talk to him for a bit before heading back to the unit.

I asked the two worker inmates to gather the carts and follow me; as we walked out of the unit, I wondered again, what kind of idiot wears cowboy boots to work anyway?

From my experience in Chicago, I had a healthy dislike of cowboys, but I was growing to really develop a deep disdain for them. So far, most cowboys I had met in the United States were not what I had expected.

I slow played like I planned, took my sweet time. I sat with Sgt. Garcia in his office until I could hear Huston on the radio asking if anyone knew my location. It was a nice sunny day out, and I took my sweet time soaking up the sun as I walked back to unit two. It was a very deliberate, slow, and purposeful walk. Petty, but fuck him.

When I arrived at the unit, Huston was waiting at the door. His face was red with anger, and his bushy mustache and sideburns were gleaming with sweat.

The door popped open, and he shoulder-bumped me as he walked past me, mumbling what I am confident was incoherent racist bullshit. I walked back into the tier and finished my shift without going into the bubble with Till.

The inmate in green comment, caught on with all the racist fucks at ESP, because that is what they started to call me, behind my back.

I worked another double shift that night, but unfortunately, not in Chico's unit. So, it was a boring shift, and I did not trust anyone there anymore. I kept to myself on the tier again. I did not go into the bubble at all. I knew my behavior was alienating the few good officers who worked at the institution and that my defensive, loner posturing affirmed their perceived biases. But I was getting past the point of caring.

When I got home just after midnight, Dacia was waiting for me. She was sitting at the kitchen table, crying.

I went to her, pulled a chair next to hers, and sat down while holding her hand. I thought there was sad news about Mike, so I asked what was wrong.

She told me she received four calls on the house phone while I was at work.

The first two were hang-ups. On the third call, a male voice said, "Tell your husband to quit," and promptly hung up. On the last call, the male voice said, "Y'all should leave town as soon as possible if you know what's good for you!"

Dacia was scared, and so was I.

Racist remarks were spouted about me at ESP; they minimized my authority. A position, I had worked just as hard as them to earn. They devalued me as person and as an authority figure in my work capacity.

The label "inmate in green" started to eat at me. I took the disrespect at work and ate it, not showing emotion. I tried not to give the racist bastards even a sliver of satisfaction their words annoyed me. Now, these racist, cowboy punk bitches, had escalated things to a level I would not allow. Threatening my wife and my kids, crossed a very specific line. A line, which made me volatile and unpredictable. I was dangerously close to responding with immediate and forceful violence.

This was clearly related to ESP, Till, and Huston specifically. I was sure of it.

I called Clem and told him. He told me he was considering filing a complaint with the Equal Employment Opportunity Commission (EEOC). He was tired of the trash thrown in his yard; he was tired of getting all the shit posts and hours at work, and most importantly, the way they denied him deserved promotions.

It was blatant racism. I told him we would talk about it in detail on the weekend. We were both fed up with what was happening.

It was getting out of hand, and now calling and threatening my family at home? Fuck that.

I could not get it out of my mind. They called my home and threatened my family. Scaring my wife. I did not know the lengths these people would go to, but I would not stick around to find out.

CHAPTER 62

I went to work the next day with a huge chip on my shoulder, pissed off at the world.

Clem talked me into not reporting the calls until we had a chance to talk. I knew who it was; it was Huston and Till. Dacia needed the car that morning, so she dropped me off at the gatehouse.

I was tasked with working in unit five that day, but at least it was not with Till. As I was making my rounds around the tier, I heard a voice from the corner cell in the bottom say, "Popeye, hey esse, come here."

I knew immediately who it was; it was Orco. I knew this day would come and had been dreading it. I was able to avoid him for months, but there was no avoiding it this time.

I walked in front of his cell, and he was waiting at his window. He was smiling, and he said, "What the fuck, homie? We heard you went back to Ecuador, came back, and went into the military. Is that true?"

"What's up, man?" I replied and continued, "Yes, that's pretty much how it happened!"

He stared at me, right into my eyes, without saying a word, trying to gauge me or discern meaning from eye contact.

Then he suddenly looked away and said, "Check this drawing out. My niece made it for me?" He slid the drawing through the side crack in the door, and I took it in my hands. We both knew the officers in the bubble had the speaker to the intercom on and could hear everything we were saying.

I commented on how cool the drawing was and asked about his family. When I picked up the drawing, a small piece of paper stuck with a dab of toothpaste on the back of the drawing was noticeable in my hand. I took it and palmed it. I do not know why. Maybe because I knew Orco? I do not know why I did it, but I regretted it instantly.

Orco took the drawing back and understood. I took his message, and he nodded and said, "Well, it's good to see one of us doing something good with their lives, esse, good for you."

He shut his light off and turned away from me.

I did not know what to do. I thought for sure the officers in the bubble had seen me palm the piece of paper, but if they did, no one said anything.

I continued to do my work and, after an hour or so, entered the bubble to use the bathroom.

I sat on the toilet and unfolded the paper. It said, "Popeye, call this number; they will give you shit to bring in for me."

A Vegas number was written on it, and by "shit," he meant drugs.

I had already rehearsed how this interaction would go, and I was not looking forward to it, but I knew it had to happen.

I returned to the tier and walked up to Orco's cell door. He switched his light on, and I stared into his eyes and said, "I don't go by Popeye anymore; I'm Officer Sullivan."

We stared intensely at each other through the small window on his cell door. He understood what I was saying because he brought his right hand up with his index finger out and slowly ran it across his throat, telling me I was a dead man.

I nodded and walked away.

When the shift ended, I saw Sgt. Garcia was in the yard, and we met up and started to walk out of the institution together.

We were on the outdoor path connecting the administration building and the prison to the gatehouse. Multiple officers walking in front of us and the same behind us, everyone leaving for the day.

I noted Huston was with a group of officers in front of us, his stupid fucking cowboy boots clacking as he walked down the cement pathway.

Sgt. Garcia and I were talking in Spanish, laughing about something I cannot recollect… when Huston, unsolicited, suddenly and aggressively turned around and said, while pointing his chubby little finger directly at me, "Why don't you just go back to whatever country you came from?"

I stared at him with obvious disdain and disrespect. Just stood there, did not flinch, did not react, just stared right into his ugly little beady eyes, as he pretended his friends held him back.

When the officers holding Huston released him momentarily, he lunged at me again, pretending he wanted to fight. I stood in place. I knew it was a show. We were still at work; his friends were "holding him back," and I just continued to stare and smile at him. Calm, not talking any shit back; he was yelling and trying to be tough; he made a big show of it.

Sgt. Garcia was finally able to diffuse the situation and asked me to wait until Huston made it through the gatehouse. I obliged. I was still quiet and calm, but inside, I was raging with barely contained violent energy.

Sgt. Garcia said we would be reporting the incident tomorrow. What Huston said was racist, and his actions were unacceptable. I just nodded my head in agreement. Sgt. Garcia could tell I was not ok, so he made sure he watched Huston leave in his truck before he let me go.

I left the gatehouse and found Dacia waiting for me with the kids in the van. They were all in car seats. "Hi, Daddy," piped from the back; I didn't respond. Dacia took one look at me, and she knew something was wrong. I said, did you see that black truck with the confederate flag flying in the back and the rifle visible against the back window? Dacia nodded. "Good, catch up to him right now."

To her credit and my surprise, Dacia took off and was on a mission with me to catch the truck. She asked me what happened, I told her, and she said, "It has to be the asshole who called our house and keyed our car!" Never threaten a mother and her kids.

Dacia was going in and out of cars, driving like a fucking formula one champion in the minivan. Our kids' heads swayed back and forth, but they were ok. Not really, what we were doing was dangerous and dumb, but fuck it, do not threaten us.

We finally saw him as he was turning right onto the main road. Dacia pulled right next to him. I had my window rolled down, and he slowed down and rolled his down; as we slowly rolled down the street, I said, "Get out, just me and you. Finish this like men."

He rolled up his window and gave me the finger. He took off at a high rate of speed, and Dacia followed. Dacia wanted accountability. I did not blame her. He had threatened our family. We got into a bit of a chase until I received a call on my Blackberry. It was Sgt. Garcia. He yelled in my ear, "Stop chasing Huston, drop your family off at home, and come back to ESP right now!"

I told Dacia to stop chasing him and to drive home. I told her what Sgt. Garcia said she knew about what Clem was planning to do; she told me I should do the same thing. Dacia loved Ely; she loved the views, the small community, and small-town life. She loved it for our kids. I did too, but not at the cost of having to deal with open racism and threats to our family.

I dropped the family off at home and drove back to ESP. Upon arriving, they wrote me up for attempting to fight another officer while off-duty and causing dangerous conditions on the roadway.

Sgt. Garcia stood up for me and told them Huston had provoked everything, but they responded, "We will deal with Officer Huston's alleged acts as well."

Huston, when confronted, got scared; when I challenged him to a fight, knowing his friends were no longer around, he reconsidered. He called from his truck to report what was happening. Huston was a typical racist bully and a snitch-ass little bitch.

I left ESP for the last time that day. I went home and called Clem, we called the EEOC and filed a complaint. Days later, Clem and I were emergency transferred out of ESP to High Desert State Prison; Sgt. Garcia followed us shortly after.

High Desert State Prison is a medium-security prison near Las Vegas. Our complaints, the evidence, and the elevated exchanges between Huston and me made it urgent for the EEOC to get us out of Ely.

The transfer was not enough for me. I wanted to see real consequences for Huston and Till and others like them. I hired an attorney, RB, and we pursued a civil suit. In the end, I agreed to take a settlement from the state, with the agreement that I would no longer seek employment with the Nevada Department of Corrections.

In retrospect, the entire settlement meeting was also questionable. I participated in the room during mediation and negotiations.

Then, suddenly, they asked me to leave the room. I was young, naive, and too trusting of people, especially my attorney; I left the room.

When allowed back into the room, the settlement was finalized, and I only needed to sign papers. I was confused and questioned my attorney. I was not happy with the amount the state was offering, and more importantly, there was no indication Huston and Till had or would receive any formal reprimand for their actions.

Months later, I learned from Chico that Huston was promoted to Sergeant. What a slap in the face. Justice never served because places like ESP were fundamentally created under institutionalized racism—just an internal example of how our Criminal Justice system fails in so many ways. Even later in life, when I became a Police Officer, I encountered so much institutionalized racism that I quit Law Enforcement. The hiring standards, particularly the psychological testing, require a major overhaul. I could not, in good conscience, be a part of any organization that displayed so much bias and behavior that directly contrasted with the mission.

To this day, the request made by the state attorneys, to have me leave the room during a critical juncture in the negotiation process, makes me feel manipulated and frankly, kind of dumb. Trusting my attorney to have my best interest at heart, and completely uneducated about the process; I believe, allowed for some back-door good-old-boy lawyering to happen behind my back, and to my detriment.

It was me and my future we were negotiating. I was the one who had the most personal stake in the negotiations. Why did they ask me to leave the room? Why was the deal reached without any input from me?

It was a hard lesson that still hurts to swallow anytime I think about it.

The whole thing took about a year. I worked at High Desert State Prison until 2001.

Right before I left, Danny (Playboy), the guy who shot Mike, transferred to High Desert, and I had the pleasure of briefly seeing him.

I wouldn't have recognized him. He could have walked right by me and never realized it was him; I would have never noticed Danny Mitchell, the inmate.

"Playboy," a man obsessed with his appearance, a flirt who charmed his way through life… The last time I saw him was when he ran out of his apartment after shooting Mike.

Now, he looked nothing like the way I remembered him. The guilt and the life behind bars had taken a heavy toll on him. I relished the person I was looking at—a defeated man. Gone was any youthful energy or vibrance for life. He had become obese. None of the once-obvious athleticism was present. Only a sad, lumbering, and sweating man, eating his way through his pain, guilt, and punishment.

It made me physically and emotionally happy to see this man become what I was currently witnessing. In a small way, I understood he was suffering for what he had done to Mike. Mike became paralyzed because of the coward I was looking at. He deserved all of it and more.

He saw me through his cell window, and we locked our eyes. His confusion caused his multiple chins to jiggle as he adjusted himself to get a better look out of the small window of his cell. "Jonny?" he asked.

I looked at him, held his gaze for a moment, and then smiled— the kind of smile that communicates every single grievance and emotion attached to what he did. It was more of a smirk, with my eyes narrowing and staring at him with an intensity and fury I had been repressing.

I wanted to open his cell door and beat the life out of him. I actually considered it, I could have walked up to his cell door, put my hand up so the bubble officer could see me, and he would have opened the cell door, without question.

It was medium security prison and a general population unit.

Somehow, no one knew of our shared past. Of his crime. Of him shooting my best friend and permanently paralyzing him, and then holding the gun to my face and nearly killing me. I was saved, only by the scream of his then pregnant girlfriend.

I resisted the urge, because I valued my freedom, but it wasn't an easy choice. I stared at his fat ass face taking up the entire window, looking like "Fat Bastard" from the Austin Powers movies. I calmed myself, and decided to do the one thing he couldn't do. The one action he could not control. The thing I knew, he wanted to do most in the world, maybe other than eating a Little Debbie pastry; I gave him the birdie and walked out of the cell block and out to a beautiful sunny day… free!

Fuck him.

EPILOGUE

Mike, thankfully, after a month in the ICU, was able to pull through and fight his way back from life-threatening injuries. In typical Mike fashion, he assimilated to his wheelchair with great enthusiasm and positive energy.

Mike is a special person. Like anyone else, not infallible and prone to mistakes. We all make mistakes; the only difference comes from socioeconomic environments and race, which place people in situations others cannot comprehend. Not understanding does not make it any less real.

Accepting people's faults, understanding they will make mistakes in life, and receiving information with a forgiving heart are human qualities missing from so many in our global community. The energy from empathy vs. the energy from apathy are the Ying's and Yang's in constant friction in our living world—this unfortunate reality, will someday result in our collective downfall.

Mike's ability to adapt and accept becoming paralyzed is an example of his mental fortitude and of someone who loves life.

Perspective is everything.

When giving up could have been easy, when fatalistic and defeated behavior could have been interpreted as a reasonable choice, Mike pushed it all away and did not allow any darkness to control his new normal or slow his forward momentum. Mike is a glass-half-full type of man, an inspiration to all who know him, and his quiet, determined choice to keep it moving, is incredibly humbling.

The multiple transitions I endured, geographically, emotionally, intellectually, and character-based, molded me into the version of the man I am today. Becoming a father and a husband was a seismic shift in my life. All my experiences with my parents fundamentally affected how I chose to be a father and a husband. The same is true for my wife. We did not want to perpetuate the same familial cycles. We wanted to start new traditions and new ways of parenting. I struggled with discipline and found myself being a calm and relaxed parent.

Sometimes, I was too understanding and allowed my kids to take advantage of my lack of boundaries. I was scared. I feared getting angry. Allowing the emotion to manifest terrified me because I feared turning into the worst version of my dad. It became a point of contention with Dacia and me because she viewed it as a lack of support from her husband. She was right.

My dad, John B. Sullivan, sadly passed away while I was overseas in Iraq in January 2019. He had been living with us at our home for a couple of years.

He moved in with us after suffering from a couple of failed attempts to take his own life. Those attempts happened while living with my mom and my brother in Ecuador. Collectively, we decided it was better for him to move in with us.

My dad did not want to live. This was obvious. He smoked as much as he could, and he started to drink again. He knew suicide was selfish and would hurt us deeply; he resorted to shortening his life with unhealthy vices.

He suffered a massive heart attack in his room, alone. When my nephew Juan Andres found him, his body was stiff and cold. Juan Andres started CPR, and an ambulance was requested.

Emergency Medical Services arrived, and on the way to the hospital, they miraculously started his heart again. In the end, they determined he had been without oxygen to his brain for at least twenty minutes, causing his brain to show no signs of life.

I left Iraq as soon as I could. I received ten days of bereavement leave to see my dad before we disconnected him from life support. When I arrived, my mom, brother, sister, and aunt Mo had also arrived. It was bitter-sweet to be together again, and a day after I arrived, we decided to take him off life support. My sister and I left the room. Neither of us wanted to see him gasping for air as his body craved oxygen.

I hope my interpretation of my dad in this memoir was congruent with the amazing man and father he was. I wish I could have included more tender moments that told a more complete story of his life. I tried to elucidate, to you, the reader, the dualism he suffered from. I hope you were able to see the side of my dad that caused so many to love and respect him.

He was my hero. He was bigger than life. I would not change anything about my life.

Thank you for immersing yourself in my story. I started this project as a therapy suggestion by my doctor to journal. I found myself unable to stop writing. I started to feel like my story could impact lives. I thought readers could find symmetry and similarities and find the courage to seek deeper perspectives and understanding via empathy.

My story could help someone find hope and fight out of similar circumstances. For me, the idea I may inadvertently, through writing about my personal experiences, possibly connect with someone who shares even the smallest similarities with my story; is an experience I hope to learn about.

Writing about one's own life is exhaustingly difficult and wonderfully therapeutic; but any time I have spent working on this project, expressing my truths, vulnerabilities and emotions, have given me renewed courage and energy, to continue to try to help. Writing helps; reading can offer the same benefit.

Thank you.

When I left my work with the Nevada Department of Corrections, I began a journey into the world of private and government security contracting. It has taken me all over the world, to places like Bosnia, Serbia, Iraq, and multiple others.

I had the most unique and incredible experience with one of the most interesting families in the world—a Middle Eastern Royal Family. The adventures and experiences of my time with them… well, that is for another story…

My dad graduating Marine Corps Bootcamp

My dad in Vietnam

My parents, my sister and me. Chicago 1975, a few months before traveling to Ecuador.

TOP: My mom, my dad, my sister and me, shortly before we left Chicago for Ecuador. BOTTOM: Me, my brother Kevin and my sister Denise. Ecuador 1984

Byung Il and I

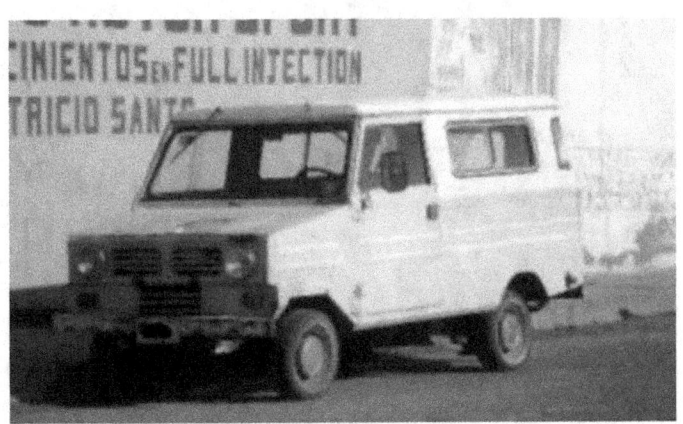

TOP: Byung and I. BOTTOM: An Andino

From L to R, 3 Cousins, my brother Kevin, sister Denise and I. In our Las Casas home and the Andino visible in the background.

Scruggs, me and Dror

Skate Park at La Carolina Park

Winning City Skate Contest, interviewed on live TV

Mike TOP LEFT: Skate Park at Carolina. TOP RIGHT: Winning City Skate Championship on live TV. BOTTOM: Mike and California Echo Park Gang Members

With Ms. Betty at my High School Graduation

With my parents at High School graduation

My wife and I Wedding photo 1995

Danny aka "Playboy"

L to R
Gina, Melissa, and Jenetti

Belinda

Gina and Melissa

Dacia and Tina

Clemons, me and Mike a few months before he was shot

Mike and me - 1992

Mike throwing up a Crip sign - 1992

Mike, Dennis and me

Mike adapting to life in a wheelchair

Big Kevin, Mike and me - 2023

Mike, happy and thankful to be alive

www.ingramcontent.com/pod-product-compliance
Lightning Source LLC
LaVergne TN
LVHW012250070526
838201LV00107B/314/J